# Anglican Daily Office

David Mathus

# FOREWORD

"Seven times a day do I praise thee; because of thy righteous judgments," the Psalmist said (119.164). This book came about as a way of conforming our prayer life to our Scriptural beliefs.

Parishioners would admit, often sheepishly, that they don't pray as often as they should, nor do they read the Bible as often as they should. In early Christian times the Bible, and especially the New Testament, was used primarily in the context of worship; prayer and liturgy help us to understand the Bible, and the Bible guides our prayer and worship. Thus, by providing a liturgical context for Scripture reading and prayer, both concerns can be met. Parishioners who do not pray often can be encouraged to start with one of the minor offices (e.g., Terce or None) as an entrance to developing a habit of regular daily prayer; as they progress and develop a habit of regular prayer, more offices (or longer offices) can be added. The short lessons provided for Noonday and Compline can be used as a starting point for Terce or None, and later on, once a habit is established, readings from the lectionary can be incorporated in their place. By following the lectionary, reading an Old Testament and a New Testament lesson each time at Morning and Evening Prayer, and the remaining New Testament lessons at other offices, a person would read the entire New Testament twice a year, and virtually the entire Old Testament once a year.

Because the Psalms are an integral part of the Daily Office, the entire Psalter is contained in this book. Collects for daily use, as well as for Holy Days, are also included. This book plus the Bible would enable a person to pray the Daily Office without need for a multitude of other resources.

One final note: the Invitatory at Morning Prayer is Psalm 95 in its entirety; those who are accustomed to saying the Venite, (part Psalm 95 and part Psalm 96) may find this strange. However, in an age when practicing Christians are increasingly a minority, the more penitential emphasis of the psalm in its final verses will remind us of our need to commend the faith that is in us.

# CONTENTS

Foreword    i

1   Lauds    1

2   Daily Morning    5
Prayer

3   Terce    23

4   Noonday    25

5   None    29

6   Daily Evening    31
Prayer

7   Compline    43

8   Psalms    49

9   Lectionary    201

10   Collects    247

# The Order for Lauds

*Psalm 5:3b: Early in the morning will I direct my prayer unto thee and will look up*

*To be said upon first rising in the morning*

✠ O God, make speed to save us.

**O Lord, make haste to help us.**

Glory be to the Father, and to the Son, and to the Holy Ghost,

**As it was in the beginning, is now, and ever shall be, world                without end. Amen.**

Praise ye the Lord.

**The Lord's Name be praised.**

*Except in Lent* **Alleluia.**

*A Psalm or Psalms is sung or said. At the end of the Psalms is sung or said*

**Glory be to the Father, and to the Son, * and to the Holy Ghost: As it was in the beginning, is now, and ever shall be, world without end. Amen.**

*One of the following is read*

Now unto the King eternal, immortal, invisible, the only wise God, be honor and glory for ever and ever. *1 Timothy 1:17*

Blessed be the God and Father of our Lord Jesus Christ! By his great mercy we have been born anew to a living hope through the resurrection of Jesus Christ from the dead. *1 Peter 1:3*

**Thanks be to God.**

The Lord be with you.

**And with thy spirit.**

Let us pray.
Lord, have mercy upon us.
  **Christ, have mercy upon us.**
Lord, have mercy upon us.

**Our Father, who art in heaven, Hallowed be thy Name. Thy kingdom come. Thy will be done, On earth as it is in heaven. Give us this day our daily bread. And forgive us our trespasses, As we forgive those who trespass against us. And lead us not into temptation but deliver us from evil.**

O Lord, arise, help us.
  **And deliver us for Thy Name's sake.**
Turn us again, O Lord God of Hosts.
  **Show the light of thy countenance, and we shall be whole.**
Hear my prayer, O Lord.
  **And let my crying come unto thee.**
Let us pray.

*The Officiant says one of the following two collects*

Lord God, almighty and everlasting Father, thou hast brought us in safety to this new day: Preserve us with thy mighty power, that we may not fall into sin, nor be overcome by adversity; and in all we do, direct us to the fulfilling of thy purpose; through Jesus Christ our Lord. **Amen.**

O Almighty Lord, vouchsafe, we beseech thee, to direct, sanctify, and govern us in the ways of thy laws; through Jesus Christ our Lord. **Amen.**

The Lord be with you.
**And with thy spirit.**

Let us bless the Lord.
**Thanks be to God.**

✠ The grace of our Lord Jesus Christ, the love of God, and the fellowship of the Holy Ghost be with us all evermore. **Amen**.

# The Order for Daily Morning Prayer

*Psalm 119:64: Seven times a day do I praise thee because of thy righteous judgments*

*The Officiant begins with one or more of these sentences of Scripture.*

*Advent*

Watch ye, for ye know not when the master of the house cometh, at even, or at midnight, or at the cock-crowing, or in the morning; lest coming suddenly he find you sleeping. *Mark 13:35, 36*

Prepare ye the way of the Lord, make straight in the desert a highway for our God. *Isaiah 40:3*

The glory of the Lord shall be revealed, and all flesh shall see it together. *Isaiah 40:5*

*Christmas*

Behold, I bring you good tidings of great joy, which shall be to all people. For unto you is born this day in the city of David a Savior, which is Christ the Lord. *Luke 2:10, 11*
Behold, the tabernacle of God is with men, and he will dwell with them, and they shall be his people, and God himself shall be with them, and be their God. *Revelation 21:3*
*Epiphany*

The Gentiles shall come to thy light, and kings to the brightness of thy rising. *Isaiah 60:3*

I will give thee for a light to the Gentiles, that thou mayest be my salvation unto the end of the earth. *Isaiah 49:6b*

From the rising of the sun even unto the going down of the same my Name shall be great among the Gentiles, and in every place incense shall be offered unto my Name, and a pure offering: for my Name shall be great among the heathen, saith the Lord of hosts. *Malachi 1:11*

*Lent*

If we say that we have no sin, we deceive ourselves, and the truth is not in us, but if we confess our sins, God is faithful and just to forgive us our sins, and to cleanse us from all unrighteousness. *1 John 1:8, 9*

Rend your heart, and not your garments, and turn unto the Lord your God; for he is gracious and merciful, slow to anger and of great kindness, and repenteth him of the evil. *Joel 2:13*

I will arise and go to my father, and will say unto him, "Father, I have sinned against heaven, and before thee, and am no more worthy to be called thy son." *Luke 15:18, 19*
To the Lord our God belong mercies and forgivenesses, though we have rebelled against him; neither have we obeyed the voice of the Lord our God, to walk in his laws which he set before us. *Daniel 9:9, 10*

Jesus said, "Whosoever will come after me, let him deny himself, and take up his cross, and follow me." *Mark 8:34*

*Holy Week*

All we like sheep have gone astray; we have turned every one to his own way; and the Lord hath laid on him the iniquity of us all. *Isaiah 53:6*

Is it nothing to you, all ye that pass by? Behold and see if there be any sorrow like unto my sorrow which is done unto me, wherewith the Lord hath afflicted me. *Lamentations 1:12*

*Easter Season, including Ascension Day and the Day of Pentecost*

Alleluia! Christ is risen.
**The Lord is risen indeed. Alleluia!**

This is the day which the Lord hath made; we will rejoice and be glad in it. *Psalm 118:24*

Thanks be to God, which giveth us the victory through our Lord Jesus Christ. *1 Corinthians 15:57*

If ye then be risen with Christ, seek those things which are above, where Christ sitteth on the right hand of God. *Colossians 3:1*

Christ is not entered into the holy places made with hands, which are the figures of the true; but into heaven itself, now to appear in the presence of God for us. *Hebrews 9:24*

Ye shall receive power, after that the Holy Ghost is come upon you; and ye shall be witnesses unto me both in Jerusalem, and in all Judaea, and in Samaria, and unto the uttermost part of the earth. *Acts 1:8*
*Trinity Sunday*

Holy, holy, holy, Lord God Almighty, which was, and is, and is to come. *Revelation 4:8*

*All Saints and other Major Saints' Days*

We give thanks unto the Father, which hath made us meet to be partakers of the inheritance of the saints in light. *Colossians 1:12*

Ye are no more strangers and foreigners, but fellow-citizens with the saints and of the household of God. *Ephesians 2:19*

Their sound is gone out into all lands, and their words into the ends of the world. *Psalm 19:4*

*Occasions of Thanksgiving*

O give thanks unto the Lord, and call upon his Name; tell the people what things he hath done. *Psalm 105:1*

*At any Time*

Grace be unto you, and peace, from God our Father, and from the Lord Jesus Christ. *Philippians 1:2*
I was glad when they said unto me, "We will go into the house of the Lord." *Psalm 122:1*

Let the words of my mouth, and the meditation of my heart, be alway acceptable in thy sight, O Lord, my strength and my redeemer. *Psalm 19:14*

O send out thy light and thy truth, that they may lead me, and bring me unto thy holy hill, and to thy dwelling. *Psalm 43:3*

The Lord is in his holy temple; let all the earth keep silence before him. *Hab. 2:20*

The hour cometh, and now is, when the true worshipers shall worship the Father in spirit and in truth; for the Father seeketh such to worship him. *John 4:23*

Thus saith the high and lofty One that inhabiteth eternity, whose name is Holy, "I dwell in the high and holy place, with him also that is of a contrite and humble spirit, to revive the spirit of the humble, and to revive the heart of the contrite ones." *Isaiah 57:15*
*The following Confession of Sin may then be said; or the Office may continue at once with "O Lord, open thou our lips."*

# Confession of Sin

Dearly beloved, we have come together in the presence of Almighty God our heavenly Father, to render thanks for the great benefits that we have received at his hands, to set forth his most worthy praise, to hear his holy Word, and to ask, for ourselves and on behalf of others, those things that are necessary for our life and our salvation. And so that we may prepare ourselves in heart and mind to worship him, let us kneel in silence, and with penitent and obedient hearts confess our sins, that we may obtain forgiveness by his infinite goodness and mercy.

*Silence may be kept.*

*Officiant and People together, all kneeling*

**Almighty and most merciful Father,**
**we have erred and strayed from thy ways like lost sheep,**
**we have followed too much the devices and desires of our own**
**hearts,**
**we have offended against thy holy laws,**
**we have left undone those things which we ought to have done,**
**and we have done those things which we ought not to have**
**done, and there is no health in us.**
**But thou, O Lord, have mercy upon us, miserable offenders;**
**spare thou those, O God, who confess their faults,**
**restore thou those who are penitent,**
**according to thy promises declared unto mankind**
**in Christ Jesus our Lord;**
**and grant, O most merciful Father, for his sake,**
**that we may hereafter live a godly, righteous, and sober life,**
**to the glory of thy holy Name. Amen.**

*The Priest alone stands and says*

The Almighty and merciful Lord grant you ✠ absolution and remission of all your sins, true repentance, amendment of life, and the grace and consolation of his Holy Spirit. **Amen.**

*A deacon or lay person using the preceding form remains kneeling, and substitutes "us" for "you" and "our" for "your."*
*All stand*

✠ O Lord, open thou our lips.

**And our mouth shall show forth thy praise.**

Glory be to the Father, and to the Son, * and to the Holy Ghost:

**As it was in the beginning, is now, and ever shall be***
**world without end. Amen.**

*Except in Lent, all may say,* **Alleluia.**

## Venite exultemus
*(Psalm 95) or Venite, Psalm 95:1-7; 96:9, 13*

**O come, let us sing unto the Lord; * let us heartily rejoice in the strength of our salvation.**

**Let us come before his presence with thanksgiving * and show ourselves glad in him with psalms.**

**For the Lord is a great God, * and a great King above all gods.**

**In his hand are all the corners of the earth, * and the strength of the hills is his also.**

**The sea is his, and he made it, * and his hands prepared the dry land.**

**O come, let us worship and fall down, * and kneel before the Lord our Maker.**

**For he is the Lord our God, * and we are the people of his pasture and the sheep of his hand.**

**Today, if ye will hear his voice, harden not your hearts * as in the provocation, and as in the day of temptation in the wilderness;**

**When your fathers tempted me, * proved me, and saw my works.**

**Forty years long was I grieved with this generation, and said, * It is a people that do err in their hearts, for they have not known my ways:**

**Unto whom I sware in my wrath, * that they should not enter into my rest.**

*In Easter Week, in place of an Invitatory Psalm, the following is sung or said. It may also be used daily until the Day of Pentecost.*

## Pascha nostrum
*1 Corinthians 5:7-8; Romans 6:9-11; 1 Corinthians 15:20-22*

**Alleluia.**
**Christ our Passover is sacrificed for us, ***
   **therefore let us keep the feast,**
**Not with old leaven,**
**neither with the leaven of malice and    wickedness, ***
   **but with the unleavened bread of sincerity and truth.**
**Alleluia.**

**Christ being raised from the dead dieth no more; ***
   **death hath no more dominion over him.**
**For in that he died, he died unto sin once; ***
   **but in that he liveth, he liveth unto God.**
**Likewise reckon ye also yourselves to be dead indeed unto sin,***
   **but alive unto God through Jesus Christ our Lord.  Alleluia.**
**Christ is risen from the dead, ***
   **and become the first fruits of them that slept.**
**For since by man came death, ***
   **by man came also the resurrection of the dead.**
**For as in Adam all die, ***
   **even so in Christ shall all be made alive.  Alleluia.**

*Then shall be sung or said the Psalm or Psalms appointed.*

*At the end of the Psalms is sung or said*

**Glory be to the Father, and to the Son, and to the Holy Ghost: ***
**As it was in the beginning, is now, and ever shall be, * world without end.   Amen.**

*Then shall be read the Lessons, as appointed, the Reader first saying,*

A Reading from _____
*A citation giving chapter and verse may be added.*
*After each Lesson the Reader says*
> The Word of the Lord.
> **Thanks be to God.**

*After the first Lesson, one of the following canticles is sung or said.*

## Benedicite, omnia opera Domini
*Song of the Three Young Men, 35-65*

I  O all ye works of the Lord, bless ye the Lord; *
  praise him and magnify him for ever.
**O ye angels of the Lord, bless ye the Lord; ***
 **praise him and magnify him for ever.**

II  O ye heavens, bless ye the Lord; *
  O ye waters that be above the firmament, bless ye the Lord;
**O all ye powers of the Lord, bless ye the Lord; ***
  **praise him and magnify him for ever.**
O ye sun and moon, bless ye the Lord; *
  O ye stars of heaven, bless ye the Lord;
**O ye showers and dew, bless ye the Lord; ***
  **praise him and magnify him for ever.**

O ye winds of God, bless ye the Lord; *
  O ye fire and heat, bless ye the Lord;
**O ye winter and summer, bless ye the Lord; ***
  **praise him and magnify him for ever.**

O ye dews and frosts, bless ye the Lord; *
  O ye frost and cold, bless ye the Lord;
**O ye ice and snow, bless ye the Lord; ***
  **praise him and magnify him for ever.**

O ye nights and days, bless ye the Lord; *
   O ye light and darkness, bless ye the Lord;
**O ye lightnings and clouds, bless ye the Lord; ***
   **praise him and magnify him for ever.**

III  O let the earth bless the Lord; *
   O ye mountains and hills, bless ye the Lord;
**O all ye green things upon the earth, bless ye the Lord; ***
   **praise him and magnify him for ever.**

O ye wells, bless ye the Lord; *
   O ye seas and floods, bless ye the Lord;
**O ye whales and all that move in the waters, bless ye the Lord;***
   **praise him and magnify him for ever.**
O all ye fowls of the air, bless ye the Lord; *
   O all ye beasts and cattle, bless ye the Lord;
**O ye children of men, bless ye the Lord; ***
   **praise him and magnify him for ever.**

IV  O ye people of God, bless ye the Lord; *
   O ye priests of the Lord, bless ye the Lord;
**O ye servants of the Lord, bless ye the Lord; ***
   **praise him and magnify him for ever.**

O ye spirits and souls of the righteous, bless ye the Lord; *
   O ye holy and humble men of heart, bless ye the Lord.
**Let us bless the Father, the Son, and the Holy Ghost; ***
   **praise him and magnify him for ever.**

*or this*

## Benedictus es, Domine
*Song of the Three Young Men, 29-34*

**Blessed art thou, O Lord God of our fathers; ***
   **praised and exalted above all for ever.**
**Blessed art thou for the name of thy Majesty; ***
   **praised and exalted above all for ever.**

13

Blessed art thou in the temple of thy holiness; *
 praised and exalted above all for ever.
Blessed art thou that beholdest the depths,
and dwellest between the Cherubim; *
 praised and exalted above all for ever.
Blessed art thou on the glorious throne of thy kingdom; *
 praised and exalted above all for ever.
Blessed art thou in the firmament of heaven; *
 praised and exalted above all for ever.
Blessed art thou, O Father, Son, and Holy Ghost; * praised
and exalted above all for ever.

*After the second Lesson one of the following canticles is sung or
said*

## Benedictus Dominus Deus
*Luke 1:68-79*

✠ Blessed be the Lord God of Israel, *
 for he hath visited and redeemed his people;
And hath raised up a mighty salvation for us *
 in the house of his servant David,
As he spake by the mouth of his holy prophets, *
 which have been since the world began:
That we should be saved from our enemies, *
 and from the hand of all that hate us;
To perform the mercy promised to our forefathers, *
 and to remember his holy covenant;
To perform the oath which he sware to our forefather
Abraham,*
 that he would give us,
That we being delivered out of the hand of our enemies *
 might serve him without fear,
In holiness and righteousness before him, *
 all the days of our life.
And thou, child, shalt be called the prophet of the Highest, *
 for thou shalt go before the face of the Lord
 to prepare his ways;

To give knowledge of salvation unto his people *
   for the remission of their sins,
Through the tender mercy of our God, *
   whereby the dayspring from on high hath visited us;
To give light to them that sit in darkness
and in the shadow of death, *
   and to guide our feet into the way of peace.
Glory be to the Father, and to the Son, and to the Holy Ghost,
* as it was in the beginning, is now, and ever shall be, world
without end. Amen.

*or this*

# Te Deum laudamus

We praise thee, O God; *
   we acknowledge thee to be the Lord.
All the earth doth worship thee, *
   the Father everlasting.
To thee all Angels cry aloud, *
   the Heavens and all the Powers therein.
To thee Cherubim and Seraphim *
   continually do cry:
Holy, holy, holy, Lord God of Sabaoth; *
   Heaven and earth are full of the majesty of thy glory.
The glorious company of the apostles praise thee: *
   the goodly fellowship of the prophets praise thee.
The noble army of martyrs praise thee: *
   The holy Church throughout all the world doth
acknowledge thee,
The Father, of an infinite majesty, thine adorable, true, and
only Son, *
   also the Holy Ghost the Comforter.
Thou art the King of glory, O Christ: *
   thou art the everlasting Son of the Father.
When thou tookest upon thee to deliver man, *
   thou didst humble thyself to be born of a Virgin.
When thou hadst overcome the sharpness of death, *

thou didst open the kingdom of heaven to all believers.
Thou sittest at the right hand of God,*
   in the glory of the Father.
We believe that thou shalt come to be our judge: *
   We therefore pray thee, halp thy servants,
    whom thou hast redeemed with thy precious blood.
Make them to be numbered with thy saints, *
   in glory everlasting.

## The Apostles' Creed

*Then, standing, all shall say*

I believe in God, the Father almighty,
   maker of heaven and earth;
And in Jesus Christ his only Son our Lord;
   who was conceived by the Holy Ghost,
   born of the Virgin Mary,
   suffered under Pontius Pilate,
   was crucified, dead, and buried.
   He descended into hell.
   The third day he rose again from the dead.
   He ascended into heaven,
   and sitteth on the right hand of God the Father almighty.
   From thence he shall come to judge the quick and the dead.
I believe in the Holy Ghost,
   the holy catholic Church,
   the communion of saints,
   the forgiveness of sins,
   the resurrection of the body,
 ✞ and the life everlasting.  Amen.

## The Prayers

*The people kneel*

   The Lord be with you.
    **And with thy spirit.**
   Let us pray.

Lord, have mercy upon us.
   **Christ, have mercy upon us.**
Lord, have mercy upon us.
**Our Father, who art in heaven,**
   **hallowed be thy Name,**
   **thy kingdom come,**
   **thy will be done,**
      **on earth as it is in heaven.**
**Give us this day our daily bread.**
**And forgive us our trespasses,**
   **as we forgive those who trespass against us.**
**And lead us not into temptation,**
   **but deliver us from evil.**
**For thine is the kingdom, and the power, and the glory,**
   **for ever and ever.  Amen.**

*Then follows one of these sets of Suffrages*

### A

O Lord, show thy mercy upon us;
   **And grant us thy salvation.**
Endue thy ministers with righteousness;
   **And make thy chosen people joyful.**
Give peace, O Lord, in all the world;
   **For only in thee can we live in safety.**
Lord, keep this nation under thy care;
   **And guide us in the way of justice and truth.**
Let thy way be known upon earth;
   **Thy saving health among all nations.**
Let not the needy, O Lord, be forgotten;
   **Nor the hope of the poor be taken away.**
Create in us clean hearts, O God;
   **And sustain us with thy Holy Spirit.**

### B

O Lord, save thy people, and bless thine heritage;
  **Govern them and lift them up for ever.**
Day by day we magnify thee;
  **And we worship thy Name ever, world without end.**
Vouchsafe, O Lord, to keep us this day without sin;
  **O Lord, have mercy upon us, have mercy upon us.**
O Lord, let thy mercy be upon us;
  **As our trust is in thee.**
O Lord, in thee have I trusted;
  **Let me never be confounded.**

## C

O Lord, show thy mercy upon us;
  **And grant us thy salvation.**
O Lord, save the State.
  **And mercifully hear us when we call upon thee.**
Endue thy ministers with righteousness;
  **And make thy chosen people joyful.**
O Lord, save thy people.
  **And bless thine inheritance.**
Give peace in our time, O Lord.
  **For it is thou, Lord, only, that makest us dwell in safety.**
O God, make clean our hearts within us.
  **And take not thy Holy Spirit from us.**

*The Officiant then says the following Collects*

*The Collect(s) of the Day*
*A Collect for Peace*

O God, who art the author of peace and lover of concord, in knowledge of whom standeth our eternal life, whose service is perfect freedom: Defend us, thy humble servants, in all assaults of our enemies; that we, surely trusting in thy defense, may not fear the power of any adversaries; through the might of Jesus Christ our Lord. **Amen**.

*A Collect for Grace*

O Lord, our heavenly Father, almighty and everlasting God, who hast safely brought us to the beginning of this day: Defend us in the same with thy mighty power; and grant that this day we fall into no sin, neither run into any kind of danger; but that we, being ordered by thy governance, may do always what is righteous in thy sight; through Jesus Christ our Lord. **Amen**.

*A Collect for Sundays*

O God, who makest us glad with the weekly remembrance of the glorious resurrection of thy Son our Lord: Grant us this day such blessing through our worship of thee, that the days to come may be spent in thy favor; through the same Jesus Christ our Lord. **Amen**.

*A Collect for Fridays*

Almighty God, whose most dear Son went not up to joy but first he suffered pain, and entered not into glory before he was crucified: Mercifully grant that we, walking in the way of the cross, may find it none other than the way of life and peace; through the same thy Son Jesus Christ our Lord. **Amen**.

*A Collect for Saturdays*

Almighty God, who after the creation of the world didst rest from all thy works and sanctify a day of rest for all thy creatures: Grant that we, putting away all earthly anxieties, may be duly prepared for the service of thy sanctuary, and that our rest here upon earth may be a preparation for the eternal rest promised to thy people in heaven; through Jesus Christ our Lord. **Amen**.

*A Collect for the Renewal of Life (Wednesday)*

O God, the King eternal, who dividest the day from the night and turnest the shadow of death into the morning: Drive far from us all wrong desires, incline our hearts to keep thy law, and guide our feet into the way of peace; that, having done thy will with cheerfulness while it was day, we may, when the night cometh, rejoice to give thee thanks; through Jesus Christ our Lord. **Amen**.

*A Collect for Guidance (Thursday)*

O heavenly Father, in whom we live and move and have our being: We humbly pray thee so to guide and govern us by thy Holy Spirit, that in all the cares and occupations of our life we may not forget thee, but may remember that we are ever walking in thy sight; through Jesus Christ our Lord. **Amen**.

*Then one of these prayers for mission is added*

Almighty and everlasting God, by whose Spirit the whole body of thy faithful people is governed and sanctified: Receive our supplications and prayers which we offer before thee for all members of thy holy Church, that in their vocation and ministry they may truly and godly serve thee; through our Lord and Savior Jesus Christ. **Amen**.

*or the following*

O God, who hast made of one blood all the peoples of the earth, and didst send thy blessed Son to preach peace to those who are far off and to those who are near: Grant that people everywhere may seek after thee and find thee; bring the nations into thy fold; pour out thy Spirit upon all flesh; and hasten the coming of thy kingdom; through the same thy Son Jesus Christ our Lord. **Amen**.

*or this*

Lord Jesus Christ, who didst stretch out thine arms of love on the hard wood of the cross that everyone might come within the reach of thy saving embrace: So clothe us in thy Spirit that we, reaching forth our hands in love, may bring those who do not know thee to the knowledge and love of thee; for the honor of thy Name. **Amen**.

*Intercessions and thanksgivings may follow.*

*Before the close of the Office one or both of the following may be used*

## The General Thanksgiving

**Almighty God, Father of all mercies,**
**we thine unworthy servants**
**do give thee most humble and hearty thanks**
**for all thy goodness and loving-kindness**
**to us and to all men.**
**We bless thee for our creation, preservation,**
**and all the blessings of this life;**
**but above all for thine inestimable love**
**in the redemption of the world by our Lord Jesus Christ,**
**for the means of grace, and for the hope of glory.**
**And, we beseech thee,**
**give us that due sense of all thy mercies,**
**that our hearts may be unfeignedly thankful;**
**and that we show forth thy praise,**
**not only with our lips, but in our lives,**
**by giving up our selves to thy service,**
**and by walking before thee**
**in holiness and righteousness all our days;**
**through Jesus Christ our Lord,**
**to whom, with thee and the Holy Ghost,**
**be all honor and glory, world without end. Amen.**

## A Prayer of St. Chrysostom

Almighty God, who hast given us grace at this time with one accord to make our common supplication unto thee; and hast promised through thy well-beloved Son that when two or three are gathered together in his Name thou wilt be in the midst of them: Fulfill now, O Lord, the desires and petitions of thy servants as may be best for us; granting us in this world knowledge of thy truth, and in the world to come life everlasting. **Amen**.

<blockquote>
The Lord be with you.
**And with thy Spirit.**

Let us bless the Lord.
**Thanks be to God.**
</blockquote>

*From Easter Day through the Day of Pentecost* "Alleluia, alleluia" *may be added to the preceding versicle and response. The Officiant then concludes with one of the following*

✠ The grace of our Lord Jesus Christ and the love of God, and the fellowship of the Holy Ghost, be with us all evermore. **Amen**. *2 Corinthians 13:14*
May the God of hope fill us with all joy and peace in believing through the power of the Holy Spirit. **Amen**. *Romans 15:13*

*The Officiant may add*

✠ May the souls of all the faithful departed, through the mercy of God, rest in peace. **Amen.**

# The Order for Terce

*Psalm 119:147: In the morning do I cry unto thee, for in thy word is my trust.*

*To be said mid-morning*

✠ O God, make speed to save us.
**O Lord, make haste to help us.**
Glory be to the Father, and to the Son, and to the Holy Ghost;
**As it was in the beginning, is now, and ever shall be, world without end. Amen.**
Praise ye the Lord.
**The Lord's Name be praised.**
*Except in Lent may be added* **Alleluia.**

*A Psalm or Psalms shall be read*

*At the end of the Psalms is sung or said*

**Glory be to the Father, and to the Son, and to the Holy Ghost; As it was in the beginning, is now, and ever shall be, world without end. Amen.**

*A reading from Scripture follows.*
**Thanks be to God.**

The Lord be with you.
**And with thy spirit.**
Let us pray.

Lord, have mercy upon us.
**Christ, have mercy upon us.**
Lord, have mercy upon us.

Our Father, who art in heaven, Hallowed be thy Name. Thy kingdom come. Thy will be done, On earth as it is in heaven. Give us this day our daily bread. And forgive us our trespasses, As we forgive those who trespass against us. And lead us not into temptation but deliver us from evil.

O Lord, arise, help us.
  **And deliver us for Thy Name's sake.**
Turn us again, O Lord God of Hosts.
  **Show the light of thy countenance, and we shall be whole.**
Hear my prayer, O Lord.
  **And let my crying come unto thee.**
The Lord be with you.
  **And with thy spirit.**

*The Officiant says one of the following two collects*

Gracious heavenly Father, we beseech thee to send thy Holy Spirit into our hearts, to direct and rule us in accordance with thy will, to comfort us in all our afflictions, to defend us from all error, and to lead us into thy truth; through Jesus Christ our Lord. **Amen.**

O Almighty God, who pourest out on all who desire it, the spirit of grace and supplication: Deliver us, when we draw nigh to thee, from coldness of heart and wanderings of mind, that with steadfast thoughts and kindled affections, we may worship thee in spirit and in truth; through Jesus Christ our Lord. **Amen**.

  The Lord be with you.
    **And with thy spirit.**
  Let us bless the Lord.
    **Thanks be to God.**

The Almighty and merciful Lord, ✠ Father, Son, and Holy Ghost, be with us all ever more. **Amen.**

# The Order for Noonday Prayer

*Acts 10:9: Peter went up upon the housetop to pray about the sixth hour:*

✠ O God, make speed to save us.
**O Lord, make haste to help us.**
Glory be to the Father, and to the Son, * and to the Holy Ghost:
**as it was in the beginning, is now, and ever shall be, * world without end.  Amen.**

Praise ye the Lord.
**The Lord's Name be praised.**

*Except in Lent may be added*     **Alleluia.**

*One or more Psalms is sung or said; at the end is said the **Gloria Patri***

**Glory be to the Father, and to the Son, * and to the Holy Ghost:**
**As it was in the beginning, is now, and ever shall be, * world without end. Amen.**

*A passage of Scripture is read*

### Sunday morning
If any man be in Christ, he is a new creation; old things are passed away; behold, all things are become new.  And all things are of God, who hath reconciled us to himself by Jesus Christ, and hath given to us the ministry of reconciliation.  *2 Corinthians 5.17-18*

### Monday morning

Hope maketh not ashamed; because the love of God is shed abroad in our hearts by the Holy Ghost which is given unto us. *Romans 5.5*

### Tuesday morning

From the rising of the sun even unto the going down of the same my name shall be great among the Gentiles; and in every place incense shall be offered unto my name, and a pure offering: for my name shall be great among the heathen, saith the Lord of hosts. *Malachi 1.11*

### Wednesday morning

Love the truth and peace, saith the Lord of hosts. *Zechariah 8.19*

### Thursday morning

The Lord by wisdom hath founded the earth; by understanding hath he established the heavens. By his knowledge the depths are broken up, and the clouds drop down the dew. *Proverbs 33.19-20*

### Friday morning

For if we be dead with him, we shall also live with him: If we suffer, we shall also reign with him. *2 Timothy 2.11b-12a*

### Saturday morning

Be sober, be vigilant; because your adversary the devil, as a roaring lion, walketh about, seeking whom he may devour: Whom resist stedfast in the faith. *1 Peter 5.8-9a*

*At the end of the Lesson is said*     **Thanks be to God.**

The Lord be with you.
 **And with thy spirit.**
Let us pray.

Lord, have mercy upon us.
 **Christ, have mercy upon us.**

Lord, have mercy upon us.

**Our Father, who art in heaven, Hallowed be thy Name. Thy kingdom come. Thy will be done, On earth as it is in heaven. Give us this day our daily bread. And forgive us our trespasses, As we forgive those who trespass against us. And lead us not into temptation but deliver us from evil.**

Send out thy light and thy truth, that they may lead me.
**And bring me unto thy holy hill, and to thy dwelling.**
Turn us again, O Lord God of Hosts.
**Show the light of thy countenance, and we shall be whole.**
The Lord be with you.
**And with thy spirit.**
Let us pray.

*The Officiant then says one of the following two collects.*

Blessed Savior, who at this hour didst hang upon the cross, stretching out thy loving arms: Grant that all the nations of the earth may look unto thee and be saved; for thy tender mercies' sake. **Amen.**

Almighty Savior, who at noonday didst call thy servant Saint Paul to be an apostle to the Gentiles: We pray thee to illumine the world with the radiance of thy glory, that all nations may come and worship thee; for thou livest and reignest for ever and ever. **Amen.**

The Lord be with you.
**And with thy spirit.**

Let us bless the Lord.
**Thanks be to God.**

✠ The grace of our Lord Jesus Christ, and the love of God, and the fellowship of the Holy Ghost, be with us all evermore. **Amen.** *2 Corinthians 13:14*

None (which rhymes with 'bone' and not with 'nun') gets its name from the Latin word 'ninth'. The Romans considered that each day was 12 hours of light and 12 hours of dark (meaning the hours varied in length depending on time of year), so Terce is the third hour of the day (midmorning), Sext (or Noonday) is the sixth hour of the day, midday, and None is the ninth hour of the day, or mid afternoon.

# The Order for None

*Acts 3:1: Now Peter and John went up together into the temple at the hour of prayer, being the ninth hour.*

*To be said mid-afternoon*

✠ O God, make speed to save us.
> **O Lord, make haste to help us.**
Glory be to the Father, and to the Son, and to the Holy Ghost;
> **As it was in the beginning, is now, and ever shall be, world without end. Amen.**
Praise ye the Lord.
> **The Lord's Name be praised.**
*Except in Lent may be added* **Alleluia.**

*A Psalm or Psalms, as appointed, shall be sung or said.*

*At the end of the Psalms is sung or said*

**Glory be to the Father, and to the Son, * and to the Holy Ghost:**
**As it was in the beginning, is now, and ever shall be, * world without end. Amen.**

*A passage of Scripture shall be read.*

*People* **Thanks be to God.**

> The Lord be with you.
> > **And with thy spirit.**
> Let us pray.

> Lord, have mercy upon us.
> > **Christ, have mercy upon us.**

29

Lord, have mercy upon us.

**Our Father, who art in heaven, Hallowed be thy Name. Thy kingdom come. Thy will be done, On earth as it is in heaven. Give us this day our daily bread. And forgive us our trespasses, As we forgive those who trespass against us. And lead us not into temptation but deliver us from evil.**

Cast me not away in the time of age.
**Forsake me not when my strength faileth me.**
Hide not thy face from me.
**Lest I be like them who go down into the pit.**
Lord, hear our prayer.
**And let our cry come unto thee.**
Let us pray.

*The Officiant says one of the following two collects.*

O Lord Jesus Christ, who saidst unto thine apostles, Peace I leave with you; my peace I give unto you: Regard not our sins, but the faith of thy Church; and grant to us the peace and unity of that heavenly City, where with the Father and the Holy Ghost thou livest and reignest, ever one God, world without end. **Amen.**

Lord Jesus, in whose perfect Kingdom no sword is known but the sword of righteousness, no strength is known but the strength of love: So mightily spread abroad thy Spirit that all peoples of the earth may know thee and be saved; for thy tender mercies' sake. **Amen.**

The Lord be with you.
**And with thy spirit.**
Let us bless the Lord.
**Thanks be to God.**

The Almighty and merciful Lord, ✠ Father, Son, and Holy Ghost, be with us all ever more. **Amen.**

# The Order for Daily Evening Prayer

*Psalm 119:105: Thy word is a lantern unto my feet, and a light unto my paths.*

*The Officiant begins the service with one or more of the following sentences of Scripture.*

Grace be unto you, and peace, from God our Father, and from the Lord Jesus Christ. *Philippians 1:2*

O worship the Lord in the beauty of holiness; let the whole earth stand in awe of him. *Psalm 96:9*

Thine is the day, O God, thine also the night; thou hast established the moon and the sun. Thou hast fixed all the boundaries of the earth; thou hast made summer and winter. *Psalm 74:15,16*

I will bless the Lord who giveth me counsel; my heart teacheth me, night after night. I have set the Lord always before me; because he is at my right hand, I shall not fall. *Psalm 16:7, 8*

Seek him that made the Pleiades and Orion, that turneth deep darkness into the morning, and darkeneth the day into night; that calleth for the waters of the sea, and poureth them out upon the face of the earth: The Lord is his Name. *Amos 5:8*

If I say, "Surely the darkness will cover me, and the light around me turn to night," darkness is not dark to thee, O Lord; the night is as bright as the day; darkness and light to thee are both alike. *Psalm 139:10, 11*

Jesus said, "I am the light of the world; he that followeth me shall not walk in darkness, but shall have the light of life." *John 8:12*

# Confession of Sin

Dearly beloved brethren, the Scripture moveth us, in sundry places, to acknowledge and confess our manifold sins and wickedness; and that we should not dissemble nor cloak them before the face of Almighty God our heavenly Father; but confess them with an humble, lowly, penitent, and obedient heart; to the end that we may obtain forgiveness of the same, by his infinite goodness and mercy. And although we ought, at all times, humbly to acknowledge our sins before God; yet ought we chiefly so to do, when we assemble and meet together to render thanks for the great benefits that we have received at his hands, to set forth his most worthy praise, to hear his most holy Word, and to ask those things which are requisite and necessary, as well for the body as the soul. Wherefore I pray and beseech you, as many as are here present, to accompany me with a pure heart, and humble voice, unto the throne of the heavenly grace, saying

*Silence may be kept.*

*Officiant and People together, all kneeling*

**Almighty and most merciful Father,**
**we have erred and strayed from thy ways like lost sheep,**
**we have followed too much the devices and desires of our own**
**hearts,**
**we have offended against thy holy laws,**
**we have left undone those things which we ought to have done,**
**and we have done those things which we ought not to have**
**done, and there is no health in us.**
**But thou, O Lord, have mercy upon us, miserable offenders;**
**spare thou those, O God, who confess their faults,**
**restore thou those who are penitent,**
**according to thy promises declared unto mankind**
**in Christ Jesus our Lord;**
**and grant, O most merciful Father, for his sake,**
**that we may hereafter live a godly, righteous, and sober life,**

**to the glory of thy holy Name.  Amen.**

*The Priest alone stands and says*

The Almighty and merciful Lord grant you ✠ absolution and remission of all your sins, true repentance, amendment of life, and the grace and consolation of his Holy Spirit.  **Amen**.

*A deacon or lay person using the preceding form remains kneeling, and substitutes "us" for "you" and "our" for "your."*

*All stand*

✠ O Lord, open thou our lips..
  **And our mouth shall show forth thy praise.**
✠ O God, make speed to save us.
  **O Lord, make haste to help us.**

Glory be to the Father, and to the Son, * and to the Holy Ghost:
**as it was in the beginning, is now, and ever shall be * world without end. Amen.**
        Praise ye the Lord.
          **The Lord's Name be praised.**

*Except in Lent, all may say* **Alleluia**

*The following, or some other suitable hymn, or an Invitatory Psalm, may be sung or said*

## Phos hilaron

**O gracious Light,**
        **pure brightness of the everliving Father in heaven,**
        **O Jesus Christ, holy and blessed!**
**Now as we come to the setting of the sun,**
        **and our eyes behold the vesper light,**

we sing thy praises, O God: Father, Son, and Holy
Spirit.
**Thou art worthy at all times**
**to be praised by happy voices,**
**O Son of God, O Giver of life,**
**and to be glorified through all the worlds.**

*Then shall be sung or said the Psalms appointed.*

*At the end of the Psalms is sung or said*

**Glory be to the Father, and to the Son, \***
**and to the Holy Ghost:**
**As it was in the beginning, is now, and ever shall be, \***
**world without end.  Amen.**

*Then shall be read the First Lesson, as appointed, the reader first
saying,*

A Reading from_____.

*A citation giving chapter and verse may be added.*

*After the Lesson the Reader says*
The Word of the Lord.
**Thanks be to God.**

*Or*  Here endeth the Lesson.

*After the Lesson the following canticle is sung or said.*


## Magnificat
*Luke 1:46-55*


**✠ My soul doth magnify the Lord, \***
**and my spirit hath rejoiced in God my Savior.**
**For he hath regarded \***

the lowliness of his handmaiden.
For behold from henceforth *
　all generations shall call me blessed.
For he that is mighty hath magnified me, *
　and holy is his Name.
And his mercy is on them that fear him *
　throughout all generations.
He hath showed strength with his arm; *
　he hath scattered the proud in the imagination of their hearts.
He hath put down the mighty from their seat, *
　and hath exalted the humble and meek.
He hath filled the hungry with good things, *
　and the rich he hath sent empty away.
He remembering his mercy hath holpen his servant Israel, *
　as he promised to our forefathers,
　Abraham and his seed for ever.
Glory be to the Father, and to the Son, *
　and to the Holy Ghost:
As it was in the beginning, is now, and ever shall be, *
　world without end.  Amen.

*Then shall be read the Second Lesson, as appointed.*
*After the Lesson the Reader says*
　　　　The Word of the Lord.
　　　　**Thanks be to God.**

*Or*　Here endeth the Lesson

*After the Lesson the following canticle is sung or said*
　　　　Nunc dimittis
　　　　*Luke 2:29-32*


✠ Lord, now lettest thou thy servant depart in peace, *
　according to thy word;
For mine eyes have seen thy salvation, *
　which thou hast prepared before the face of all people,
To be a light to lighten the Gentiles, *

and to be the glory of thy people Israel.
Glory be to the Father, and to the Son, *
    and to the Holy Ghost: *
As it was in the beginning, is now, and ever shall be, *
    world without end.  Amen.

## The Apostles' Creed

*Then, standing, all shall say*

I believe in God, the Father almighty,
    maker of heaven and earth;
And in Jesus Christ his only Son our Lord;
    who was conceived by the Holy Ghost,
    born of the Virgin Mary,
    suffered under Pontius Pilate,
    was crucified, dead, and buried.
    He descended into hell.
    The third day he rose again from the dead.
    He ascended into heaven,
    and sitteth on the right hand of God the Father almighty.
    From thence he shall come to judge the quick and the dead.
I believe in the Holy Ghost,
    the holy catholic Church,
    the communion of saints,
    the forgiveness of sins,
    the resurrection of the body,
✠ and the life everlasting.  Amen.

## The Prayers

*The People kneel*

The Lord be with you.
    **And with thy spirit.**
Let us pray.

Lord, have mercy upon us.
**Christ, have mercy upon us.**
Lord, have mercy upon us.

**Our Father, who art in heaven,**
   **hallowed be thy Name,**
   **thy kingdom come,**
   **thy will be done,**
      **on earth as it is in heaven.**
**Give us this day our daily bread.**
**And forgive us our trespasses,**
   **as we forgive those who trespass against us.**
**And lead us not into temptation,**
   **but deliver us from evil.**
**For thine is the kingdom, and the power, and the glory,**
   **for ever and ever. Amen.**

*Then follows one of these sets of Suffrages*

## A

O Lord, show thy mercy upon us;
   **And grant us thy salvation.**
Endue thy ministers with righteousness;
   **And make thy chosen people joyful.**
Give peace, O Lord, in all the world;
   **For only in thee can we live in safety.**
Lord, keep this nation under thy care;
   **And guide us in the way of justice and truth.**
Let thy way be known upon earth;
   **Thy saving health among all nations.**
Let not the needy, O Lord, be forgotten;
   **Nor the hope of the poor be taken away.**
Create in us clean hearts, O God;
   **And sustain us with thy Holy Spirit.**

## B

That this evening may be holy, good, and peaceful,

**We entreat thee, O Lord.**

That thy holy angels may lead us in paths of peace and goodwill,
**We entreat thee, O Lord.**

That we may be pardoned and forgiven for our sins and offenses,
**We entreat thee, O Lord.**

That there may be peace to thy Church and to the whole world,
**We entreat thee, O Lord.**

That we may depart this life in thy faith and fear, and not be condemned before the great judgment seat of Christ,
**We entreat thee, O Lord.**

That we may be bound together by thy Holy Spirit in the Communion of the Blessed Virgin Mary, [Blessed _____] and all thy saints, entrusting one another and all our life to Christ,
**We entreat thee, O Lord.**

### C

O Lord, show thy mercy upon us.
  **And grant us thy salvation.**
O Lord, save the State.
  **And mercifully hear us when we call upon thee.**
Endue thy Ministers with righteousness.
  **And make thy chosen people joyful.**
O Lord, save thy people.
  **And bless thine inheritance.**
Give peace in our time, O Lord.
  **For it is thou, Lord, only, that makest us dwell in safety.**
O God, make clean our hearts within us.
  **And take not thy Holy Spirit from us.**

*The Officiant then says the following Collects*

*The Collect(s) of the Day*
*A Collect for Peace*

O God, from whom all holy desires, all good counsels, and all just works do proceed: Give unto thy servants that peace which the world cannot give, that our hearts may be set to obey thy commandments, and also that by thee, we, being defended from the fear of all enemies, may pass our time in rest and quietness; through the merits of Jesus Christ our Savior. **Amen**.

*A Collect for Aid against Perils*

Lighten our darkness, we beseech thee, O Lord; and by thy great mercy defend us from all perils and dangers of this night; for the love of thy only Son, our Savior Jesus Christ. **Amen**.

*The following, or other additional collects may be added, if desired*

*A Collect for Sundays*

Lord God, whose Son our Savior Jesus Christ triumphed over the powers of death and prepared for us our place in the new Jerusalem: Grant that we, who have this day given thanks for his resurrection, may praise thee in that City of which he is the light; and where he liveth and reigneth for ever and ever. **Amen**.

*A Collect for Fridays*

O Lord Jesus Christ, who by thy death didst take away the sting of death: Grant unto us thy servants so to follow in faith where thou hast led the way, that we may at length fall asleep peacefully in thee, and awake up after thy likeness; for thy tender mercies' sake. **Amen**.

*A Collect for Saturdays*

O God, the source of eternal light: Shed forth thine unending day upon us who watch for thee, that our lips may praise thee, our lives may bless thee, and our worship on the morrow may give thee glory; through Jesus Christ our Lord. **Amen**.

*A Collect for Protection (Wednesdays)*

O God, who art the life of all who live, the light of the faithful, the strength of those who labor, and the repose of the dead: We thank thee for the timely blessings of the day, and humbly beseech thy merciful protection all the night. Bring us, we pray thee, in safety to the morning hours; through him who died for us and rose again, thy Son our Savior Jesus Christ. **Amen**.

*A Collect for the Presence of Christ (Thursdays)*

Lord Jesus, stay with us, for evening is at hand and the day is past; be our companion in the way, kindle our hearts, and awaken hope, that we may know thee as thou art revealed in Scripture and the breaking of bread. Grant this for the sake of thy love. **Amen**.

*Then one of these prayers for mission is added*

O God and Father of all, whom the whole heavens adore: Let the whole earth also worship thee, all nations obey thee, all tongues confess and bless thee, and men and women everywhere love thee and serve thee in peace; through Jesus Christ our Lord. **Amen**.

*or the following*

Keep watch, dear Lord, with those who work, or watch, or weep this night, and give thine angels charge over those who sleep. Tend the sick, Lord Christ; give rest to the weary, bless the dying, soothe the suffering, pity the afflicted, shield the joyous; and all for thy love's sake. **Amen**.

*or this*

O God, who dost manifest in thy servants the signs of thy presence: Send forth upon us the Spirit of love, that in companionship with one another thine abounding grace may increase among us; through Jesus Christ our Lord. **Amen**.

*Intercessions and thanksgivings may follow.*

*Before the close of the Office one or both of the following may be used*

# The General Thanksgiving

*Officiant and People*

**Almighty God, Father of all mercies, we thine unworthy servants do give thee most humble and hearty thanks for all thy goodness and lovingkindness to us and to all men. We bless thee for our creation, preservation, and all the blessings of this life; but above all for thine inestimable love in the redemption of the world by our Lord Jesus Christ, for the means of grace, and for the hope of glory.**
**And, we beseech thee, give us that due sense of all thy mercies, that our hearts may be unfeignedly thankful; and that we show forth thy praise, not only with our lips, but in our lives, by giving up our selves to thy service, and by walking before thee in holiness and righteousness all our days; through Jesus Christ our Lord, to whom, with thee and the Holy Ghost, be all honor and glory, world without end. Amen.**

# A Prayer of St. Chrysostom

Almighty God, who hast given us grace at this time with one accord to make our common supplication unto thee; and hast promised through thy well-beloved Son that when two or three are gathered together in his Name thou wilt be in the midst of them: Fulfill now, O Lord, the desires and petitions of thy servants as may be best for us; granting us in this world knowledge of thy truth, and in the world to come life everlasting. **Amen**.

The Lord be with you.
**And with thy spirit.**

Let us bless the Lord.
**Thanks be to God.**

*From Easter Day through the Day of Pentecost* "Alleluia, alleluia" *may be added to the preceding versicle and response.*

*The Officiant then concludes with one of the following*

✠ The grace of our Lord Jesus Christ, and the love of God, and the fellowship of the Holy Ghost, be with us all evermore. **Amen**. *2 Corinthians 13:14*

May the God of hope fill us with all joy and peace in believing through the power of the Holy Spirit. **Amen**. *Romans 15:13*

*The Officiant may add*

✠ May the souls of all the faithful departed, through the mercy of God, rest in peace. **Amen.**

# The Order for Compline

*Psalm 119:55a: I have thought upon thy Name, O Lord, in the night season.*

✠ The Lord Almighty grant us a quiet night and a perfect end. **Amen.**

Brethren: Be sober, be vigilant, because your adversary the devil, as a roaring lion, walketh about, seeking whom he may devour: whom resist, steadfast in the faith.

But thou, O Lord, have mercy upon us. **Thanks be to God.**

Our help is in the Name of the Lord; **Who hath made heaven and earth.**

Let us humbly confess our sins unto Almighty God.

**Almighty God, our heavenly Father: We have sinned against thee, through our own fault, in thought, word, and deed, and in those things which we have left undone. For these offenses we are truly sorry and we humbly repent. For the sake of thy Son our Lord Jesus Christ, forgive us all our offenses; and grant that we may serve thee in newness of life, to the glory of thy Name. Amen.**

May the Almighty God grant us ✠ forgiveness of all our sins, amendment of life, and the grace and comfort of the Holy Ghost. **Amen.**

✠ O God, make speed to save us. **O Lord, make haste to help us.**

Glory be to the Father, and to the Son,* and to the Holy Ghost:

**As it was in the beginning, is now, and ever shall be,\* world without end. Amen.**

Praise ye the Lord.
**The Lord's Name be praised.**

*Except in Lent, all may say,* **Alleluia**

*One or more Psalms are sung or said.*

*At the end of the Psalms is sung or said*

**Glory be to the Father, and to the Son,\* and to the Holy Ghost: As it was in the beginning, is now, and ever shall be,\* world without end. Amen.**

*A passage of scripture is read.*

**Sunday evening**
Thou, O Lord, art in the midst of us, and we are called by Thy name; leave us not. *Jeremiah 14.9*

**Monday evening**
Come unto me, all ye that labor and are heavy laden, and I will give you rest. Take my yoke upon you, and learn of me; for I am meek and lowly in heart: and ye shall find rest unto your souls. For my yoke is easy, and my burden is light. *Matthew 11.28-30*

**Tuesday evening**
Now the God of peace, that brought again from the dead our Lord Jesus, that great shepherd of the sheep, through the blood of the everlasting covenant, make you perfect in every good work to do his will, working in you that which is well pleasing in his sight, through Jesus Christ, to whom be glory for ever and ever. *Hebrews 13.20-21*

**Wednesday evening**

For we preach not ourselves, but Christ Jesus the Lord; and ourselves your servants for Jesus' sake. For God, who commanded the light to shine out of darkness, hath shined in our hearts, to give the light of the knowledge of the glory of God in the face of Jesus Christ. *2 Corinthians 4.5-6*

## Thursday evening
O God, thou wilt keep in perfect peace those whose minds are fixed on thee; for in returning and rest we shall be saved; in quietness and trust shall be our strength. *Isaiah 26.3; 30.15*

## Friday evening
If I say, Peradventure the darkness shall cover me, then shall my night be turned to day. Yea, the darkness is no darkness with thee, but the night is as clear as the day; * the darkness and light to thee are both alike.
*Psalm 139.10-11*

## Saturday evening
Ye are the light of the world. A city that is set on a hill cannot be hid. Neither do men light a candle, and put it under a bushel, but put it on a candlestick; and it giveth light unto all that are in the house. Let your light so shine before men, that they may see your good works, and glorify your Father which is in heaven. *Matthew 5.14-16*

**Thanks be to God.**

Into thy hands I commend my spirit.
  **For thou hast redeemed me, O Lord, thou God of truth.**
Keep me as an apple of an eye;
  **Hide me under the shadow of thy wings.**
Lord, have mercy upon us.
  **Christ have mercy upon us.**
Lord, have mercy upon us.

**Our Father, who art in heaven, hallowed be thy Name, thy kingdom come, thy will be done, on earth as it is in heaven. Give us this day our daily bread. And forgive us our**

trespasses, as we forgive those who trespass against us. **And lead us not into temptation, but deliver us from evil.**

> O Lord, hear my prayer;
> **And let my cry come unto thee.**
> Let us pray.

*The Officiant says one of the following prayers.*

Visit, we beseech thee, O Lord, this habitation: Drive far from it all snares of the enemy; let thy holy angels dwell herein to preserve us in peace, and let thy blessing be ever upon us. Through Jesus Christ our Lord. **Amen.**

Lighten our darkness, we beseech thee, O Lord; and by thy great mercy defend us from all perils and dangers of this night; for the love of thy only Son, our Savior Jesus Christ. **Amen.**

Be present, O merciful God, and protect us through the silent hours of this night, so that we who are wearied by the changes and chances of this fleeting world may rest in thy eternal changelessness; through Jesus Christ our Lord. **Amen.**

*Silence may be kept. Intercessions and thanksgivings may be offered.*

*The service concludes with the following Antiphon and Nunc dimittis, which is sung or said by all.*

**Guide us waking, O Lord, and guard us sleeping;\* that awake we may watch with Christ, and asleep we may rest in peace.**

*In Easter Season, add* **Alleluia, alleluia, alleluia.**

**Lord, now lettest thou thy servant depart in peace, according to thy word;**
**For mine eyes have seen thy salvation, which thou hast prepared before the face of all people,**

To be a light to lighten the Gentiles, and to be the glory of thy people Israel.
Glory be to the Father, and to the Son, and to the Holy Ghost: As it was in the beginning, is now, and ever shall be, world without end. Amen.

Guide us waking, O Lord, and guard us sleeping; that awake we may watch with Christ, and asleep we may rest in peace.

*In Easter Season, add* **Alleluia, alleluia, alleluia.**

> The Lord be with you.
> **And with thy spirit.**
>
> Let us bless the Lord.
> **Thanks be to God.**

The Almighty and merciful Lord, ✠ Father, Son, and Holy Ghost, bless us and keep us. **Amen**

Regular reading of the psalms forms an essential and central element of the Daily Office. Whether one follows the 30-day cycle established by Cranmer for Morning and Evening Prayer, the six week cycle in the Book of Common Prayer, or some other, a regular program of reading the Psalms is important.

# Psalms

**Psalm 1.** *Beatus vir qui non abiit.*
BLESSED is the man that hath not walked in the counsel of the
ungodly, nor stood in the way of sinners, * and hath not sat in the
seat of the scornful.
2 But his delight is in the law of the LORD; * and in his law will he
exercise himself day and night.
3 And he shall be like a tree planted by the water-side, * that will
bring forth his fruit in due season.
4 His leaf also shall not wither; * and look, whatsoever he doeth, it
shall prosper.
5 As for the ungodly, it is not so with them; * but they are like the
chaff, which the wind scattereth away from the face of the earth.
6 Therefore the ungodly shall not be able to stand in the judgment,
* neither the sinners in the congregation of the righteous.
7 But the LORD knoweth the way of the righteous; * and the way
of the ungodly shall perish.


**Psalm 2.** *Quare fremuerunt gentes?*
WHY do the heathen so furiously rage together? * and why do the
people imagine a vain thing?
2 The kings of the earth stand up, and the rulers take counsel
together * against the LORD, and against his Anointed:
3 Let us break their bonds asunder, * and cast away their cords
from us.
4 He that dwelleth in heaven shall laugh them to scorn: * the Lord
shall have them in derision.
5 Then shall he speak unto them in his wrath, * and vex them in his
sore displeasure:
6 Yet have I set my King * upon my holy hill of Sion.
7 I will rehearse the decree; * the LORD hath said unto me, Thou

art my Son, this day have I begotten thee.
8 Desire of me, and I shall give thee the nations for thine inheritance, * and the utmost parts of the earth for thy possession.
9 Thou shalt bruise them with a rod of iron, * and break them in pieces like a potter's vessel.
10 Be wise now therefore, O ye kings; * be instructed, ye that are judges of the earth.
11 Serve the LORD in fear, * and rejoice unto him with reverence.
12 Kiss the Son, lest he be angry, and so ye perish from the right way, if his wrath be kindled, yea but a little. * Blessed are all they that put their trust in him.

**Psalm 3.** *Domine, quid multiplicati?*
LORD, how are they increased that trouble me! * many are they that rise against me.
2 Many one there be that say of my soul, * There is no help for him in his God.
3 But thou, O LORD, art my defender; * thou art my worship, and the lifter up of my head.
4 I did call upon the LORD with my voice, * and he heard me out of his holy hill.
5 I laid me down and slept, and rose up again; * for the LORD sustained me.
6 I will not be afraid for ten thousands of the people, * that have set themselves against me round about.
7 Up, LORD, and help me, O my God, * for thou smitest all mine enemies upon the cheek-bone; thou hast broken the teeth of the ungodly.
8 Salvation belongeth unto the LORD; * and thy blessing is upon thy people.

**Psalm 4.** *Cum invocarem.*
HEAR me when I call, O God of my righteousness: * thou hast set me at liberty when I was in trouble; have mercy upon me, and hearken unto my prayer.
2 O ye sons of men, how long will ye blaspheme mine honor, * and have such pleasure in vanity, and seek after falsehood?

3 Know this also, that the LORD hath chosen to himself the man that is godly; * when I call upon the LORD he will hear me.
4 Stand in awe, and sin not; * commune with your own heart, and in your chamber, and be still.
5 Offer the sacrifice of righteousness, * and put your trust in the LORD.
6 There be many that say, * Who will show us any good?
7 LORD, lift thou up* the light of thy countenance upon us.
8 Thou hast put gladness in my heart; * yea, more than when their corn and wine and oil increase.
9 I will lay me down in peace, and take my rest; * for it is thou, LORD, only, that makest me dwell in safety.

**Psalm**     **5.**     *Verba*     *mea*     *auribus.*
PONDER my words, O LORD, * consider my meditation.
2 O hearken thou unto the voice of my calling, my King and my God: * for unto thee will I make my prayer.
3 My voice shalt thou hear betimes, O LORD; * early in the morning will I direct my prayer unto thee, and will look up.
4 For thou art the God that hast no pleasure in wickedness; * neither shall any evil dwell with thee.
5 Such as be foolish shall not stand in thy sight; * for thou hatest all them that work iniquity.
6 Thou shalt destroy them that speak lies: * the LORD will abhor both the blood-thirsty and deceitful man.
7 But as for me, in the multitude of thy mercy I will come into thine house; * and in thy fear will I worship toward thy holy temple.
8 Lead me, O LORD, in thy righteousness, because of mine enemies; * make thy way plain before my face.
9 For there is no faithfulness in their mouth; * their inward parts are very wickedness.
10 Their throat is an open sepulcher; * they flatter with their tongue
11 Destroy thou them, O God; let them perish through their own imaginations; * cast them out in the multitude of their ungodliness; for they have rebelled against thee.
12 And let all them that put their trust in thee rejoice: * they shall

ever be giving of thanks, because thou defendest them; they that love thy Name shall be joyful in thee;
13 For thou, LORD, wilt give thy blessing unto the righteous, * and with thy favorable kindness wilt thou defend him as with a shield.

**Psalm 6.** *Domine, ne in furore.*
O LORD, rebuke me not in thine indignation, * neither chasten me in thy displeasure.
2 Have mercy upon me, O LORD, for I am weak; * O LORD, heal me, for my bones are vexed.
3 My soul also is sore troubled: * but, LORD, how long wilt thou punish me?
4 Turn thee, O LORD, and deliver my soul; * O save me, for thy mercy's sake.
5 For in death no man remembereth thee; * and who will give thee thanks in the pit?
6 I am weary of my groaning; * every night wash I my bed, and water my couch with my tears.
7 My beauty is gone for very trouble, * and worn away because of all mine enemies.
8 Away from me, all ye that work iniquity; * for the LORD hath heard the voice of my weeping.
9 The LORD hath heard my petition; * the LORD will receive my prayer.
10 All mine enemies shall be confounded, and sore vexed; * they shall be turned back, and put to shame suddenly.

**Psalm 7.** *Domine, Deus meus.*
O LORD my God, in thee have I put my trust: * save me from all them that persecute me, and deliver me;
2 Lest he devour my soul like a lion, and tear it in pieces, * while there is none to help.
3 O LORD my God, if I have done any such thing; * or if there be any wickedness in my hands;
4 If I have rewarded evil unto him that dealt friendly with me; * (yea, I have delivered him that without any cause is mine enemy;)
5 Then let mine enemy persecute my soul, and take me; * yea, let

him tread my life down upon the earth, and lay mine honor in the dust.

6 Stand up, O LORD, in thy wrath, and lift up thyself, because of the indignation of mine enemies; * arise up for me in the judgment that thou hast commanded.

7 And so shall the congregation of the peoples come about thee: * for their sakes therefore lift up thyself again.

8 The LORD shall judge the peoples: give sentence with me, O LORD, * according to my righteousness, and according to the innocency that is in me.

9 O let the wickedness of the ungodly come to an end; * but guide thou the just.

10 For the righteous God * trieth the very hearts and reins.

11 My help cometh of God, * who preserveth them that are true of heart.

12 God is a righteous Judge, strong, and patient; * and God is provoked every day.

13 If a man will not turn, he will whet his sword; * he hath bent his bow, and made it ready.

14 He hath prepared for him the instruments of death; * he ordaineth his arrows against the persecutors.

15 Behold, the ungodly travaileth with iniquity; * he hath conceived mischief, and brought forth falsehood.

16 He hath graven and digged up a pit, * and is fallen himself into the destruction that he made for other.

17 For his travail shall come upon his own head, * and his wickedness shall fall on his own pate.

18 I will give thanks unto the LORD, according to his righteousness; * and I will praise the Name of the LORD Most High.

**Psalm 8.** *Domine, Dominus noster.*

O LORD our Governor, how excellent is thy Name in all the world; * thou that hast set thy glory above the heavens!

2 Out of the mouth of very babes and sucklings hast thou ordained strength, because of thine enemies, * that thou mightest still the enemy and the avenger.

3 When I consider thy heavens, even the work of thy fingers; * the moon and the stars which thou hast ordained;

4 What is man, that thou art mindful of him? * and the son of man,

that        thou        visitest        him?
5 Thou madest him lower than the angels, * to crown him with
glory           and         worship.
6 Thou makest him to have dominion of the works of thy hands; *
and thou hast put all things in subjection under his feet:
7 All sheep and oxen; * yea, and the beasts of the field;
8 The fowls of the air, and the fishes of the sea; * and whatsoever
walketh    through    the    paths    of    the    seas.
9 O LORD our Governor, * how excellent is thy Name in all the
world!

**Psalm**        **9**.        *Confitebor*        *tibi.*
I WILL give thanks unto thee, O LORD, with my whole heart; * I
will    speak    of    all    thy    marvelous    works.
2 I will be glad and rejoice in thee; * yea, my songs will I make of
thy    Name,    O    thou    Most    Highest.
3 While mine enemies are driven back, * they shall fall and perish
at        thy        presence.
4 For thou hast maintained my right and my cause; * thou art set in
the    throne    that    judgest    right.
5 Thou hast rebuked the heathen, and destroyed the ungodly; *
thou    hast    put    out    their    name    for    ever    and    ever.
6 O thou enemy, thy destructions are come to a perpetual end; *
even as the cities which thou hast destroyed, whose memorial is
perished        with        them.
7 But the LORD shall endure for ever; * he hath also prepared his
seat        for        judgment.
8 For he shall judge the world in righteousness, * and minister true
judgment    unto    the    people.
9 The LORD also will be a defense for the oppressed, * even a
refuge    in    due    time    of    trouble.
10 And they that know thy Name will put their trust in thee; * for
thou,    LORD,    hast    never    failed    them    that    seek    thee.
11 O praise the LORD which dwelleth in Sion; * show the people
of        his        doings.
12 For when he maketh inquisition for blood, he remembereth
them,    *    and    forgetteth    not    the    complaint    of    the    poor.
13 Have mercy upon me, O LORD; consider the trouble which I
suffer of them that hate me, * thou that liftest me up from the gates

of                                                                      death;
14 That I may show all thy praises within the gates of the daughter
of     Sion:     *     I     will     rejoice     in     thy     salvation.
15 The heathen are sunk down in the pit that they made; * in the
same net which they hid privily is their foot taken.
16 The LORD is known to execute judgment; * the ungodly is
trapped     in     the     work     of     his     own     hands.
17 The wicked shall be turned to destruction, * and all the people
that                              forget                              God.
18 For the poor shall not alway be forgotten; * the patient abiding
of     the     meek     shall     not     perish     for     ever.
19 Up, LORD, and let not man have the upper hand; * let the
heathen     be     judged     in     thy     sight.
20 Put them in fear, O LORD, * that the heathen may know
themselves              to              be              but              men.

**Psalm 10**. *Ut quid, Domine ?*
WHY standest thou so far off, O LORD, * and hidest thy face in
the          needful          time          of          trouble?
2 The ungodly, for his own lust, doth persecute the poor: * let them
be     taken     in     the     crafty     wiliness     that     they     have     imagined.
3 For the ungodly hath made boast of his own heart's desire, * and
speaketh     good     of     the     covetous,     whom     the     LORD     abhorreth.
4 The ungodly is so proud, that he careth not for God, * neither is
God          in          all          his          thoughts.
5 His ways are alway grievous; * thy judgments are far above out
of     his     sight,     and     therefore     defieth     he     all     his     enemies.
6 For he hath said in his heart, Tush, I shall never be cast down, *
there     shall     no     harm     happen     unto     me.
7 His mouth is full of cursing, deceit, and fraud; * under his tongue
is              ungodliness              and              vanity.
8 He sitteth lurking in the thievish corners of the streets, * and
privily in his lurking dens doth he murder the innocent; his eyes
are          set          against          the          poor.
9 For he lieth waiting secretly; even as a lion lurketh he in his den,
*          that          he          may          ravish          the          poor.
10 He doth ravish the poor, * when he getteth him into his net.
11 He falleth down, and humbleth himself, * that the congregation
of     the     poor     may     fall     into     the     hands     of     his     captains.

12 He hath said in his heart, Tush, God hath forgotten; * he hideth away his face, and he will never see it.
13 Arise, O LORD God, and lift up thine hand; * forget not the poor.
14 Wherefore should the wicked blaspheme God, * while he doth say in his heart, Tush, thou God carest not for it?
15 Surely thou hast seen it; * for thou beholdest ungodliness and wrong, that thou mayest take the matter into thy hand.
16 The poor committeth himself unto thee; * for thou art the helper of the friendless.
17 Break thou the power of the ungodly and malicious; * search out his ungodliness, until thou find none.
18 The LORD is King for ever and ever, * and the heathen are perished out of the land.
19 LORD, thou hast heard the desire of the poor; * thou preparest their heart, and thine ear hearkeneth;
20 To help the fatherless and poor unto their right, * that the man of the earth be no more exalted against them.

**Psalm 11.** *In Domino confido.*
IN the LORD put I my trust; * how say ye then to my soul, that she should flee as a bird unto the hill?
2 For lo, the ungodly bend their bow, and make ready their arrows within the quiver, * that they may privily shoot at them which are true of heart.
3 If the foundations be destroyed, * what can the righteous do?
4 The LORD is in his holy temple; * the LORD's seat is in heaven.
5 His eyes consider the poor, * and his eyelids try the children of men.
6 The LORD approveth the righteous: * but the ungodly, and him that delighteth in wickedness, doth his soul abhor.
7 Upon the ungodly he shall rain snares, fire and brimstone, storm and tempest: * this shall be their portion to drink.
8 For the righteous LORD loveth righteousness; * his countenance will behold the thing that is just.

**Psalm 12.** *Salvum me fac.*
HELP me, LORD, for there is not one godly man left; * for the faithful are minished from among the children of men.

2 They talk of vanity every one with his neighbor; * they do but flatter with their lips, and dissemble in their double heart.
3 The LORD shall root out all deceitful lips, * and the tongue that speaketh proud things;
4 Which have said, With our tongue will we prevail; * we are they that ought to speak; who is lord over us?
5 Now, for the comfortless troubles' sake of the needy, * and because of the deep sighing of the poor,
6 I will up, saith the LORD; * and will help every one from him that swelleth against him, and will set him at rest.
7 The words of the LORD are pure words; * even as the silver which from the earth is tried, and purified seven times in the fire.
8 Thou shalt keep them, O LORD; * thou shalt preserve them from this generation for ever.
9 The ungodly walk on every side: * when they are exalted, the children of men are put to rebuke.

**Psalm 13.** *Usquequo, Domine?*
HOW long wilt thou forget me, O LORD; for ever? * how long wilt thou hide thy face from me?
2 How long shall I seek counsel in my soul, and be so vexed in my heart? * how long shall mine enemy triumph over me?
3 Consider, and hear me, O LORD my God; * lighten mine eyes, that I sleep not in death;
4 Lest mine enemy say, I have prevailed against him: * for if I be cast down, they that trouble me will rejoice at it.
5 But my trust is in thy mercy, * and my heart is joyful in thy salvation.
6 I will sing of the LORD, because he hath dealt so lovingly with me; * yea, I will praise the Name of the Lord Most Highest.

**Psalm 14.** *Dixit insipiens.*
THE fool hath said in his heart, * There is no God.
2 They are corrupt, and become abominable in their doings; * there is none that doeth good, no not one.
3 The LORD looked down from heaven upon the children of men, * to see if there were any that would understand, and seek after God.
4 But they are all gone out of the way, they are altogether become

abominable; * there is none that doeth good, no not one.
5 Have they no knowledge, that they are all such workers of mischief, * eating up my people as it were bread, and call not upon the LORD?
6 There were they brought in great fear, even where no fear was; * for God is in the generation of the righteous.
7 As for you, ye have made a mock at the counsel of the poor; * because he putteth his trust in the LORD.
8 Who shall give salvation unto Israel out of Sion? * When the LORD turneth the captivity of his people, then shall Jacob rejoice, and Israel shall be glad.

**Psalm 15.** *Domine, quis habitabit?*
LORD, who shall dwell in thy tabernacle? * or who shall rest upon thy holy hill?
2 Even he that leadeth an uncorrupt life, * and doeth the thing which is right, and speaketh the truth from his heart.
3 He that hath used no deceit in his tongue, nor done evil to his neighbor, * and hath not slandered his neighbor.
4 He that setteth not by himself, but is lowly in his own eyes, * and maketh much of them that fear the LORD.
5 He that sweareth unto his neighbor, and disappointeth him not, * though it were to his own hindrance.
6 He that hath not given his money upon usury, * nor taken reward against the innocent.
7 Whoso doeth these things * shall never fall.

**Psalm 16.** *Conserva me, Domine.*
PRESERVE me, O God; * for in thee have I put my trust.
2 O my soul, thou hast said unto the LORD, * Thou art my God; I have no good like unto thee.
3 All my delight is upon the saints that are in the earth, * and upon such as excel in virtue.
4 But they that run after another god * shall have great trouble.
5 Their drink-offerings of blood will I not offer, * neither make mention of their names within my lips.
6 The LORD himself is the portion of mine inheritance, and of my cup; * thou shalt maintain my lot.
7 The lot is fallen unto me in a fair ground; * yea, I have a goodly

heritage.

8 I will thank the LORD for giving me warning; * my reins also chasten me in the night season.

9 I have set the LORD alway before me; * for he is on my right hand, therefore I shall not fall.

10 Wherefore my heart is glad, and my glory rejoiceth: * my flesh also shall rest in hope.

11 For why? thou shalt not leave my soul in hell; * neither shalt thou suffer thy Holy One to see corruption.

12 Thou shalt show me the path of life: in thy presence is the fulness of joy, * and at thy right hand there is pleasure for evermore.

**Psalm** **17.** *Exaudi,* *Domine.*

HEAR the right, O LORD, consider my complaint, * and hearken unto my prayer, that goeth not out of feigned lips.

2 Let my sentence come forth from thy presence; * and let thine eyes look upon the thing that is equal.

3 Thou hast proved and visited mine heart in the night season; thou hast tried me, and shalt find no wickedness in me; * for I am utterly purposed that my mouth shall not offend.

4 As for the works of men, * by the word of thy lips I have kept me from the ways of the destroyer.

5 O hold thou up my goings in thy paths, * that my footsteps slip not.

6 I have called upon thee, O God, for thou shalt hear me: * incline thine ear to me, and hearken unto my words.

7 Show thy marvelous loving-kindness, thou that art the Savior of them which put their trust in thee, * from such as resist thy right hand.

8 Keep me as the apple of an eye; * hide me under the shadow of thy wings,

9 From the ungodly, that trouble me; * mine enemies compass me round about, to take away my soul.

10 They are inclosed in their own fat, * and their mouth speaketh proud things.

11 They lie waiting in our way on every side, * watching to cast us down to the ground;

12 Like as a lion that is greedy of his prey, * and as it were a lion's

whelp         lurking        in        secret        places.
13 Up, LORD, disappoint him, and cast him down; * deliver my
soul      from      the      ungodly,      by      thine      own      sword;
14 Yea, by thy hand, O LORD; from the men of the evil world; *
which have their portion in this life, whose bellies thou fillest with
thy                         hid                         treasure.
15 They have children at their desire, * and leave the rest of their
substance             for             their             babes.
16 But as for me, I shall behold thy presence in righteousness; *
and when I awake up after thy likeness, I shall be satisfied.

**Psalm         18**.      *Diligam         te,         Domine.*
I WILL love thee, O LORD, my strength. * The LORD is my stony
rock,                and                my                defense;
2 My Savior, my God, and my might, in whom I will trust; * my
buckler,      the      horn      also      of      my      salvation,      and      my      refuge.
3 I will call upon the LORD, which is worthy to be praised; * so
shall      I      be      safe      from      mine      enemies.
4 The sorrows of death compassed me, * and the overflowings of
ungodliness             made             me             afraid.
5 The pains of hell came about me; * the snares of death overtook
me.
6 In my trouble I called upon the LORD, * and complained unto my
God:
7 So he heard my voice out of his holy temple, * and my complaint
came      before      him;      it      entered      even      into      his      ears.
8 The earth trembled and quaked, * the very foundations also of
the hills shook, and were removed, because he was wroth.
9 There went a smoke out in his presence, * and a consuming fire
out    of    his    mouth,    so    that    coals    were    kindled    at    it.
10 He bowed the heavens also, and came down, * and it was dark
under                         his                         feet.
11 He rode upon the Cherubim, and did fly; * he came flying upon
the             wings             of             the             wind.
12 He made darkness his secret place, * his pavilion round about
him    with    dark    water,    and    thick    clouds    to    cover    him.
13 At the brightness of his presence his clouds removed; *
hailstones             and             coals             of             fire.
14 The LORD also thundered out of heaven, and the Highest gave

his thunder; * hailstones and coals of fire.
15 He sent out his arrows, and scattered them; * he cast forth lightnings, and destroyed them.
16 The springs of waters were seen, and the foundations of the round world
were discovered, * at thy chiding, O LORD, at the blasting of the breath of thy displeasure.
17 He sent down from on high to fetch me, * and took me out of many waters.
18 He delivered me from my strongest enemy, and from them which hate me; * for they were too mighty for me.
19 They came upon me in the day of my trouble; * but the LORD was my upholder.
20 He brought me forth also into a place of liberty; * he brought me forth, even because he had a favor unto me.
21 The LORD rewarded me after my righteous dealing, * according to the cleanness of my hands did he recompense me.
22 Because I have kept the ways of the LORD, * and have not forsaken my God, as the wicked doth.
23 For I have an eye unto all his laws, * and will not cast out his commandments from me.
24 I was also uncorrupt before him, * and eschewed mine own wickedness.
25 Therefore the LORD rewarded me after my righteous dealing, * and according unto the cleanness of my hands in his eyesight.
26 With the holy thou shalt be holy, * and with a perfect man thou shalt be perfect.
27 With the clean thou shalt be clean, * and with the froward thou shalt be froward.
28 For thou shalt save the people that are in adversity, and shalt bring down the high looks of the proud.
29 Thou also shalt light my candle; * the LORD my God shall make my darkness to be light.
30 For in thee I shall discomfit an host of men, * and with the help of my God I shall leap over the wall.
31 The way of God is an undefiled way: * the word of the LORD also is tried in the fire; he is the defender of all them that put their trust in him.
32 For who is God, but the LORD? * or who hath any strength,

except                         our                         God?
33 It is God that girdeth me with strength of war, * and maketh my
way                                                         perfect.
34 He maketh my feet like harts' feet, * and setteth me up on high.
35 He teacheth mine hands to fight, * and mine arms shall bend
even          a          bow          of          steel.
36 Thou hast given me the defense of thy salvation; * thy right
hand also shall hold me up, and thy loving correction shall make
me                                                          great.
37 Thou shalt make room enough under me for to go, * that my
footsteps          shall          not          slide.
38 I will follow upon mine enemies, and overtake them; * neither
will I turn again till I have destroyed them.
39 I will smite them, that they shall not be able to stand, * but fall
under                         my                         feet.
40 Thou hast girded me with strength unto the battle; * thou shalt
throw     down     mine     enemies     under     me.
41 Thou hast made mine enemies also to turn their backs upon me,
*     and     I     shall     destroy     them     that     hate     me.
42 They shall cry, but there shall be none to help them; * yea, even
unto the LORD shall they cry, but he shall not hear them.
43 I will beat them as small as the dust before the wind: * I will
cast     them     out     as     the     clay     in     the     streets.
44 Thou shalt deliver me from the strivings of the people, * and
thou shalt make me the head of the nations; a people whom I have
not          known          shall          serve          me.
45 As soon as they hear of me, they shall obey me; * the strangers
shall          feign          obedience          unto          me.
46 The strangers shall fail, * and come trembling out of their
strongholds.
47 The LORD liveth; and blessed be my strong helper, * and
praised     be     the     God     of     my     salvation;
48 Even the God that seeth that I be avenged, * and subdueth the
people                         unto                         me.
49 It is he that delivereth me from my cruel enemies, and setteth
me up above mine adversaries: * thou shalt rid me from the wicked
man.
50 For this cause will I give thanks unto thee, O LORD, among the
Gentiles,     *     and     sing     praises     unto     thy     Name.

51 Great prosperity giveth he unto his King, * and showeth loving-kindness unto David his anointed, and unto his seed for evermore.

**Psalm**        **19**.        *Caeli*        *enarrant.*
THE heavens declare the glory of God; * and the firmament showeth        his        handy-work.
2 One day telleth another; * and one night certifieth another.
3 There is neither speech nor language; * but their voices are heard among        them.
4 Their sound is gone out into all lands; * and their words into the ends of the world.
5 In them hath he set a tabernacle for the sun; * which cometh forth as a bridegroom out of his chamber, and rejoiceth as a giant to        run        his        course.
6 It goeth forth from the uttermost part of the heaven, and runneth about unto the end of it again; * and there is nothing hid from the heat        thereof.
7 The law of the LORD is an undefiled law, converting the soul; * the testimony of the LORD is sure, and giveth wisdom unto the simple.
8 The statutes of the LORD are right, and rejoice the heart; * the commandment of the LORD is pure, and giveth light unto the eyes.
9 The fear of the LORD is clean, and endureth for ever; * the judgments of the LORD are true, and righteous altogether.
10 More to be desired are they than gold, yea, than much fine gold; * sweeter also than honey, and the honeycomb.
11 Moreover, by them is thy servant taught; * and in keeping of them        there        is        great        reward.
12 Who can tell how oft he offendeth? * O cleanse thou me from my        secret        faults.
13 Keep thy servant also from presumptuous sins, lest they get the dominion over me; * so shall I be undefiled, and innocent from the great        offense.
14 Let the words of my mouth, and the meditation of my heart, be alway acceptable in thy sight, * O LORD, my strength and my redeemer.

**Psalm**        **20**.        *Exaudiat*        *te*        *Dominus.*
THE LORD hear thee in the day of trouble; * the Name of the God

of          Jacob          defend          thee:
2 Send thee help from the sanctuary, * and strengthen thee out of Sion:
3 Remember all thy offerings, * and accept thy burnt-sacrifice:
4 Grant thee thy heart's desire, * and fulfill all thy mind.
5 We will rejoice in thy salvation, and triumph in the Name of the Lord   our   God:   *   the   LORD   perform   all   thy   petitions.
6 Now know I that the LORD helpeth his anointed, and will hear him from his holy heaven, * even with the wholesome strength of his right hand.
7 Some put their trust in chariots, and some in horses; * but we will   remember   the   Name   of   the   LORD   our   God.
8 They are brought down and fallen; * but we are risen and stand upright.
9 Save, LORD; and hear us, O King of heaven, * when we call upon                                                              thee.

**Psalm   21**.   *Domine,   in   virtute   tua.*
THE King shall rejoice in thy strength, O LORD; * exceeding glad shall       he       be       of       thy       salvation.
2 Thou hast given him his heart's desire, * and hast not denied him the          request          of          his          lips.
3 For thou shalt meet him with the blessings of goodness, * and shalt set a crown of pure gold upon his head.
4 He asked life of thee; and thou gavest him a long life, * even for ever                       and                       ever.
5 His honor is great in thy salvation; * glory and great worship shalt          thou          lay          upon          him.
6 For thou shalt give him everlasting felicity, * and make him glad with       the       joy       of       thy       countenance.
7 And why? because the King putteth his trust in the LORD; * and in the   mercy   of   the   Most   Highest   he   shall   not   miscarry.
8 All thine enemies shall feel thine hand; * thy right hand shall find        out        them        that        hate        thee.
9 Thou shalt make them like a fiery oven in time of thy wrath: * the LORD shall destroy them in his displeasure, and the fire shall consume                                                          them.
10 Their fruit shalt thou root out of the earth, * and their seed from

among the children of men.
11 For they intended mischief against thee, * and imagined such a device as they are not able to perform.
12 Therefore shalt thou put them to flight, * and the strings of thy bow shalt thou make ready against the face of them.
13 Be thou exalted, LORD, in thine own strength; * so will we sing, and praise thy power.

**Psalm 22.** *Deus, Deus meus.*
MY God, my God, look upon me; why hast thou forsaken me? * and art so far from my health, and from the words of my complaint?
2 O my God, I cry in the day-time, but thou hearest not; * and in the night season also I take no rest.
3 And thou continuest holy, * O thou Worship of Israel.
4 Our fathers hoped in thee; * they trusted in thee, and thou didst deliver them.
5 They called upon thee, and were holpen; * they put their trust in thee, and were not confounded.
6 But as for me, I am a worm, and no man; * a very scorn of men, and the outcast of the people.
7 All they that see me laugh me to scorn; * they shoot out their lips, and shake their heads, saying,
8 He trusted in the LORD, that he would deliver him; * let him deliver him, if he will have him.
9 But thou art he that took me out of my mother's womb; * thou wast my hope, when I hanged yet upon my mother's breasts.
10 I have been left unto thee ever since I was born; * thou art my God even from my mother's womb.
11 O go not from me; for trouble is hard at hand, * and there is none to help me.
12 Many oxen are come about me; * fat bulls of Bashan close me in on every side.
13 They gape upon me with their mouths, * as it were a ramping and a roaring lion.
14 I am poured out like water, and all my bones are out of joint; * my heart also in the midst of my body is even like melting wax.
15 My strength is dried up like a potsherd, and my tongue cleaveth to my gums, * and thou bringest me into the dust of death.

16 For many dogs are come about me, * and the council of the
wicked          layeth          siege          against          me.
17 They pierced my hands and my feet: I may tell all my bones: *
they     stand     staring     and     looking     upon     me.
18 They part my garments among them, * and cast lots upon my
vesture.
19 But be not thou far from me, O LORD; * thou art my succor,
haste          thee          to          help          me.
20 Deliver my soul from the sword, * my darling from the power
of                          the                          dog.
21 Save me from the lion's mouth; * thou hast heard me also from
among     the     horns     of     the     unicorns.
22 I will declare thy Name unto my brethren; * in the midst of the
congregation          will          I          praise          thee.
23 O praise the LORD, ye that fear him: * magnify him, all ye of
the  seed  of  Jacob;  and  fear  him,  all  ye  seed  of  Israel.
24 For he hath not despised nor abhorred the low estate of the
poor; * he hath not hid his face from him; but when he called unto
him          he          heard          him.
25 My praise is of thee in the great congregation; * my vows will I
perform     in     the     sight     of     them     that     fear     him.
26 The poor shall eat, and be satisfied; they that seek after the
LORD shall praise him: * your heart shall live for ever.
27 All the ends of the world shall remember themselves, and be
turned unto the LORD; * and all the kindreds of the nations shall
worship                    before                    him.
28 For the kingdom is the LORD's, * and he is the Governor among
the                                                  nations.
29 All such as be fat upon earth * have eaten, and worshipped.
30 All they that go down into the dust shall kneel before him; *
and     no     man     hath     quickened     his     own     soul.
31 My seed shall serve him: * they shall be counted unto the Lord
for                          a                          generation.
32 They shall come, and shall declare his righteousness * unto a
people that shall be born, whom the Lord hath made.

**Psalm          23.**          *Dominus          regit          me.*
THE LORD is my shepherd; * therefore can I lack nothing.
2 He shall feed me in a green pasture, * and lead me forth beside

the                 waters                 of                 comfort.
3 He shall convert my soul, * and bring me forth in the paths of
righteousness for his Name's sake.
4 Yea, though I walk through the valley of the shadow of death, I
will fear no evil; * for thou art with me; thy rod and thy staff
comfort                                                               me.
5 Thou shalt prepare a table before me in the presence of them that
trouble me; * thou hast anointed my head with oil, and my cup
shall                         be                         full.
6 Surely thy loving-kindness and mercy shall follow me all the
days of my life; * and I will dwell in the house of the LORD for
ever.

**Psalm                 24.**                 *Domini            est            terra.*
THE earth is the LORD's, and all that therein is; * the compass of
the       world,       and       they       that       dwell       therein.
2 For he hath founded it upon the seas, * and stablished it upon the
floods.
3 Who shall ascend into the hill of the LORD? * or who shall rise
up                 in                 his                 holy                 place?
4 Even he that hath clean hands, and a pure heart; * and that hath
not lift up his mind unto vanity, nor sworn to deceive his neighbor.
5 He shall receive the blessing from the LORD, * and righteousness
from       the       God       of       his       salvation.
6 This is the generation of them that seek him; * even of them that
seek       thy       face,       O       God       of       Jacob.
7 Lift up your heads, O ye gates; and be ye lift up, ye everlasting
doors;       *       and       the       King       of       glory       shall       come       in.
8 Who is this King of glory? * It is the LORD strong and mighty,
even the LORD mighty in battle.
9 Lift up your heads, O ye gates; and be ye lift up, ye everlasting
doors;       *       and       the       King       of       glory       shall       come       in.
10 Who is this King of glory? * Even the LORD of hosts, he is the
King of glory.

**Psalm                 25.**                 *Ad            te,            Domine,            levavi.*
UNTO thee, O LORD, will I lift up my soul; my God, I have put
my trust in thee: * O let me not be confounded, neither let mine
enemies                 triumph                 over                 me.

2 For all they that hope in thee shall not be ashamed; * but such as transgress without a cause shall be put to confusion.
3 Show me thy ways, O LORD, * and teach me thy paths.
4 Lead me forth in thy truth, and learn me: * for thou art the God of my salvation; in thee hath been my hope all the day long.
5 Call to remembrance, O LORD, thy tender mercies, * and thy loving-kindnesses, which have been ever of old.
6 O remember not the sins and offenses of my youth; * but according to thy mercy think thou upon me, O LORD, for thy goodness.
7 Gracious and righteous is the LORD; * therefore will he teach sinners in the way.
8 Them that are meek shall he guide in judgment; * and such as are gentle, them shall he learn his way.
9 All the paths of the LORD are mercy and truth, * unto such as keep his covenant and his testimonies.
10 For thy Name's sake, O LORD, * be merciful unto my sin; for it is great.
11 What man is he that feareth the LORD? * him shall he teach in the way that he shall choose.
12 His soul shall dwell at ease, * and his seed shall inherit the land.
13 The secret of the LORD is among them that fear him; * and he will show them his covenant.
14 Mine eyes are ever looking unto the LORD; * for he shall pluck my feet out of the net.
15 Turn thee unto me, and have mercy upon me; * for I am desolate, and in misery.
16 The sorrows of my heart are enlarged: * O bring thou me out of my troubles.
17 Look upon my adversity and misery, * and forgive me all my sin.
18 Consider mine enemies, how many they are; * and they bear a tyrannous hate against me.
19 O keep my soul, and deliver me: * let me not be confounded, for I have put my trust in thee.
20 Let perfectness and righteous dealing wait upon me; * for my hope hath been in thee.
21 Deliver Israel, O God, * out of all his troubles.

**Psalm 26.** *Judica me, Domine.*

BE thou my Judge, O LORD, for I have walked innocently: * my trust hath been also in the LORD, therefore shall I not fall.

2 Examine me, O LORD, and prove me; * try out my reins and my heart.

3 For thy loving-kindness is ever before mine eyes; * and I will walk in thy truth.

4 I have not dwelt with vain persons; * neither will I have fellowship with the deceitful.

5 I have hated the congregation of the wicked; * and will not sit among the ungodly.

6 I will wash my hands in innocency, O LORD; * and so will I go to thine altar;

7 That I may show the voice of thanksgiving, * and tell of all thy wondrous works.

8 LORD, I have loved the habitation of thy house, * and the place where thine honor dwelleth.

9 O shut not up my soul with the sinners, * nor my life with the blood-thirsty;

10 In whose hands is wickedness, * and their right hand is full of gifts.

11 But as for me, I will walk innocently: * O deliver me, and be merciful unto me.

12 My foot standeth right: * I will praise the LORD in the congregations.

**Psalm 27.** *Dominus illuminatio.*

THE LORD is my light and my salvation; whom then shall I fear? * the LORD is the strength of my life; of whom then shall I be afraid?

2 When the wicked, even mine enemies and my foes, came upon me to eat up my flesh, * they stumbled and fell.

3 Though an host of men were laid against me, yet shall not my heart be afraid; * and though there rose up war against me, yet will I put my trust in him.

4 One thing have I desired of the LORD, which I will require; * even that I may dwell in the house of the LORD all the days of my life, to behold the fair beauty of the LORD, and to visit his temple.

5 For in the time of trouble he shall hide me in his tabernacle; * yea, in the secret place of his dwelling shall he hide me, and set me

up upon a rock of stone.

6 And now shall he lift up mine head * above mine enemies round about me.

7 Therefore will I offer in his dwelling an oblation, with great gladness: * I will sing and speak praises unto the LORD.

8 Hearken unto my voice, O LORD, when I cry unto thee; * have mercy upon me, and hear me.

9 My heart hath talked of thee, Seek ye my face: * Thy face, LORD, will I seek.

10 O hide not thou thy face from me, * nor cast thy servant away in displeasure.

11 Thou hast been my succor; * leave me not, neither forsake me, O God of my salvation.

12 When my father and my mother forsake me, * the LORD taketh me up.

13 Teach me thy way, O LORD, * and lead me in the right way, because of mine enemies.

14 Deliver me not over into the will of mine adversaries: * for there are false witnesses risen up against me, and such as speak wrong.

15 I should utterly have fainted, * but that I believe verily to see the goodness of the LORD in the land of the living.

16 O tarry thou the LORD's leisure; * be strong, and he shall comfort thine heart; and put thou thy trust in the LORD.

**Psalm 28.** *Ad te, Domine.*

UNTO thee will I cry, O LORD, my strength: * think no scorn of me; lest, if thou make as though thou hearest not, I become like them that go down into the pit.

2 Hear the voice of my humble petitions, when I cry unto thee; * when I hold up my hands towards the mercy seat of thy holy temple.

3 O pluck me not away, neither destroy me with the ungodly and wicked doers, * which speak friendly to their neighbors, but imagine mischief in their hearts.

4 Reward them according to their deeds, * and according to the wickedness of their own inventions.

5 Recompense them after the work of their hands; * pay them that they have deserved.

6 For they regard not in their mind the works of the LORD, nor the operation of his hands; * therefore shall he break them down, and not build them up.

7 Praised be the LORD; * for he hath heard the voice of my humble                                                                  petitions.

8 The LORD is my strength, and my shield; my heart hath trusted in him, and I am helped; * therefore my heart danceth for joy, and in my           song           will           I           praise           him.

9 The LORD is my strength, * and he is the wholesome defense of his                                                                  anointed.

10 O save thy people, and give thy blessing unto thine inheritance: * feed them, and set them up for ever.

**Psalm           29.**           *Afferte*           *Domino.*

ASCRIBE unto the LORD, O ye mighty, * ascribe unto the LORD worship                             and                             strength.

2 Ascribe unto the LORD the honor due unto his Name; * worship the           LORD           with           holy           worship.

3 The voice of the LORD is upon the waters; * it is the glorious God           that           maketh           the           thunder.

4 It is the LORD that ruleth the sea; the voice of the LORD is mighty in operation; * the voice of the LORD is a glorious voice.

5 The voice of the LORD breaketh the cedar-trees; * yea, the LORD breaketh           the           cedars           of           Lebanon.

6 He maketh them also to skip like a calf; * Lebanon also, and Sirion,           like           a           young           unicorn.

7 The voice of the LORD divideth the flames of fire; the voice of the LORD shaketh the wilderness; * yea, the LORD shaketh the wilderness                             of                             Kadesh.

8 The voice of the LORD maketh the hinds to bring forth young, and strippeth bare the forests: * in his temple doth every thing speak           of           his           honor.

9 The LORD sitteth above the water-flood, * and the LORD remaineth           a           King           for           ever.

10 The LORD shall give strength unto his people; * the LORD shall give his people the blessing of peace.

**Psalm           30.**           *Exaltabo           te,           Domine.*

I WILL magnify thee, O LORD; for thou hast set me up, * and not

made my foes to triumph over me.
2 O LORD my God, I cried unto thee; * and thou hast healed me.
3 Thou, LORD, hast brought my soul out of hell: * thou hast kept my life, that I should not go down into the pit.
4 Sing praises unto the LORD, O ye saints of his; * and give thanks unto him, for a remembrance of his holiness.
5 For his wrath endureth but the twinkling of an eye, and in his pleasure is life; * heaviness may endure for a night, but joy cometh in the morning.
6 And in my prosperity I said, I shall never be removed: * thou, LORD, of thy goodness, hast made my hill so strong.
7 Thou didst turn thy face from me, * and I was troubled.
8 Then cried I unto thee, O LORD; * and gat me to my LORD right humbly.
9 What profit is there in my blood, * when I go down into the pit?
10 Shall the dust give thanks unto thee? * or shall it declare thy truth?
11 Hear, O LORD, and have mercy upon me; * LORD, be thou my helper.
12 Thou hast turned my heaviness into joy; * thou hast put off my sackcloth, and girded me with gladness:
13 Therefore shall every good man sing of thy praise without ceasing. * O my God, I will give thanks unto thee for ever.

**Psalm 31.** *In te, Domine, speravi.*
IN thee, O LORD, have I put my trust; let me never be put to confusion; * deliver me in thy righteousness.
2 Bow down thine ear to me; * make haste to deliver me.
3 And be thou my strong rock, and house of defense, * that thou mayest save me.
4 For thou art my strong rock, and my castle: * be thou also my guide, and lead me for thy Name's sake.
5 Draw me out of the net that they have laid privily for me; * for thou art my strength.
6 Into thy hands I commend my spirit; * for thou hast redeemed me, O LORD, thou God of truth.
7 I have hated them that hold of lying vanities, * and my trust hath been in the LORD.
8 I will be glad and rejoice in thy mercy; * for thou hast considered

my trouble, and hast known my soul in adversities.
9 Thou hast not shut me up into the hand of the enemy; * but hast set my feet in a large room.
10 Have mercy upon me, O LORD, for I am in trouble, * and mine eye is consumed for very heaviness; yea, my soul and my body.
11 For my life is waxen old with heaviness, * and my years with mourning.
12 My strength faileth me, because of mine iniquity, * and my bones are consumed.
13 I became a reproach among all mine enemies, but especially among my neighbors; * and they of mine acquaintance were afraid of me; and they that did see me without, conveyed themselves from me.
14 I am clean forgotten as a dead man out of mind; * I am become like a broken vessel.
15 For I have heard the blasphemy of the multitude, and fear is on every side; * while they conspire together against me, and take their counsel to take away my life.
16 But my hope hath been in thee, O LORD; * I have said, Thou art my God.
17 My times are in thy hand; deliver me from the hand of mine enemies, * and from them that persecute me.
18 Show thy servant the light of thy countenance, * and save me for thy mercy's sake.
19 Let me not be confounded, O LORD, for I have called upon thee; * let the ungodly be put to confusion, and be put to silence in the grave.
20 Let the lying lips be put to silence, * which cruelly, disdainfully, and despitefully speak against the righteous.
21 O how plentiful is thy goodness, which thou hast laid up for them that fear thee, * and that thou hast prepared for them that put their trust in thee, even before the sons of men!
22 Thou shalt hide them in the covert of thine own presence from the plottings of men: * thou shalt keep them secretly in thy tabernacle from the strife of tongues.
23 Thanks be to the LORD; * for he hath showed me marvelous great kindness in a strong city.
24 But in my haste I said, * I am cast out of the sight of thine eyes.
25 Nevertheless, thou heardest the voice of my prayer, * when I

cried                               unto                               thee.
26 O love the LORD, all ye his saints; * for the LORD preserveth
them that are faithful, and plenteously rewardeth the proud doer.
27 Be strong, and he shall establish your heart, * all ye that put
your trust in the LORD.

**Psalm                         32.**                    *Beati                          quorum.*
BLESSED is he whose unrighteousness is forgiven, * and whose
sin                               is                               covered.
2 Blessed is the man unto whom the LORD imputeth no sin, * and
in        whose        spirit        there        is        no        guile.
3 For whilst I held my tongue, * my bones consumed away
through             my             daily             complaining.
4 For thy hand was heavy upon me day and night, * and my
moisture      was      like      the      drought      in      summer.
5 I acknowledged my sin unto thee; * and mine unrighteousness
have                     I                     not                     hid.
6 I said, I will confess my sins unto the LORD; * and so thou
forgavest      the      wickedness      of      my      sin.
7 For this shall every one that is godly make his prayer unto thee,
in a time when thou mayest be found; * surely the great water-
floods      shall      not      come      nigh      him.
8 Thou art a place to hide me in; thou shalt preserve me from
trouble; * thou shalt compass me about with songs of deliverance.
9 I will inform thee, and teach thee in the way wherein thou shalt
go;        *        and        I        will        guide        thee        with        mine        eye.
10 Be ye not like to horse and mule, which have no understanding;
* whose mouths must be held with bit and bridle, else they will not
obey                                                             thee.
11 Great plagues remain for the ungodly; * but whoso putteth his
trust in the LORD, mercy embraceth him on every side.
12 Be glad, O ye righteous, and rejoice in the LORD; * and be
joyful,      all      ye      that      are      true      of      heart.

**Psalm                         33.**                    *Exultate,                          justi.*
REJOICE in the LORD, O ye righteous; * for it becometh well the
just                     to                     be                     thankful.
2 Praise the LORD with harp; * sing praises unto him with the lute,

and instrument of ten strings.
3 Sing unto the Lord a new song; * sing praises lustily unto him with a good courage.
4 For the word of the LORD is true; * and all his works are faithful.
5 He loveth righteousness and judgment; * the earth is full of the goodness of the LORD.
6 By the word of the LORD were the heavens made; * and all the host of them by the breath of his mouth.
7 He gathereth the waters of the sea together, as it were upon an heap; * and layeth up the deep, as in a treasure-house.
8 Let all the earth fear the LORD: * stand in awe of him, all ye that dwell in the world.
9 For he spake, and it was done; * he commanded, and it stood fast.
10 The LORD bringeth the counsel of the heathen to nought, * and maketh the devices of the people to be of none effect, and casteth out the counsels of princes.
11 The counsel of the LORD shall endure for ever, * and the thoughts of his heart from generation to generation.
12 Blessed are the people whose God is the Lord JEHOVAH; * and blessed are the folk that he hath chosen to him, to be his inheritance.
13 The LORD looketh down from heaven, and beholdeth all the children of men; * from the habitation of his dwelling, he considereth all them that dwell on the earth.
14 He fashioneth all the hearts of them, * and understandeth all their works.
15 There is no king that can be saved by the multitude of an host; * neither is any mighty man delivered by much strength.
16 A horse is counted but a vain thing to save a man; * neither shall he deliver any man by his great strength.
17 Behold, the eye of the LORD is upon them that fear him, * and upon them that put their trust in his mercy;
18 To deliver their soul from death, * and to feed them in the time of dearth.
19 Our soul hath patiently tarried for the LORD; * for he is our help and our shield.
20 For our heart shall rejoice in him; * because we have hoped in his holy Name.

21 Let thy merciful kindness, O LORD, be upon us, * like as we do put our trust in thee.

**Psalm 34.** *Benedicam Dominum.*

I WILL alway give thanks unto the LORD; * his praise shall ever be in my mouth.

2 My soul shall make her boast in the LORD; * the humble shall hear thereof, and be glad.

3 O praise the LORD with me, * and let us magnify his Name together.

4 I sought the LORD, and he heard me; * yea, he delivered me out of all my fear.

5 They had an eye unto him, and were lightened; * and their faces were not ashamed.

6 Lo, the poor crieth, and the LORD heareth him; * yea, and saveth him out of all his troubles.

7 The angel of the LORD tarrieth round about them that fear him, * and delivereth them.

8 O taste, and see, how gracious the LORD is: * blessed is the man that trusteth in him.

9 O fear the LORD, ye that are his saints; * for they that fear him lack nothing.

10 The lions do lack, and suffer hunger; * but they who seek the LORD shall want no manner of thing that is good.

11 Come, ye children, and hearken unto me; * I will teach you the fear of the LORD.

12 What man is he that lusteth to live, * and would fain see good days?

13 Keep thy tongue from evil, * and thy lips, that they speak no guile.

14 Eschew evil, and do good; * seek peace, and ensue it.

15 The eyes of the LORD are over the righteous, * and his ears are open unto their prayers.

16 The countenance of the LORD is against them that do evil, * to root out the remembrance of them from the earth.

17 The righteous cry, and the LORD heareth them, * and delivereth them out of all their troubles.

18 The LORD is nigh unto them that are of a contrite heart, * and will save such as be of an humble spirit.

19 Great are the troubles of the righteous; * but the LORD delivereth him out of all.
20 He keepeth all his bones, * so that not one of them is broken.
21 But misfortune shall slay the ungodly; * and they that hate the righteous shall be desolate.
22 The LORD delivereth the souls of his servants; * and all they that put their trust in him shall not be destitute.

**Psalm**      **35**.      *Judica,*      *Domine.*
PLEAD thou my cause, O LORD, with them that strive with me, * and fight thou against them that fight against me.
2 Lay hand upon the shield and buckler, * and stand up to help me.
3 Bring forth the spear, and stop the way against them that pursue me: * say unto my soul, I am thy salvation.
4 Let them be confounded, and put to shame, that seek after my soul; * let them be turned back, and brought to confusion, that imagine mischief for me.
5 Let them be as the dust before the wind, * and the angel of the LORD scattering them.
6 Let their way be dark and slippery, * and let the angel of the LORD pursue them.
7 For they have privily laid their net to destroy me without a cause; * yea, even without a cause have they made a pit for my soul.
8 Let a sudden destruction come upon him unawares, and his net that he hath laid privily catch himself; * that he may fall into his own mischief.
9 And my soul shall be joyful in the LORD; * it shall rejoice in his salvation.
10 All my bones shall say, LORD, who is like unto thee, who deliverest the poor from him that is too strong for him; * yea, the poor, and him that is in misery, from him that spoileth him?
11 False witnesses did rise up: * they laid to my charge things that I knew not.
12 They rewarded me evil for good, * to the great discomfort of my soul.
13 Nevertheless, when they were sick, I put on sackcloth, and humbled my soul with fasting; * and my prayer shall turn into mine own bosom.
14 I behaved myself as though it had been my friend or my

brother; * I went heavily, as one that mourneth for his mother.
15 But in mine adversity they rejoiced, and gathered themselves together; * yea, the very abjects came together against me unawares, making mouths at me, and ceased not.
16 With the flatterers were busy mockers, * who gnashed upon me with their teeth.
17 Lord, how long wilt thou look upon this? * O deliver my soul from the calamities which they bring on me, and my darling from the                                                                                              lions.
18 So will I give thee thanks in the great congregation; * I will praise            thee            among            much            people.
19 O let not them that are mine enemies triumph over me ungodly; * neither let them wink with their eyes, that hate me without a cause.
20 And why? their communing is not for peace; * but they imagine deceitful words against them that are quiet in the land.
21 They gaped upon me with their mouths, and said, * Fie on thee! fie      on      thee!      we      saw      it      with      our      eyes.
22 This thou hast seen, O LORD; * hold not thy tongue then; go not far            from            me,            O            Lord.
23 Awake, and stand up to judge my quarrel; * avenge thou my cause,            my            God            and            my            Lord.
24 Judge me, O LORD my God, according to thy righteousness; * and      let      them      not      triumph      over      me.
25 Let them not say in their hearts, There! there! so would we have it;      *      neither      let      them      say,      We      have      devoured      him.
26 Let them be put to confusion and shame together, that rejoice at my trouble; * let them be clothed with rebuke and dishonor, that boast            themselves            against            me.
27 Let them be glad and rejoice, that favor my righteous dealing; * yea, let them say alway, Blessed be the LORD, who hath pleasure in            the            prosperity            of            his            servant.
28 And as for my tongue, it shall be talking of thy righteousness, * and of thy praise, all the day long.

**Psalm            36.**            *Dixit            injustus.*
MY heart showeth me the wickedness of the ungodly, * that there is      no      fear      of      God      before      his      eyes.
2 For he flattereth himself in his own sight, * until his abominable

sin                 be                 found                out.
3 The words of his mouth are unrighteous and full of deceit: * he
hath left off to behave himself wisely, and to do good.
4 He imagineth mischief upon his bed, and hath set himself in no
good way; * neither doth he abhor any thing that is evil.
5 Thy mercy, O LORD, reacheth unto the heavens, * and thy
faithfulness             unto             the             clouds.
6 Thy righteousness standeth like the strong mountains: * thy
judgments         are         like         the         great         deep.
7 Thou, LORD, shalt save both man and beast: how excellent is thy
mercy, O God! * and the children of men shall put their trust under
the             shadow             of             thy             wings.
8 They shall be satisfied with the plenteousness of thy house; * and
thou shalt give them drink of thy pleasures, as out of the river.
9 For with thee is the well of life; * and in thy light shall we see
light.
10 O continue forth thy loving-kindness unto them that know thee,
* and thy righteousness unto them that are true of heart.
11 O let not the foot of pride come against me; * and let not the
hand     of     the     ungodly     cast     me     down.
12 There are they fallen, all that work wickedness; * they are cast
down, and shall not be able to stand.

**Psalm**               **37.**               *Noli*               *aemulari.*
FRET not thyself because of the ungodly; * neither be thou
envious             against             the             evil             doers.
2 For they shall soon be cut down like the grass, * and be withered
even             as             the             green             herb.
3 Put thou thy trust in the LORD, and be doing good; * dwell in the
land,     and     verily     thou     shalt     be     fed.
4 Delight thou in the LORD, * and he shall give thee thy heart's
desire.
5 Commit thy way unto the LORD, and put thy trust in him, * and
he         shall         bring         it         to         pass.
6 He shall make thy righteousness as clear as the light, * and thy
just         dealing         as         the         noon-day.
7 Hold thee still in the LORD, and abide patiently upon him: * but
grieve not thyself at him whose way doth prosper, against the man
that doeth after evil counsels.

8 Leave off from wrath, and let go displeasure: * fret not thyself, else shalt thou be moved to do evil.

9 Wicked doers shall be rooted out; * and they that patiently abide the LORD, those shall inherit the land.

10 Yet a little while, and the ungodly shall be clean gone: * thou shalt look after his place, and he shall be away.

11 But the meek-spirited shall possess the earth, * and shall be refreshed in the multitude of peace.

12 The ungodly seeketh counsel against the just, * and gnasheth upon him with his teeth.

13 The Lord shall laugh him to scorn; * for he hath seen that his day is coming.

14 The ungodly have drawn out the sword, and have bent their bow, * to cast down the poor and needy, and to slay such as be upright in their ways.

15 Their sword shall go through their own heart, * and their bow shall be broken.

16 A small thing that the righteous hath, * is better than great riches of the ungodly.

17 For the arms of the ungodly shall be broken, * and the LORD upholdeth the righteous.

18 The LORD knoweth the days of the godly; * and their inheritance shall endure for ever.

19 They shall not be confounded in the perilous time; * and in the days of dearth they shall have enough.

20 As for the ungodly, they shall perish, and the enemies of the LORD shall consume as the fat of lambs: * yea, even as the smoke shall they consume away.

21 The ungodly borroweth, and payeth not again; * but the righteous is merciful and liberal.

22 Such as are blessed of God, shall possess the land; * and they that are cursed of him, shall be rooted out.

23 The LORD ordereth a good man's going, * and maketh his way acceptable to himself.

24 Though he fall, he shall not be cast away; * for the LORD upholdeth him with his hand.

25 I have been young, and now am old; * and yet saw I never the righteous forsaken, nor his seed begging their bread.

26 The righteous is ever merciful, and lendeth; * and his seed is

blessed.

27 Flee from evil, and do the thing that is good; * and dwell for evermore.

28 For the LORD loveth the thing that is right; * he forsaketh not his that be godly, but they are preserved for ever.

29 The unrighteous shall be punished; * as for the seed of the ungodly, it shall be rooted out.

30 The righteous shall inherit the land, * and dwell therein for ever.

31 The mouth of the righteous is exercised in wisdom, * and his tongue will be talking of judgment.

32 The law of his God is in his heart, * and his goings shall not slide.

33 The ungodly watcheth the righteous, * and seeketh occasion to slay him.

34 The LORD will not leave him in his hand, * nor condemn him when he is judged.

35 Hope thou in the LORD, and keep his way, and he shall promote thee, that thou shalt possess the land: * when the ungodly shall perish, thou shalt see it.

36 I myself have seen the ungodly in great power, * and flourishing like a green bay-tree.

37 I went by, and lo, he was gone: * I sought him, but his place could no where be found.

38 Keep innocency, and take heed unto the thing that is right; * for that shall bring a man peace at the last.

39 As for the transgressors, they shall perish together; * and the end of the ungodly is, they shall be rooted out at the last.

40 But the salvation of the righteous cometh of the LORD; * who is also their strength in the time of trouble.

41 And the LORD shall stand by them, and save them: * he shall deliver them from the ungodly, and shall save them, because they put their trust in him.

**Psalm 38**. *Domine, ne in furore.*
PUT me not to rebuke, O LORD, in thine anger; * neither chasten me in thy heavy displeasure:

2 For thine arrows stick fast in me, * and thy hand presseth me sore.

3 There is no health in my flesh, because of thy displeasure; * neither is there any rest in my bones, by reason of my sin.
4 For my wickednesses are gone over my head, * and are like a sore burden, too heavy for me to bear.
5 My wounds stink, and are corrupt, * through my foolishness.
6 I am brought into so great trouble and misery, * that I go mourning all the day long.
7 For my loins are filled with a sore disease, * and there is no whole part in my body.
8 I am feeble and sore smitten; * I have roared for the very disquietness of my heart.
9 Lord, thou knowest all my desire; * and my groaning is not hid from thee.
10 My heart panteth, my strength hath failed me, * and the light of mine eyes is gone from me.
11 My lovers and my neighbors did stand looking upon my trouble, * and my kinsmen stood afar off.
12 They also that sought after my life laid snares for me; * and they that went about to do me evil talked of wickedness, and imagined deceit all the day long.
13 As for me, I was like a deaf man, and heard not; * and as one that is dumb, who doth not open his mouth.
14 I became even as a man that heareth not, * and in whose mouth are no reproofs.
15 For in thee, O LORD, have I put my trust; * thou shalt answer for me, O Lord my God.
16 I have required that they, even mine enemies, should not triumph over me; * for when my foot slipt, they rejoiced greatly against me.
17 And I truly am set in the plague, * and my heaviness is ever in my sight.
18 For I will confess my wickedness, * and be sorry for my sin.
19 But mine enemies live, and are mighty; * and they that hate me wrongfully are many in number.
20 They also that reward evil for good are against me; * because I follow the thing that good is.
21 Forsake me not, O LORD my God; * be not thou far from me.

**Psalm**        **39**.        *Dixi,*        *Custodiam.*

I SAID, I will take heed to my ways, * that I offend not in my tongue.

2 I will keep my mouth as it were with a bridle, * while the ungodly is in my sight.

3 I held my tongue, and spake nothing: * I kept silence, yea, even from good words; but it was pain and grief to me.

4 My heart was hot within me: and while I was thus musing the fire kindled, * and at the last I spake with my tongue:

5 LORD, let me know mine end, and the number of my days; * that I may be certified how long I have to live.

6 Behold, thou hast made my days as it were a span long, and mine age is even as nothing in respect of thee; * and verily every man living is altogether vanity.

7 For man walketh in a vain shadow, and disquieteth himself in vain; * he heapeth up riches, and cannot tell who shall gather them.

8 And now, Lord, what is my hope? * truly my hope is even in thee.

9 Deliver me from all mine offenses; * and make me not a rebuke unto the foolish.

10 I became dumb, and opened not my mouth; * for it was thy doing.

11 Take thy plague away from me: * I am even consumed by the means of thy heavy hand.

12 When thou with rebukes dost chasten man for sin, thou makest his beauty to consume away, like as it were a moth fretting a garment: * every man therefore is but vanity.

13 Hear my prayer, O LORD, and with thine ears consider my calling; * hold not thy peace at my tears;

14 For I am a stranger with thee, and a sojourner, * as all my fathers were.

15 O spare me a little, that I may recover my strength, * before I go hence, and be no more seen.


**Psalm**        **40**.        *Expectans*        *expectavi.*

I WAITED patiently for the LORD, * and he inclined unto me, and heard my calling.

2 He brought me also out of the horrible pit, out of the mire and clay, * and set my feet upon the rock, and ordered my goings.

3 And he hath put a new song in my mouth, * even a thanksgiving unto our God.

4 Many shall see it, and fear, * and shall put their trust in the LORD.

5 Blessed is the man that hath set his hope in the LORD, * and turned not unto the proud, and to such as go about with lies.

6 O LORD my God, great are the wondrous works which thou hast done, like as be also thy thoughts, which are to us-ward; * and yet there is no man that ordereth them unto thee.

7 If I should declare them, and speak of them, * they should be more than I am able to express.

8 Sacrifice and offering thou wouldest not, * but mine ears hast thou opened.

9 Burnt-offering and sacrifice for sin hast thou not required: * then said I, Lo, I come;

10 In the volume of the book it is written of me, that I should fulfill thy will, O my God: * I am content to do it; yea, thy law is within my heart.

11 I have declared thy righteousness in the great congregation: * lo, I will not refrain my lips, O LORD, and that thou knowest.

12 I have not hid thy righteousness within my heart; * my talk hath been of thy truth, and of thy salvation.

13 I have not kept back thy loving mercy and truth * from the great congregation.

14 Withdraw not thou thy mercy from me, O LORD; * let thy loving-kindness and thy truth alway preserve me.

15 For innumerable troubles are come about me; my sins have taken such hold upon me, that I am not able to look up; * yea, they are more in number than the hairs of my head, and my heart hath failed me.

16 O LORD, let it be thy pleasure to deliver me; * make haste, O LORD, to help me.

17 Let them be ashamed, and confounded together, that seek after my soul to destroy it; * let them be driven backward, and put to rebuke, that wish me evil.

18 Let them be desolate, and rewarded with shame, * that say unto me, Fie upon thee! fie upon thee!

19 Let all those that seek thee, be joyful and glad in thee; * and let such as love thy salvation, say alway, The LORD be praised.

20 As for me, I am poor and needy; * but the Lord careth for me.

21 Thou art my helper and redeemer; * make no long tarrying, O my God.

**Psalm 41.** *Beatus qui intelligit.*
BLESSED is he that considereth the poor and needy; * the LORD shall deliver him in the time of trouble.

2 The LORD preserve him, and keep him alive, that he may be blessed upon earth; * and deliver not thou him into the will of his enemies.

3 The LORD comfort him when he lieth sick upon his bed; * make thou all his bed in his sickness.

4 I said, LORD, be merciful unto me; * heal my soul, for I have sinned against thee.

5 Mine enemies speak evil of me, * When shall he die, and his name perish?

6 And if he come to see me, he speaketh vanity, * and his heart conceiveth falsehood within himself; and when he cometh forth, he telleth it.

7 All mine enemies whisper together against me; * even against me do they imagine this evil.

8 An evil disease, say they, cleaveth fast unto him; * and now that he lieth, he shall rise up no more.

9 Yea, even mine own familiar friend whom I trusted, * who did also eat of my bread, hath laid great wait for me.

10 But be thou merciful unto me, O LORD; * raise thou me up again, and I shall reward them.

11 By this I know thou favorest me, * that mine enemy doth not triumph against me.

12 And in my innocency thou upholdest me, * and shalt set me before thy face for ever.

13 Blessed be the LORD God of Israel, * world without end. Amen.

**Psalm 42.** *Quemadmodum.*
LIKE as the hart desireth the water-brooks, * so longeth my soul after thee, O God.

2 My soul is athirst for God, yea, even for the living God: * when shall I come to appear before the presence of God?

3 My tears have been my meat day and night, * while they daily say unto me, Where is now thy God?
4 Now when I think thereupon, I pour out my heart by myself; * for I went with the multitude, and brought them forth into the house of God;
5 In the voice of praise and thanksgiving, * among such as keep holy-day.
6 Why art thou so full of heaviness, O my soul? * and why art thou so disquieted within me?
7 O put thy trust in God; * for I will yet thank him, which is the help of my countenance, and my God.
8 My soul is vexed within me; * therefore will I remember thee from the land of Jordan, from Hermon and the little hill.
9 One deep calleth another, because of the noise of thy water-floods; * all thy waves and storms are gone over me.
10 The LORD will grant his loving-kindness in the daytime; * and in the night season will I sing of him, and make my prayer unto the God of my life.
11 I will say unto the God of my strength, Why hast thou forgotten me? * why go I thus heavily, while the enemy oppresseth me?
12 My bones are smitten asunder as with a sword, * while mine enemies that trouble me cast me in the teeth;
13 Namely, while they say daily unto me, * Where is now thy God?
14 Why art thou so vexed, O my soul? * and why art thou so disquieted within me?
15 O put thy trust in God; * for I will yet thank him, which is the help of my countenance, and my God.

**Psalm 43.** *Judica me, Deus.*
GIVE sentence with me, O God, and defend my cause against the ungodly people; * O deliver me from the deceitful and wicked man.
2 For thou art the God of my strength; why hast thou put me from thee? * and why go I so heavily, while the enemy oppresseth me?
3 O send out thy light and thy truth, that they may lead me, * and bring me unto thy holy hill, and to thy dwelling;
4 And that I may go unto the altar of God, even unto the God of

my joy and gladness; * and upon the harp will I give thanks unto thee, O God, my God.
5 Why art thou so heavy, O my soul? * and why art thou so disquieted within me?
6 O put thy trust in God; * for I will yet give him thanks, which is the help of my countenance, and my God.

**Psalm 44.** *Deus, auribus.*
WE have heard with our ears, O God, our fathers have told us * what thou hast done in their time of old:
2 How thou hast driven out the heathen with thy hand, and planted our fathers in; * how thou hast destroyed the nations, and made thy people to flourish.
3 For they gat not the land in possession through their own sword, * neither was it their own arm that helped them;
4 But thy right hand, and thine arm, and the light of thy countenance; * because thou hadst a favor unto them.
5 Thou art my King, O God; * send help unto Jacob.
6 Through thee will we overthrow our enemies, * and in thy Name will we tread them under that rise up against us.
7 For I will not trust in my bow, * it is not my sword that shall help me;
8 But it is thou that savest us from our enemies, * and puttest them to confusion that hate us.
9 We make our boast of God all day long, * and will praise thy Name for ever.
10 But now thou art far off, and puttest us to confusion, * and goest not forth with our armies.
11 Thou makest us to turn our backs upon our enemies, * so that they which hate us spoil our goods.
12 Thou lettest us be eaten up like sheep, * and hast scattered us among the heathen.
13 Thou sellest thy people for nought, * and takest no money for them.
14 Thou makest us to be rebuked of our neighbors, * to be laughed to scorn, and had in derision of them that are round about us.
15 Thou makest us to be a by-word among the nations, * and that the peoples shake their heads at us.
16 My confusion is daily before me, * and the shame of my face

hath                         covered                              me;
17 For the voice of the slanderer and blasphemer, * for the enemy
and                                                              avenger.
18 And though all this be come upon us, yet do we not forget thee,
*   nor   behave   ourselves   frowardly   in   thy   covenant.
19 Our heart is not turned back, * neither our steps gone out of thy
way;
20 No, not when thou hast smitten us into the place of dragons, *
and   covered   us   with   the   shadow   of   death.
21 If we have forgotten the Name of our God, and holden up our
hands to any strange god, * shall not God search it out? for he
knoweth   the   very   secrets   of   the   heart.
22 For thy sake also are we killed all the day long, * and are
counted   as   sheep   appointed   to   be   slain.
23 Up, Lord, why sleepest thou? * awake, and be not absent from
us                         for                              ever.
24 Wherefore hidest thou thy face, * and forgettest our misery and
trouble?
25 For our soul is brought low, even unto the dust; * our belly
cleaveth         unto         the         ground.
26 Arise, and help us, * and deliver us, for thy mercy's sake.


**Psalm         45.**         *Eructavit         cor         meum.*
MY heart overfloweth with a good matter; I speak the things which
I have made concerning the King. * My tongue is the pen of a
ready                                                         writer.
2 Thou art fairer than the children of men; * full of grace are thy
lips,   because   God   hath   blessed   thee   for   ever.
3 Gird thee with thy sword upon thy thigh, O thou Most Mighty, *
according   to   thy   worship   and   renown.
4 Good luck have thou with thine honor: * ride on, because of the
word of truth, of meekness, and righteousness; and thy right hand
shall         teach         thee         terrible         things.
5 Thy arrows are very sharp in the heart of the King's enemies, *
and   the   people   shall   be   subdued   unto   thee.
6 Thy seat, O God, endureth for ever; * the scepter of thy kingdom
is                 a                 right                 scepter.
7 Thou hast loved righteousness, and hated iniquity; * wherefore

88

God, even thy God, hath anointed thee with the oil of gladness above thy fellows.
8 All thy garments smell of myrrh, aloes, and cassia; * out of the ivory palaces, whereby they have made thee glad.
9 Kings' daughters are among thy honorable women; * upon thy right hand doth stand the queen in a vesture of gold, wrought about with divers colors.
10 Hearken, O daughter, and consider; incline thine ear; * forget also thine own people, and thy father's house.
11 So shall the King have pleasure in thy beauty; * for he is thy Lord, and worship thou him.
12 And the daughter of Tyre shall be there with a gift; * like as the rich also among the people shall make their supplication before thee.
13 The King's daughter is all glorious within; * her clothing is of wrought gold.
14 She shall be brought unto the King in raiment of needlework: * the virgins that be her fellows shall bear her company, and shall be brought unto thee.
15 With joy and gladness shall they be brought, * and shall enter into the King's palace.
16 Instead of thy fathers, thou shalt have children, * whom thou mayest make princes in all lands.
17 I will make thy Name to be remembered from one generation to another; * therefore shall the people give thanks unto thee, world without end.

**Psalm 46.** *Deus noster refugium.*
GOD is our hope and strength, * a very present help in trouble.
2 Therefore will we not fear, though the earth be moved, * and though the hills be carried into the midst of the sea;
3 Though the waters thereof rage and swell, * and though the mountains shake at the tempest of the same.
4 There is a river, the streams whereof make glad the city of God; * the holy place of the tabernacle of the Most Highest.
5 God is in the midst of her, therefore shall she not be removed; * God shall help her, and that right early.
6 The nations make much ado, and the kingdoms are moved; * but God hath showed his voice, and the earth shall melt away.

7 The LORD of hosts is with us; * the God of Jacob is our refuge.
8 O come hither, and behold the works of the LORD, * what destruction he hath brought upon the earth.
9 He maketh wars to cease in all the world; * he breaketh the bow, and knappeth the spear in sunder, and burneth the chariots in the fire.
10 Be still then, and know that I am God: * I will be exalted among the nations, and I will be exalted in the earth.
11 The LORD of hosts is with us; * the God of Jacob is our refuge.

**Psalm 47.** *Omnes gentes, plaudite.*
CLAP your hands together, all ye peoples: * O sing unto God with the voice of melody.
2 For the LORD is high, and to be feared; * he is the great King upon all the earth.
3 He shall subdue the peoples under us, * and the nations under our feet.
4 He shall choose out an heritage for us, * even the excellency of Jacob, whom he loved.
5 God is gone up with a merry noise, * and the LORD with the sound of the trump.
6 O sing praises, sing praises unto our God; * O sing praises, sing praises unto our King.
7 For God is the King of all the earth: * sing ye praises with understanding.
8 God reigneth over the nations; * God sitteth upon his holy seat.
9 The princes of the peoples are joined unto the people of the God of Abraham; * for God, which is very high exalted, doth defend the earth, as it were with a shield.

**Psalm 48.** *Magnus Dominus.*
GREAT is the LORD, and highly to be praised * in the city of our God, even upon his holy hill.
2 The hill of Sion is a fair place, and the joy of the whole earth; * upon the north side lieth the city of the great King: God is well known in her palaces as a sure refuge.
3 For lo, the kings of the earth * were gathered, and gone by together.
4 They marveled to see such things; * they were astonished, and

suddenly                              cast                              down.
5 Fear came there upon them; and sorrow, * as upon a woman in her                                                                 travail.
6 Thou dost break the ships of the sea * through the east-wind.
7 Like as we have heard, so have we seen in the city of the LORD of hosts, in the city of our God; * God upholdeth the same for ever.
8 We wait for thy loving-kindness, O God, * in the midst of thy temple.
9 O God, according to thy Name, so is thy praise unto the world's end;    *    thy    right    hand    is    full    of    righteousness.
10 Let the Mount Sion rejoice, and the daughters of Judah be glad, *           because            of            thy            judgments.
11 Walk about Sion, and go round about her; * and tell the towers thereof.
12 Mark well her bulwarks, consider her palaces, * that ye may tell them                    that                    come                    after.
13 For this God is our God for ever and ever: * he shall be our guide                              unto                              death.


**Psalm          49**.          *Audite          haec,          omnes.*
O HEAR ye this, all ye people; * ponder it with your ears, all ye that              dwell              in              the              world;
2   High   and   low,   rich   and   poor,   *   one   with   another.
3 My mouth shall speak of wisdom, * and my heart shall muse of understanding.
4 I will incline mine ear to the parable, * and show my dark speech upon                              the                              harp.
5 Wherefore should I fear in the days of evil, * when wickedness at my        heels        compasseth        me        round        about?
6 There be some that put their trust in their goods, * and boast themselves        in        the        multitude        of        their        riches.
7 But no man may deliver his brother, * nor give a ransom unto God                              for                              him,
8 (For it cost more to redeem their souls, * so that he must let that alone                              for                              ever;)
9   That   he   shall   live   alway,   *   and   not   see   the   grave.
10 For he seeth that wise men also die and perish together, * as well as the ignorant and foolish, and leave their riches for other.

11 And yet they think that their houses shall continue for ever, and that their dwelling-places shall endure from one generation to another; * and call the lands after their own names.

12 Nevertheless, man being in honor abideth not, * seeing he may be compared unto the beasts that perish;

13 This their way is very foolishness; * yet their posterity praise their saying.

14 They lie in the grave like sheep; death is their shepherd; and the righteous shall have dominion over them in the morning: * their beauty shall consume in the sepulcher, and have no abiding.

15 But God hath delivered my soul from the power of the grave; * for he shall receive me.

16 Be not thou afraid, though one be made rich, * or if the glory of his house be increased;

17 For he shall carry nothing away with him when he dieth, * neither shall his pomp follow him.

18 For while he lived, he counted himself an happy man; * and so long as thou doest well unto thyself, men will speak good of thee.

19 He shall follow the generation of his fathers, * and shall never see light.

20 Man that is in honor but hath no understanding * is compared unto the beasts that perish.


**Psalm**     **50**.     *Deus*     *deorum.*

THE LORD, even the Most Mighty God, hath spoken, * and called the world, from the rising up of the sun unto the going down thereof.

2 Out of Sion hath God appeared * in perfect beauty.

3 Our God shall come, and shall not keep silence; * there shall go before him a consuming fire, and a mighty tempest shall be stirred up round about him.

4 He shall call the heaven from above, * and the earth, that he may judge his people.

5 Gather my saints together unto me; * those that have made a covenant with me with sacrifice.

6 And the heavens shall declare his righteousness; * for God is Judge himself.

7 Hear, O my people, and I will speak; * I myself will testify against thee, O Israel; for I am God, even thy God.

8 I will not reprove thee because of thy sacrifices; * as for thy burnt-offerings,     they     are     alway     before     me.
9 I will take no bullock out of thine house, * nor he-goats out of thy                                                                      folds.
10 For all the beasts of the forest are mine, * and so are the cattle upon     a     thousand     hills.
11 I know all the fowls upon the mountains, * and the wild beasts of     the     field     are     in     my     sight.
12 If I be hungry, I will not tell thee; * for the whole world is mine, and     all     that     is     therein.
13 Thinkest thou that I will eat bulls' flesh, * and drink the blood of                                                                      goats?
14 Offer unto God thanksgiving, * and pay thy vows unto the Most Highest.
15 And call upon me in the time of trouble; * so will I hear thee, and     thou     shalt     praise     me.
16 But unto the ungodly saith God, * Why dost thou preach my laws,     and     takest     my     covenant     in     thy     mouth;
17 Whereas thou hatest to be reformed, * and hast cast my words behind                                                                      thee?
18 When thou sawest a thief, thou consentedst unto him; * and hast been     partaker     with     the     adulterers.
19 Thou hast let thy mouth speak wickedness, * and with thy tongue     thou     hast     set     forth     deceit.
20 Thou sattest and spakest against thy brother; * yea, and hast slandered     thine     own     mother's     son.
21 These things hast thou done, and I held my tongue, and thou thoughtest wickedly, that I am even such a one as thyself; * but I will reprove thee, and set before thee the things that thou hast done.
22 O consider this, ye that forget God, * lest I pluck you away, and there     be     none     to     deliver     you.
23 Whoso offereth me thanks and praise, he honoreth me; * and to him that ordereth his way aright, will I show the salvation of God.

**Psalm     51**.     *Miserere     mei,     Deus.*
HAVE mercy upon me, O God, after thy great goodness; * according to the multitude of thy mercies do away mine offenses.
2 Wash me throughly from my wickedness, * and cleanse me from

my                                                                                    sin.
3 For I acknowledge my faults, * and my sin is ever before me.
4 Against thee only have I sinned, and done this evil in thy sight; *
that thou mightest be justified in thy saying, and clear when thou
shalt                                                                                 judge.
5 Behold, I was shapen in wickedness, * and in sin hath my mother
conceived                                                                               me.
6 But lo, thou requirest truth in the inward parts, * and shalt make
me          to          understand          wisdom          secretly.
7 Thou shalt purge me with hyssop, and I shall be clean; * thou
shalt    wash    me,    and    I    shall    be    whiter    than    snow.
8 Thou shalt make me hear of joy and gladness, * that the bones
which        thou        hast        broken        may        rejoice.
9 Turn thy face from my sins, * and put out all my misdeeds.
10 Make me a clean heart, O God, * and renew a right spirit within
me.
11 Cast me not away from thy presence, * and take not thy holy
Spirit                              from                              me.
12 O give me the comfort of thy help again, * and stablish me with
thy                              free                              Spirit.
13 Then shall I teach thy ways unto the wicked, * and sinners shall
be              converted              unto              thee.
14 Deliver me from blood-guiltiness, O God, thou that art the God
of my health; * and my tongue shall sing of thy righteousness.
15 Thou shalt open my lips, O Lord, * and my mouth shall show
thy                                                                                   praise.
16 For thou desirest no sacrifice, else would I give it thee; * but
thou        delightest        not        in        burnt-offerings.
17 The sacrifice of God is a troubled spirit: * a broken and contrite
heart,        O        God,        shalt        thou        not        despise.
18 O be favorable and gracious unto Sion; * build thou the walls of
Jerusalem.
19 Then shalt thou be pleased with the sacrifice of righteousness,
with the burnt-offerings and oblations; * then shall they offer
young bullocks upon thine altar.


**Psalm**                    **52**.                    *Quid*                    *gloriaris?*
WHY boastest thou thyself, thou tyrant, * that thou canst do
mischief;

2 Whereas the goodness of God * endureth yet daily?
3 Thy tongue imagineth wickedness, * and with lies thou cuttest like a sharp razor.
4 Thou hast loved unrighteousness more than goodness, * and falsehood more than righteousness.
5 Thou hast loved to speak all words that may do hurt, * O thou false tongue.
6 Therefore shall God destroy thee for ever; * he shall take thee, and pluck thee out of thy dwelling, and root thee out of the land of the living.
7 The righteous also shall see this, and fear, * and shall laugh him to scorn:
8 Lo, this is the man that took not God for his strength; * but trusted unto the multitude of his riches, and strengthened himself in his wickedness.
9 As for me, I am like a green olive-tree in the house of God; * my trust is in the tender mercy of God for ever and ever.
10 I will alway give thanks unto thee for that thou hast done; * and I will hope in thy Name, for thy saints like it well.

**Psalm**          **53**.          *Dixit*          *insipiens.*
THE foolish body hath said in his heart, * There is no God.
2 Corrupt are they, and become abominable in their wickedness; * there is none that doeth good.
3 God looked down from heaven upon the children of men, * to see if there were any that would understand, and seek after God.
4 But they are all gone out of the way, they are altogether become abominable; * there is also none that doeth good, no not one.
5 Are not they without understanding that work wickedness, * eating up my people as if they would eat bread? they have not called upon God.
6 They were afraid where no fear was; * for God hath broken the bones of him that besieged thee; thou hast put them to confusion, because God hath despised them.
7 O that the salvation were given unto Israel out of Sion! * O that the Lord would deliver his people out of captivity!
8 Then should Jacob rejoice, * and Israel should be right glad.

**Psalm**     **54**.     *Deus,*     *in*     *Nomine.*

SAVE me, O God, for thy Name's sake, * and avenge me in thy strength.

2 Hear my prayer, O God, * and hearken unto the words of my mouth.

3 For strangers are risen up against me; * and tyrants, which have not God before their eyes, seek after my soul.

4 Behold, God is my helper; * the Lord is with them that uphold my soul.

5 He shall reward evil unto mine enemies: * destroy thou them in thy truth.

6 An offering of a free heart will I give thee, and praise thy Name, O LORD; * because it is so comfortable.

7 For he hath delivered me out of all my trouble; * and mine eye hath seen his desire upon mine enemies.


**Psalm**     **55**.     *Exaudi,*     *Deus.*

HEAR my prayer, O God, * and hide not thyself from my petition.

2 Take heed unto me, and hear me, * how I mourn in my prayer, and am vexed;

3 The enemy crieth so, and the ungodly cometh on so fast; * for they are minded to do me some mischief, so maliciously are they set against me.

4 My heart is disquieted within me, * and the fear of death is fallen upon me.

5 Fearfulness and trembling are come upon me, * and an horrible dread hath overwhelmed me.

6 And I said, O that I had wings like a dove! * for then would I flee away, and be at rest.

7 Lo, then would I get me away far off, * and remain in the wilderness.

8 I would make haste to escape, * because of the stormy wind and tempest.

9 Destroy their tongues, O Lord, and divide them; * for I have spied unrighteousness and strife in the city.

10 Day and night they go about within the walls thereof: * mischief also and sorrow are in the midst of it.

11 Wickedness is therein; * deceit and guile go not out of her

streets.

12 For it is not an open enemy that hath done me this dishonor; * for then I could have borne it;

13 Neither was it mine adversary that did magnify himself against me; * for then peradventure I would have hid myself from him;

14 But it was even thou, my companion, * my guide, and mine own familiar friend.

15 We took sweet counsel together, * and walked in the house of God as friends.

16 Let death come hastily upon them, and let them go down alive into the pit; * for wickedness is in their dwellings, and among them.

17 As for me, I will call upon God, * and the LORD shall save me.

18 In the evening, and morning, and at noon-day will I pray, and that instantly; * and he shall hear my voice.

19 It is he that hath delivered my soul in peace from the battle that was against me; * for there were many that strove with me.

20 Yea, even God, that endureth for ever, shall hear me, and bring them down; * for they will not turn, nor fear God.

21 He laid his hands upon such as be at peace with him, * and he brake his covenant.

22 The words of his mouth were softer than butter, having war in his heart; * his words were smoother than oil, and yet be they very swords.

23 O cast thy burden upon the LORD, and he shall nourish thee, * and shall not suffer the righteous to fall for ever.

24 And as for them, * thou, O God, shalt bring them into the pit of destruction.

25 The blood-thirsty and deceitful men shall not live out half their days: * nevertheless, my trust shall be in thee, O Lord.

**Psalm 56.** *Miserere mei, Deus.*
BE merciful unto me, O God, for man goeth about to devour me; * he is daily fighting, and troubling me.

2 Mine enemies are daily at hand to swallow me up; * for they be many that fight against me, O thou Most Highest.

3 Nevertheless, though I am sometime afraid, * yet put I my trust in thee.

4 I will praise God, because of his word: * I have put my trust in

God, and will not fear what flesh can do unto me.
5 They daily mistake my words; * all that they imagine is to do me evil.
6 They hold all together, and keep themselves close, * and mark my steps, when they lay wait for my soul.
7 Shall they escape for their wickedness? * thou, O God, in thy displeasure shalt cast them down.
8 Thou tellest my wanderings; put my tears into thy bottle: * are not these things noted in thy book?
9 Whensoever I call upon thee, then shall mine enemies be put to flight: * this I know; for God is on my side.
10 In God's word will I rejoice; * in the LORD's word will I comfort me.
11 Yea, in God have I put my trust; * I will not be afraid what man can do unto me.
12 Unto thee, O God, will I pay my vows; * unto thee will I give thanks.
13 For thou hast delivered my soul from death, and my feet from falling, * that I may walk before God in the light of the living.

**Psalm 57.** *Miserere mei, Deus.*
BE merciful unto me, O God, be merciful unto me; for my soul trusteth in thee; * and under the shadow of thy wings shall be my refuge, until this tyranny be overpast.
2 I will call unto the Most High God, * even unto the God that shall perform the cause which I have in hand.
3 He shall send from heaven, * and save me from the reproof of him that would eat me up.
4 God shall send forth his mercy and truth: * my soul is among lions;
5 And I lie even among the children of men, that are set on fire, * whose teeth are spears and arrows, and their tongue a sharp sword.
6 Set up thyself, O God, above the heavens; * and thy glory above all the earth.
7 They have laid a net for my feet, and pressed down my soul; * they have digged a pit before me, and are fallen into the midst of it themselves.
8 My heart is fixed, O God, my heart is fixed; * I will sing and

give praise.
9 Awake up, my glory; awake, lute and harp: * I myself will awake right early.
10 I will give thanks unto thee, O Lord, among the peoples; * and I will sing unto thee among the nations.
11 For the greatness of thy mercy reacheth unto the heavens, * and thy truth unto the clouds.
12 Set up thyself, O God, above the heavens; * and thy glory above all the earth.

**Psalm 58.** *Si vere utique.*
ARE your minds set upon righteousness, O ye congregation? * and do ye judge the thing that is right, O ye sons of men?
2 Yea, ye imagine mischief in your heart upon the earth, * and your hands deal with wickedness.
3 The ungodly are froward, even from their mother's womb; * as soon as they are born, they go astray, and speak lies.
4 They are as venomous as the poison of a serpent, * even like the deaf adder, that stoppeth her ears;
5 Which refuseth to hear the voice of the charmer, * charm he never so wisely.
6 Break their teeth, O God, in their mouths; * smite the jaw-bones of the lions, O LORD.
7 Let them fall away like water that runneth apace; * when they shoot their arrows, let them be rooted out.
8 Let them consume away like a snail, and be like the untimely fruit of a woman; * and let them not see the sun.
9 Or ever your pots be made hot with thorns, * he shall take them away with a whirlwind, the green and the burning alike.
10 The righteous shall rejoice when he seeth the vengeance; * he shall wash his footsteps in the blood of the ungodly.
11 So that a man shall say, Verily there is a reward for the righteous; * doubtless there is a God that judgeth the earth.

**Psalm 59.** *Eripe me de inimicis.*
DELIVER me from mine enemies, O God; * defend me from them that rise up against me.
2 O deliver me from the wicked doers, * and save me from the blood-thirsty men.

3 For lo, they lie waiting for my soul; * the mighty men are gathered against me, without any offense or fault of me, O LORD.
4 They run and prepare themselves without my fault; * arise thou therefore to help me, and behold.
5 Stand up, O LORD God of hosts, thou God of Israel, to visit all the heathen, * and be not merciful unto them that offend of malicious wickedness.
6 They go to and fro in the evening, * they grin like a dog, and run about through the city.
7 Behold, they speak with their mouth, and swords are in their lips; * for who doth hear?
8 But thou, O LORD, shalt have them in derision, * and thou shalt laugh all the heathen to scorn.
9 My strength will I ascribe unto thee; * for thou art the God of my refuge.
10 God showeth me his goodness plenteously; * and God shall let me see my desire upon mine enemies.
11 Slay them not, lest my people forget it; * but scatter them abroad among the people, and put them down, O Lord our defense.
12 For the sin of their mouth, and for the words of their lips, they shall be taken in their pride: * and why? their talk is of cursing and lies.
13 Consume them in thy wrath, consume them, that they may perish; * and know that it is God that ruleth in Jacob, and unto the ends of the world.
14 And in the evening they will return, * grin like a dog, and will go about the city.
15 They will run here and there for meat, * and grudge if they be not satisfied.
16 As for me, I will sing of thy power, and will praise thy mercy betimes in the morning; * for thou hast been my defense and refuge in the day of my trouble.
17 Unto thee, O my strength, will I sing; * for thou, O God, art my refuge, and my merciful God.


**Psalm** **60.** *Deus,* *repulisti* *nos.*
O GOD, thou hast cast us out, and scattered us abroad; * thou hast also been displeased: O turn thee unto us again.

100

2 Thou hast moved the land, and divided it: * heal the sores thereof, for it shaketh.
3 Thou hast showed thy people heavy things; * thou hast given us a drink of deadly wine.
4 Thou hast given a token for such as fear thee, * that they may triumph because of the truth.
5 Therefore were thy beloved delivered; * help me with thy right hand, and hear me.
6 God hath spoken in his holiness, I will rejoice, and divide Shechem, * and mete out the valley of Succoth.
7 Gilead is mine, and Manasseh is mine; * Ephraim also is the strength of my head; Judah is my law-giver;
8 Moab is my wash-pot; over Edom will I cast out my shoe; * Philistia, be thou glad of me.
9 Who will lead me into the strong city? * who will bring me into Edom?
10 Hast not thou cast us out, O God? * wilt not thou, O God, go out with our hosts?
11 O be thou our help in trouble; * for vain is the help of man.
12 Through God will we do great acts; * for it is he that shall tread down our enemies.

**Psalm** **61**. *Exaudi,* *Deus.*
HEAR my crying, O God, * give ear unto my prayer.
2 From the ends of the earth will I call upon thee, * when my heart is in heaviness.
3 O set me up upon the rock that is higher than I; * for thou hast been my hope, and a strong tower for me against the enemy.
4 I will dwell in thy tabernacle for ever, * and my trust shall be under the covering of thy wings.
5 For thou, O Lord, hast heard my desires, * and hast given an heritage unto those that fear thy Name.
6 Thou shalt grant the King a long life, * that his years may endure throughout all generations.
7 He shall dwell before God for ever: * O prepare thy loving mercy and faithfulness, that they may preserve him.
8 So will I alway sing praise unto thy Name, * that I may daily perform my vows.

**Psalm**      **62.**      *Nonne*      *Deo?*

MY soul truly waiteth still upon God; * for of him cometh my salvation.

2 He verily is my strength and my salvation; * he is my defense, so that I shall not greatly fall.

3 How long will ye imagine mischief against every man? * Ye shall be slain all the sort of you; yea, as a tottering wall shall ye be, and like a broken hedge.

4 Their device is only how to put him out whom God will exalt; * their delight is in lies; they give good words with their mouth, but curse with their heart.

5 Nevertheless, my soul, wait thou still upon God; * for my hope is in him.

6 He truly is my strength and my salvation; * he is my defense, so that I shall not fall.

7 In God is my health and my glory; * the rock of my might; and in God is my trust.

8 O put your trust in him alway, ye people; * pour out your hearts before him, for God is our hope.

9 As for the children of men, they are but vanity; the children of men are deceitful; * upon the weights they are altogether lighter than vanity itself.

10 O trust not in wrong and robbery; give not yourselves unto vanity: * if riches increase, set not your heart upon them.

11 God spake once, and twice I have also heard the same, * that power belongeth unto God;

12 And that thou, Lord, art merciful; * for thou rewardest every man according to his work.


**Psalm**      **63.**      *Deus,*      *Deus*      *meus.*

O GOD, thou art my God; * early will I seek thee.

2 My soul thirsteth for thee, my flesh also longeth after thee, * in a barren and dry land where no water is.

3 Thus have I looked for thee in the sanctuary, * that I might behold thy power and glory.

4 For thy loving-kindness is better than the life itself: * my lips shall praise thee.

5 As long as I live will I magnify thee in this manner, * and lift up

my hands in thy Name.
6 My soul shall be satisfied, even as it were with marrow and fatness, * when my mouth praiseth thee with joyful lips.
7 Have I not remembered thee in my bed, * and thought upon thee when I was waking?
8 Because thou hast been my helper; * therefore under the shadow of thy wings will I rejoice.
9 My soul hangeth upon thee; * thy right hand hath upholden me.
10 These also that seek the hurt of my soul, * they shall go under the earth.
11 Let them fall upon the edge of the sword, * that they may be a portion for foxes.
12 But the King shall rejoice in God; all they also that swear by him shall be commended; * for the mouth of them that speak lies shall be stopped.

**Psalm** **64**. *Exaudi,* *Deus*.
HEAR my voice, O God, in my prayer; * preserve my life from fear of the enemy.
2 Hide me from the gathering together of the froward, * and from the insurrection of wicked doers;
3 Who have whet their tongue like a sword, * and shoot out their arrows, even bitter words;
4 That they may privily shoot at him that is perfect: * suddenly do they hit him, and fear not.
5 They encourage themselves in mischief, * and commune among themselves, how they may lay snares; and say, that no man shall see them.
6 They imagine wickedness, and practice it; * that they keep secret among themselves, every man in the deep of his heart.
7 But God shall suddenly shoot at them with a swift arrow, * that they shall be wounded.
8 Yea, their own tongues shall make them fall; * insomuch that whoso seeth them shall laugh them to scorn.
9 And all men that see it shall say, This hath God done; * for they shall perceive that it is his work.
10 The righteous shall rejoice in the LORD, and put his trust in him; * and all they that are true of heart shall be glad.

**Psalm**      **65**.      *Te*      *decet*      *hymnus.*

THOU, O God, art praised in Sion; * and unto thee shall the vow be performed in Jerusalem.

2 Thou that hearest the prayer, * unto thee shall all flesh come.

3 My misdeeds prevail against me: * O be thou merciful unto our sins.

4 Blessed is the man whom thou choosest, and receivest unto thee: * he shall dwell in thy court, and shall be satisfied with the pleasures of thy house, even of thy holy temple.

5 Thou shalt show us wonderful things in thy righteousness, O God of our salvation; * thou that art the hope of all the ends of the earth, and of them that remain in the broad sea.

6 Who in his strength setteth fast the mountains, * and is girded about with power.

7 Who stilleth the raging of the sea, * and the noise of his waves, and the madness of the peoples.

8 They also that dwell in the uttermost parts of the earth shall be afraid at thy tokens, * thou that makest the out-goings of the morning and evening to praise thee.

9 Thou visitest the earth, and blessest it; * thou makest it very plenteous.

10 The river of God is full of water: * thou preparest their corn, for so thou providest for the earth.

11 Thou waterest her furrows; thou sendest rain into the little valleys thereof; * thou makest it soft with the drops of rain, and blessest the increase of it.

12 Thou crownest the year with thy goodness; * and thy clouds drop fatness.

13 They shall drop upon the dwellings of the wilderness; * and the little hills shall rejoice on every side.

14 The folds shall be full of sheep; * the valleys also shall stand so thick with corn, that they shall laugh and sing.


**Psalm**      **66**.      *Jubilate*      *Deo.*

O BE joyful in God, all ye lands; * sing praises unto the honor of his Name; make his praise to be glorious.

2 Say unto God, O how wonderful art thou in thy works! * through the greatness of thy power shall thine enemies bow down unto thee.

3 For all the world shall worship thee, * sing of thee, and praise thy Name.

4 O come hither, and behold the works of God; * how wonderful he is in his doing toward the children of men.

5 He turned the sea into dry land, * so that they went through the water on foot; there did we rejoice thereof.

6 He ruleth with his power for ever; his eyes behold the nations: * and such as will not believe shall not be able to exalt themselves.

7 O praise our God, ye peoples, * and make the voice of his praise to be heard;

8 Who holdeth our soul in life; * and suffereth not our feet to slip.

9 For thou, O God, hast proved us; * thou also hast tried us, like as silver is tried.

10 Thou broughtest us into the snare; * and laidest trouble upon our loins.

11 Thou sufferedst men to ride over our heads; * we went through fire and water, and thou broughtest us out into a wealthy place.

12 I will go into thine house with burnt-offerings, and will pay thee my vows, * which I promised with my lips, and spake with my mouth, when I was in trouble.

13 I will offer unto thee fat burnt-sacrifices, with the incense of rams; * I will offer bullocks and goats.

14 O come hither, and hearken, all ye that fear God; * and I will tell you what he hath done for my soul.

15 I called unto him with my mouth, * and gave him praises with my tongue.

16 If I incline unto wickedness with mine heart, * the Lord will not hear me.

17 But God hath heard me; * and considered the voice of my prayer.

18 Praised be God, who hath not cast out my prayer, * nor turned his mercy from me.


**Psalm** **67.** *Deus* *misereatur.*

GOD be merciful unto us, and bless us, * and show us the light of his countenance, and be merciful unto us;

2 That thy way may be known upon earth, * thy saving health among all nations.

3 Let the peoples praise thee, O God; * yea, let all the peoples

praise                                                    thee.
4 O let the nations rejoice and be glad; * for thou shalt judge the
folk   righteously,   and   govern   the   nations   upon   earth.
5 Let the peoples praise thee, O God; * yea, let all the peoples
praise                                                    thee.
6 Then shall the earth bring forth her increase; * and God, even our
own      God,      shall      give      us      his      blessing.
7 God shall bless us; * and all the ends of the world shall fear him.

**Psalm**                    **68**.              *Exsurgat*           *Deus*.
LET God arise, and let his enemies be scattered; * let them also
that      hate      him      flee      before      him.
2 Like as the smoke vanisheth, so shalt thou drive them away; *
and like as wax melteth at the fire, so let the ungodly perish at the
presence                        of                        God.
3 But let the righteous be glad, and rejoice before God; * let them
also         be         merry         and         joyful.
4 O sing unto God, and sing praises unto his Name; magnify him
that rideth upon the heavens; * praise him in his Name JAH, and
rejoice                        before                        him.
5 He is a Father of the fatherless, and defendeth the cause of the
widows;      *      even      God      in      his      holy      habitation.
6 He is the God that maketh men to be of one mind in an house,
and bringeth the prisoners out of captivity; * but letteth the
runagates          continue          in          scarceness.
7 O God, when thou wentest forth before the people; * when thou
wentest          through          the          wilderness,
8 The earth shook, and the heavens dropped at the presence of
God; * even as Sinai also was moved at the presence of God, who
is          the          God          of          Israel.
9 Thou, O God, sentest a gracious rain upon thine inheritance, *
and      refreshedst      it      when      it      was      weary.
10 Thy congregation shall dwell therein; * for thou, O God, hast of
thy      goodness      prepared      for      the      poor.
11 The Lord gave the word; * great was the company of women
that          bare          the          tidings.
12 Kings with their armies did flee, and were discomfited, * and
they   of   the   household   divided   the   spoil.
13 Though ye have lain among the sheep-folds, yet shall ye be as

the wings of a dove * that is covered with silver wings, and her feathers like gold.

14 When the Almighty scattered kings for their sake, * then were they as white as snow in Salmon.

15 As the hill of Bashan, so is God's hill; * even an high hill, as the hill of Bashan.

16 Why mock ye so, ye high hills? this is God's hill, in the which it pleaseth him to dwell; * yea, the LORD will abide in it for ever.

17 The chariots of God are twenty thousand, even thousands of angels; * and the Lord is among them as in the holy place of Sinai.

18 Thou art gone up on high, thou hast led captivity captive, and received gifts from men; * yea, even from thine enemies, that the LORD God might dwell among them.

19 Praised be the Lord daily, * even the God who helpeth us, and poureth his benefits upon us.

20 He is our God, even the God of whom cometh salvation: * God is the Lord, by whom we escape death.

21 God shall wound the head of his enemies, * and the hairy scalp of such a one as goeth on still in his wickedness.

22 The Lord hath said, I will bring my people again, as I did from Bashan; * mine own will I bring again, as I did sometime from the deep of the sea.

23 That thy foot may be dipped in the blood of thine enemies, * and that the tongue of thy dogs may be red through the same.

24 It is well seen, O God, how thou goest; * how thou, my God and King, goest in the sanctuary.

25 The singers go before, the minstrels follow after, * in the midst of the damsels playing with the timbrels.

26 Give thanks unto God the Lord in the congregation, * ye that are of the fountain of Israel.

27 There is little Benjamin their ruler, and the princes of Judah their council; * the princes of Zebulon, and the princes of Naphthali.

28 Thy God hath sent forth strength for thee; * stablish the thing, O God, that thou hast wrought in us,

29 For thy temple's sake at Jerusalem; * so shall kings bring presents unto thee.

30 Rebuke thou the dragon and the bull, with the leaders of the heathen, so that they humbly bring pieces of silver; * scatter thou

the          peoples          that          delight          in          war;
31 Then shall the princes come out of Egypt; * the Morians' land
shall     soon     stretch     out     her     hands     unto     God.
32 Sing unto God, O ye kingdoms of the earth; * O sing praises
unto                          the                          Lord;
33 Who sitteth in the heavens over all, from the beginning: * lo, he
doth   send   out   his   voice;   yea,   and   that   a   mighty   voice.
34 Ascribe ye the power to God over Israel; * his worship and
strength          is          in          the          clouds.
35 O God, wonderful art thou in thy holy places: * even the God of
Israel, he will give strength and power unto his people. Blessed be
God.

**Psalm          69.**          *Salvum          me          fac.*
SAVE me, O God; * for the waters are come in, even unto my
soul.
2 I stick fast in the deep mire, where no ground is; * I am come
into   deep   waters,   so   that   the   floods   run   over   me.
3 I am weary of crying; my throat is dry; * my sight faileth me for
waiting          so          long          upon          my          God.
4 They that hate me without a cause are more than the hairs of my
head; * they that are mine enemies, and would destroy me
guiltless,                          are                          mighty.
5 I paid them the things that I never took: * God, thou knowest my
simpleness,   and   my   faults   are   not   hid   from   thee.
6 Let not them that trust in thee, O Lord God of hosts, be ashamed
for my cause; * let not those that seek thee be confounded through
me,          O          Lord          God          of          Israel.
7 And why? for thy sake have I suffered reproof; * shame hath
covered                          my                          face.
8 I am become a stranger unto my brethren, * even an alien unto
my                          mother's                          children.
9 For the zeal of thine house hath even eaten me; * and the rebukes
of   them   that   rebuked   thee   are   fallen   upon   me.
10 I wept, and chastened myself with fasting, * and that was turned
to                          my                          reproof.
11 I   put   on   sackcloth   also,   *   and   they   jested   upon   me.
12 They that sit in the gate speak against me, * and the drunkards

make songs upon me.
13 But, LORD, I make my prayer unto thee * in an acceptable time.
14 Hear me, O God, in the multitude of thy mercy, * even in the truth of thy salvation.
15 Take me out of the mire, that I sink not; * O let me be delivered from them that hate me, and out of the deep waters.
16 Let not the water-flood drown me, neither let the deep swallow me up; * and let not the pit shut her mouth upon me.
17 Hear me, O LORD, for thy loving-kindness is comfortable; * turn thee unto me according to the multitude of thy mercies.
18 And hide not thy face from thy servant; for I am in trouble: * O haste thee, and hear me.
19 Draw nigh unto my soul, and save it; * O deliver me, because of mine enemies.
20 Thou hast known my reproach, my shame, and my dishonor: * mine adversaries are all in thy sight.
21 Reproach hath broken my heart; I am full of heaviness: * I looked for some to have pity on me, but there was no man, neither found I any to comfort me.
22 They gave me gall to eat; * and when I was thirsty they gave me vinegar to drink.
23 Let their table be made a snare to take themselves withal; * and let the things that should have been for their wealth be unto them an occasion of falling.
24 Let their eyes be blinded, that they see not; * and ever bow thou down their backs.
25 Pour out thine indignation upon them, * and let thy wrathful displeasure take hold of them.
26 Let their habitation be void, * and no man to dwell in their tents.
27 For they persecute him whom thou hast smitten; * and they talk how they may vex them whom thou hast wounded.
28 Let them fall from one wickedness to another, * and not come into thy righteousness.
29 Let them be wiped out of the book of the living, * and not be written among the righteous.
30 As for me, when I am poor and in heaviness, * thy help, O God, shall lift me up.
31 I will praise the Name of God with a song, * and magnify it

with thanksgiving.

32 This also shall please the LORD * better than a bullock that hath horns and hoofs.

33 The humble shall consider this, and be glad: * seek ye after God, and your soul shall live.

34 For the LORD heareth the poor, * and despiseth not his prisoners.

35 Let heaven and earth praise him: * the sea, and all that moveth therein.

36 For God will save Sion, and build the cities of Judah, * that men may dwell there, and have it in possession.

37 The posterity also of his servants shall inherit it; * and they that love his Name shall dwell therein.


**Psalm** **70.** *Deus,* *in* *adjutorium.*

HASTE thee, O God, to deliver me; * make haste to help me, O LORD.

2 Let them be ashamed and confounded that seek after my soul; * let them be turned backward and put to confusion that wish me evil.

3 Let them for their reward be soon brought to shame, * that cry over me, There! there!

4 But let all those that seek thee be joyful and glad in thee: * and let all such as delight in thy salvation say alway, The Lord be praised.

5 As for me, I am poor and in misery: * haste thee unto me, O God.

6 Thou art my helper, and my redeemer: * O LORD, make no long tarrying.


**Psalm** **71.** *In* *te,* *Domine,* *speravi.*

IN thee, O LORD, have I put my trust; let me never be put to confusion, * but rid me and deliver me in thy righteousness; incline thine ear unto me, and save me.

2 Be thou my stronghold, whereunto I may alway resort: * thou hast promised to help me, for thou art my house of defense, and my castle.

3 Deliver me, O my God, out of the hand of the ungodly, * out of the hand of the unrighteous and cruel man.

4 For thou, O Lord God, art the thing that I long for: * thou art my hope, even from my youth.
5 Through thee have I been holden up ever since I was born: * thou art he that took me out of my mother's womb: my praise shall be alway of thee.
6 I am become as it were a monster unto many, * but my sure trust is in thee.
7 O let my mouth be filled with thy praise, * that I may sing of thy glory and honor all the day long.
8 Cast me not away in the time of age; * forsake me not when my strength faileth me.
9 For mine enemies speak against me; * and they that lay wait for my soul take their counsel together, saying,
10 God hath forsaken him; * persecute him, and take him, for there is none to deliver him.
11 Go not far from me, O God; * my God, haste thee to help me.
12 Let them be confounded and perish that are against my soul; * let them be covered with shame and dishonor that seek to do me evil.
13 As for me, I will patiently abide alway, * and will praise thee more and more.
14 My mouth shall daily speak of thy righteousness and salvation; * for I know no end thereof.
15 I will go forth in the strength of the Lord God, * and will make mention of thy righteousness only.
16 Thou, O God, hast taught me from my youth up until now; * therefore will I tell of thy wondrous works.
17 Forsake me not, O God, in mine old age, when I am gray-headed, * until I have showed thy strength unto this generation, and thy power to all them that are yet for to come.
18 Thy righteousness, O God, is very high, * and great things are they that thou hast done: O God, who is like unto thee!
19 O what great troubles and adversities hast thou showed me, and yet didst thou turn and refresh me; * yea, and broughtest me from the deep of the earth again.
20 Thou hast brought me to great honor, * and comforted me on every side:
21 Therefore will I praise thee, and thy faithfulness, O God, playing upon an instrument of music: * unto thee will I sing upon

the     harp,     O     thou     Holy     One     of     Israel.
22 My lips will be glad when I sing unto thee; * and so will my soul     whom     thou     hast     delivered.
23 My tongue also shall talk of thy righteousness all the day long; * for they are confounded and brought unto shame that seek to do me evil.

**Psalm               72**.               *Deus,               judicium.*
GIVE the King thy judgments, O God, * and thy righteousness unto               the               King's               son.
2 Then shall he judge thy people according unto right, * and defend               the               poor.
3 The mountains also shall bring peace, * and the little hills righteousness               unto               the               people.
4 He shall keep the simple folk by their right, * defend the children of     the     poor,     and     punish     the     wrong     doer.
5 They shall fear thee, as long as the sun and moon endureth, * from          one          generation          to          another.
6 He shall come down like the rain upon the mown grass, * even as the     drops     that     water     the     earth.
7 In his time shall the righteous flourish; * yea, and abundance of peace,     so     long     as     the     moon     endureth.
8 His dominion shall be also from the one sea to the other, * and from     the     River     unto     the     world's     end.
9 They that dwell in the wilderness shall kneel before him; * his enemies     shall     lick     the     dust.
10 The kings of Tarshish and of the isles shall give presents; * the kings     of     Arabia     and     Saba     shall     bring     gifts.
11 All kings shall fall down before him; * all nations shall do him service.
12 For he shall deliver the poor when he crieth; * the needy also, and     him     that     hath     no     helper.
13 He shall be favorable to the simple and needy, * and shall preserve     the     souls     of     the     poor.
14 He shall deliver their souls from falsehood and wrong; * and dear     shall     their     blood     be     in     his     sight.
15 He shall live, and unto him shall be given of the gold of Arabia; * prayer shall be made ever unto him, and daily shall he be praised.
16 There shall be an heap of corn in the earth, high upon the hills ;

112

the fruit thereof shall shake like Lebanon: * and they of the city shall flourish like grass upon the earth.

17 His Name shall endure for ever; his Name shall remain under the sun among the posterities, which shall be blessed in him; * and all the nations shall praise him.

18 Blessed be the LORD God, even the God of Israel, * which only doeth wondrous things;

19 And blessed be the Name of his majesty for ever: * and all the earth shall be filled with his majesty. Amen, Amen.

**Psalm      73**.      *Quam      bonus      Israel!*
TRULY God is loving unto Israel: * even unto such as are of a clean heart.

2 Nevertheless, my feet were almost gone, * my treadings had well-nigh slipped.

3 And why? I was grieved at the wicked: * I do also see the ungodly in such prosperity.

4 For they are in no peril of death; * but are lusty and strong.

5 They come in no misfortune like other folk; * neither are they plagued like other men.

6 And this is the cause that they are so holden with pride, * and cruelty covereth them as a garment.

7 Their eyes swell with fatness, * and they do even what they lust.

8 They corrupt other, and speak of wicked blasphemy; * their talking is against the Most High.

9 For they stretch forth their mouth unto the heaven, * and their tongue goeth through the world.

10 Therefore fall the people unto them, * and thereout suck they no small advantage.

11 Tush, say they, how should God perceive it? * is there knowledge in the Most High?

12 Lo, these are the ungodly, * these prosper in the world, and these have riches in possession:

13 And I said, Then have I cleansed my heart in vain, * and washed my hands in innocency.

14 All the day long have I been punished, * and chastened every morning.

15 Yea, and I had almost said even as they; * but lo, then I should have condemned the generation of thy children.

16 Then thought I to understand this; * but it was too hard for me,
17 Until I went into the sanctuary of God: * then understood I the
end          of          these          men;
18 Namely, how thou dost set them in slippery places, * and
castest      them      down,      and      destroyest      them.
19 O how suddenly do they consume, * perish, and come to a
fearful                                                    end!
20 Yea, even like as a dream when one awaketh; * so shalt thou
make      their      image      to      vanish      out      of      the      city.
21 Thus my heart was grieved, * and it went even through my
reins.
22 So foolish was I, and ignorant, * even as it were a beast before
thee.
23 Nevertheless, I am alway by thee; * for thou hast holden me by
my                            right                            hand.
24 Thou shalt guide me with thy counsel, * and after that receive
me                          with                          glory.
25 Whom have I in heaven but thee? * and there is none upon earth
that      I      desire      in      comparison      of      thee.
26 My flesh and my heart faileth; * but God is the strength of my
heart,      and      my      portion      for      ever.
27 For lo, they that forsake thee shall perish; * thou hast destroyed
all      them      that      are      unfaithful      unto      thee.
28 But it is good for me to hold me fast by God, to put my trust in
the Lord God, * and to speak of all thy works in the gates of the
daughter of Sion.


**Psalm          74.          *Ut          quid,          Deus?*
O GOD, wherefore art thou absent from us so long? * why is thy
wrath      so      hot      against      the      sheep      of      thy      pasture?
2 O think upon thy congregation, * whom thou hast purchased, and
redeemed                            of                            old.
3 Think upon the tribe of thine inheritance, * and Mount Sion,
wherein                  thou                  hast                  dwelt.
4 Lift up thy feet, that thou mayest utterly destroy every enemy, *
which      hath      done      evil      in      thy      sanctuary.
5 Thine adversaries roar in the midst of thy congregations, * and
set          up          their          banners          for          tokens.

6 He that hewed timber afore out of the thick trees, * was known to bring it to an excellent work.
7 But now they break down all the carved work thereof * with axes and hammers.
8 They have set fire upon thy holy places, * and have defiled the dwelling-place of thy Name, even unto the ground.
9 Yea, they said in their hearts, Let us make havoc of them altogether: * thus have they burnt up all the houses of God in the land.
10 We see not our tokens; there is not one prophet more; * no, not one is there among us, that understandeth any more.
11 O God, how long shall the adversary do this dishonor? * shall the enemy blaspheme thy Name for ever?
12 Why withdrawest thou thy hand? * why pluckest thou not thy right hand out of thy bosom to consume the enemy?
13 For God is my King of old; * the help that is done upon earth, he doeth it himself.
14 Thou didst divide the sea through thy power; * thou breakest the heads of the dragons in the waters.
15 Thou smotest the heads of leviathan in pieces, * and gavest him to be meat for the people of the wilderness.
16 Thou broughtest out fountains and waters out of the hard rocks; * thou driedst up mighty waters.
17 The day is thine, and the night is thine; * thou hast prepared the light and the sun.
18 Thou hast set all the borders of the earth; * thou hast made summer and winter.
19 Remember this, O LORD, how the enemy hath rebuked; * and how the foolish people hath blasphemed thy Name.
20 O deliver not the soul of thy turtle-dove unto the multitude of the enemies; * and forget not the congregation of the poor for ever.
21 Look upon the covenant; * for all the earth is full of darkness and cruel habitations.
22 O let not the simple go away ashamed; * but let the poor and needy give praise unto thy Name.
23 Arise, O God, maintain thine own cause; * remember how the foolish man blasphemeth thee daily.
24 Forget not the voice of thine enemies: * the presumption of them that hate thee increaseth ever more and more.

**Psalm**      **75.**      *Confitebimur*      *tibi.*

UNTO thee, O God, do we give thanks; * yea, unto thee do we give thanks.

2 Thy Name also is so nigh; * and that do thy wondrous works declare.

3 In the appointed time, saith God, * I shall judge according unto right.

4 The earth is weak, and all the inhabiters thereof: * I bear up the pillars of it.

5 I said unto the fools, Deal not so madly; * and to the ungodly, Set not up your horn.

6 Set not up your horn on high, * and speak not with a stiff neck.

7 For promotion cometh neither from the east, nor from the west, * nor yet from the south.

8 And why? God is the Judge; * he putteth down one, and setteth up another.

9 For in the hand of the LORD there is a cup, and the wine is red; * it is full mixed, and he poureth out of the same.

10 As for the dregs thereof, * all the ungodly of the earth shall drink them, and suck them out.

11 But I will talk of the God of Jacob, * and praise him for ever.

12 All the horns of the ungodly also will I break, * and the horns of the righteous shall be exalted.

**Psalm**      **76.**      *Notus*      *in*      *Judaea.*

IN Judah is God known; * his Name is great in Israel.

2 At Salem is his tabernacle, * and his dwelling in Sion.

3 There brake he the arrows of the bow, * the shield, the sword, and the battle.

4 Thou art glorious in might, * when thou comest from the hills of the robbers.

5 The proud are robbed, they have slept their sleep; * and all the men whose hands were mighty have found nothing.

6 At thy rebuke, O God of Jacob, * both the chariot and horse are fallen.

7 Thou, even thou art to be feared; * and who may stand in thy sight when thou art angry?

8 Thou didst cause thy judgment to be heard from heaven; * the earth trembled, and was still,

9 When God arose to judgment, * and to help all the meek upon earth.

10 The fierceness of man shall turn to thy praise; * and the fierceness     of     them     shalt     thou     refrain.

11 Promise unto the LORD your God, and keep it, all ye that are round about him; * bring presents unto him that ought to be feared.

12 He shall refrain the spirit of princes, * and is wonderful among the kings of the earth.

**Psalm      77.      *Voce      mea      ad      Dominum.*

I WILL cry unto God with my voice; * even unto God will I cry with     my     voice,     and     he     shall     hearken     unto     me.

2 In the time of my trouble I sought the Lord: * I stretched forth my hands unto him, and ceased not in the night season; my soul refused                                                                                comfort.

3 When I am in heaviness, I will think upon God; * when my heart is          vexed,          I          will          complain.

4 Thou holdest mine eyes waking: * I am so feeble that I cannot speak.

5 I have considered the days of old, * and the years that are past.

6 I call to remembrance my song, * and in the night I commune with     mine     own     heart,     and     search     out     my     spirit.

7 Will the Lord absent himself for ever? * and will he be no more intreated?

8 Is his mercy clean gone for ever? * and is his promise come utterly          to          an          end          for          evermore?

9 Hath God forgotten to be gracious? * and will he shut up his loving-kindness                    in                    displeasure?

10 And I said, It is mine own infirmity; * but I will remember the years     of     the     right     hand     of     the     Most     Highest.

11 I will remember the works of the LORD, * and call to mind thy wonders                    of                    old                    time.

12 I will think also of all thy works, * and my talking shall be of thy                                                                                doings.

13 Thy way, O God, is holy: * who is so great a God as our God?

14 Thou art the God that doest wonders, * and hast declared thy power                    among                    the                    peoples.

15 Thou hast mightily delivered thy people, * even the sons of Jacob                    and                    Joseph.

16 The waters saw thee, O God, the waters saw thee, and were afraid; * the depths also were troubled.
17 The clouds poured out water, the air thundered, * and thine arrows went abroad.
18 The voice of thy thunder was heard round about: * the lightnings shone upon the ground; the earth was moved, and shook withal.
19 Thy way is in the sea, and thy paths in the great waters, * and thy footsteps are not known.
20 Thou leddest thy people like sheep, * by the hand of Moses and Aaron.

**Psalm**        **78**.        *Attendite,*        *popule.*
HEAR my law, O my people; * incline your ears unto the words of my mouth.
2 I will open my mouth in a parable; * I will declare hard sentences of old;
3 Which we have heard and known, * and such as our fathers have told us;
4 That we should not hide them from the children of the generations to come; * but to show the honor of the LORD, his mighty and wonderful works that he hath done.
5 He made a covenant with Jacob, and gave Israel a law, * which he commanded our forefathers to teach their children;
6 That their posterity might know it, * and the children which were yet unborn;
7 To the intent that when they came up, * they might show their children the same;
8 That they might put their trust in God; * and not to forget the works of God, but to keep his commandments;
9 And not to be as their forefathers, a faithless and stubborn generation; * a generation that set not their heart aright, and whose spirit clave not steadfastly unto God;
10 Like as the children of Ephraim; * who being harnessed, and carrying bows, turned themselves back in the day of battle.
11 They kept not the covenant of God, * and would not walk in his law;
12 But forgat what he had done, * and the wonderful works that he had showed for them.

13 Marvelous things did he in the sight of our forefathers, in the land of Egypt, * even in the field of Zoan.
14 He divided the sea, and let them go through; * he made the waters to stand on an heap.
15 In the day-time also he led them with a cloud, * and all the night through with a light of fire.
16 He clave the hard rocks in the wilderness, * and gave them drink thereof, as it had been out of the great depth.
17 He brought waters out of the stony rock, * so that it gushed out like the rivers.
18 Yet for all this they sinned more against him, * and provoked the Most Highest in the wilderness.
19 They tempted God in their hearts, * and required meat for their lust.
20 They spake against God also, saying, * Shall God prepare a table in the wilderness?
21 He smote the stony rock indeed, that the water gushed out, and the streams flowed withal; * but can he give bread also, or provide flesh for his people?
22 When the LORD heard this, he was wroth; * so the fire was kindled in Jacob, and there came up heavy displeasure against Israel;
23 Because they believed not in God, * and put not their trust in his help.
24 So he commanded the clouds above, * and opened the doors of heaven.
25 He rained down manna also upon them for to eat, * and gave them food from heaven.
26 So man did eat angels' food; * for he sent them meat enough.
27 He caused the east-wind to blow under heaven; * and through his power he brought in the southwest-wind.
28 He rained flesh upon them as thick as dust, * and feathered fowls like as the sand of the sea.
29 He let it fall among their tents, * even round about their habitation.
30 So they did eat, and were well filled; for he gave them their own desire: * they were not disappointed of their lust.
31 But while the meat was yet in their mouths, the heavy wrath of God came upon them, and slew the wealthiest of them; * yea, and

smote down the chosen men that were in Israel.
32 But for all this they sinned yet more, * and believed not his wondrous works.
33 Therefore their days did he consume in vanity, * and their years in trouble.
34 When he slew them, they sought him, * and turned them early, and inquired after God.
35 And they remembered that God was their strength, * and that the High God was their redeemer.
36 Nevertheless, they did but flatter him with their mouth, * and dissembled with him in their tongue.
37 For their heart was not whole with him, * neither continued they stedfast in his covenant.
38 But he was so merciful, that he forgave their misdeeds, * and destroyed them not.
39 Yea, many a time turned he his wrath away, * and would not suffer his whole displeasure to arise.
40 For he considered that they were but flesh, * and that they were even a wind that passeth away, and cometh not again.
41 Many a time did they provoke him in the wilderness, * and grieved him in the desert.
42 They turned back, and tempted God, * and provoked the Holy One in Israel.
43 They thought not of his hand, * and of the day when he delivered them from the hand of the enemy;
44 How he had wrought his miracles in Egypt, * and his wonders in the field of Zoan.
45 He turned their waters into blood, * so that they might not drink of the rivers.
46 He sent flies among them, and devoured them up; * and frogs to destroy them.
47 He gave their fruit unto the caterpillar, * and their labor unto the grasshopper.
48 He destroyed their vines with hailstones, * and their mulberry-trees with the frost.
49 He smote their cattle also with hailstones, * and their flocks with hot thunderbolts.
50 He cast upon them the furiousness of his wrath, anger, displeasure, and trouble: * and sent evil angels among them.

51 He made a way to his indignation, and spared not their soul from death; * but gave their life over to the pestilence;

52 And smote all the firstborn in Egypt, * the most principal and mightiest in the dwellings of Ham.

53 But as for his own people, he led them forth like sheep, * and carried them in the wilderness like a flock.

54 He brought them out safely, that they should not fear, * and overwhelmed their enemies with the sea.

55 And brought them within the borders of his sanctuary, * even to this mountain, which he purchased with his right hand.

56 He cast out the heathen also before them, * caused their land to be divided among them for an heritage, and made the tribes of Israel to dwell in their tents.

57 Yet they tempted and displeased the Most High God, * and kept not his testimonies.

58 They turned their backs, and fell away like their forefathers; * starting aside like a broken bow.

59 For they grieved him with their hill-altars, * and provoked him to displeasure with their images.

60 When God heard this, he was wroth, * and took sore displeasure at Israel;

61 So that he forsook the tabernacle in Shiloh, * even the tent that he had pitched among men.

62 He delivered their power into captivity, * and their beauty into the enemy's hand

63 He gave his people over also unto the sword, * and was wroth with his inheritance.

64 The fire consumed their young men, * and their maidens were not given in marriage.

65 Their priests were slain with the sword, * and there were no widows to make lamentation.

66 So the Lord awaked as one out of sleep, * and like a giant refreshed with wine.

67 He drave his enemies backward, * and put them to a perpetual shame.

68 He refused the tabernacle of Joseph, * and chose not the tribe of Ephraim;

69 But chose the tribe of Judah, * even the hill of Sion which he loved.

70 And there he built his temple on high, * and laid the foundation of it like the ground which he hath made continually.
71 He chose David also his servant, * and took him away from the sheep-folds:
72 As he was following the ewes with their young he took him, * that he might feed Jacob his people, and Israel his inheritance.
73 So he fed them with a faithful and true heart, * and ruled them prudently with all his power.

**Psalm**            **79**.          *Deus,*           *venerunt.*

O GOD, the heathen are come into thine inheritance; * thy holy temple have they defiled, and made Jerusalem an heap of stones.
2 The dead bodies of thy servants have they given to be meat unto the fowls of the air, * and the flesh of thy saints unto the beasts of the                                    land.
3 Their blood have they shed like water on every side of Jerusalem, * and there was no man to bury them.
4 We are become an open shame to our enemies, * a very scorn and derision unto them that are round about us.
5 LORD, how long wilt thou be angry? * shall thy jealousy burn like           fire           for            ever?
6 Pour out thine indignation upon the heathen that have not known thee; * and upon the kingdoms that have not called upon thy Name.
7 For they have devoured Jacob, * and laid waste his dwelling-place.
8 O remember not our old sins, but have mercy upon us, and that soon;    *    for    we    are    come    to    great    misery.
9 Help us, O God of our salvation, for the glory of thy Name: * O deliver us, and be merciful unto our sins, for thy Name's sake.
10 Wherefore do the heathen say, * Where is now their God?
11 O let the vengeance of thy servants' blood that is shed, * be openly    showed    upon    the    heathen,    in    our    sight.
12 O let the sorrowful sighing of the prisoners come before thee; * according to the greatness of thy power, preserve thou those that are           appointed          to           die.
13 And for the blasphemy wherewith our neighbors have blasphemed thee, * reward thou them, O Lord, sevenfold into their bosom.

14 So we, that are thy people, and sheep of thy pasture, shall give thee thanks for ever, * and will alway be showing forth thy praise from generation to generation.

**Psalm 80.** *Qui regis Israel.*

HEAR, O thou Shepherd of Israel, thou that leadest Joseph like a flock; * show thyself also, thou that sittest upon the Cherubim.

2 Before Ephraim, Benjamin, and Manasseh, * stir up thy strength, and come and help us.

3 Turn us again, O God; * show the light of thy countenance, and we shall be whole.

4 O LORD God of hosts, * how long wilt thou be angry with thy people that prayeth?

5 Thou feedest them with the bread of tears, * and givest them plenteousness of tears to drink.

6 Thou hast made us a very strife unto our neighbors, * and our enemies laugh us to scorn.

7 Turn us again, thou God of hosts; * show the light of thy countenance, and we shall be whole.

8 Thou hast brought a vine out of Egypt; * thou hast cast out the heathen, and planted it.

9 Thou madest room for it; * and when it had taken root, it filled the land.

10 The hills were covered with the shadow of it, * and the boughs thereof were like the goodly cedar-trees.

11 She stretched out her branches unto the sea, * and her boughs unto the River.

12 Why hast thou then broken down her hedge, * that all they that go by pluck off her grapes?

13 The wild boar out of the wood doth root it up, * and the wild beasts of the field devour it.

14 Turn thee again, thou God of hosts, look down from heaven, * behold, and visit this vine;

15 And the place of the vineyard that thy right hand hath planted, * and the branch that thou madest so strong for thyself.

16 It is burnt with fire, and cut down; * and they shall perish at the rebuke of thy countenance.

17 Let thy hand be upon the man of thy right hand, * and upon the

son of man, whom thou madest so strong for thine own self.
18 And so will not we go back from thee: * O let us live, and we
shall call upon thy Name.
19 Turn us again, O LORD God of hosts; * show the light of thy
countenance, and we shall be whole.

**Psalm**          **81.**          *Exultate*          *Deo.*
SING we merrily unto God our strength; * make a cheerful noise
unto the God of Jacob.
2 Take the psalm, bring hither the tabret, * the merry harp with the
lute.
3 Blow up the trumpet in the new moon, * even in the time
appointed, and upon our solemn feast-day.
4 For this was made a statute for Israel, * and a law of the God of
Jacob.
5 This he ordained in Joseph for a testimony, * when he came out
of the land of Egypt, and had heard a strange language.
6 I eased his shoulder from the burden, * and his hands were
delivered from making the pots.
7 Thou calledst upon me in troubles, and I delivered thee; * and
heard thee what time as the storm fell upon thee.
8 I proved thee also * at the waters of strife.
9 Hear, O my people; and I will assure thee, O Israel, * if thou wilt
hearken unto me,
10 There shall no strange god be in thee, * neither shalt thou
worship any other god.
11 I am the LORD thy God, who brought thee out of the land of
Egypt: * open thy mouth wide, and I shall fill it.
12 But my people would not hear my voice; * and Israel would not
obey me;
13 So I gave them up unto their own hearts' lusts, * and let them
follow their own imaginations.
14 O that my people would have hearkened unto me! * for if Israel
had walked in my ways,
15 I should soon have put down their enemies, * and turned my
hand against their adversaries.
16 The haters of the LORD should have submitted themselves unto
him; * but their time should have endured for ever.

17 I would have fed them also with the finest wheatflour; * and with honey out of the stony rock would I have satisfied thee.

**Psalm** **82**. *Deus* *stetit.*
GOD standeth in the congregation of princes; * he is a Judge among gods.
2 How long will ye give wrong judgment, * and accept the persons of the ungodly?
3 Defend the poor and fatherless; * see that such as are in need and necessity have right.
4 Deliver the outcast and poor; * save them from the hand of the ungodly.
5 They know not, neither do they understand, but walk on still in darkness: * all the foundations of the earth are out of course.
6 I have said, Ye are gods, * and ye are all the children of the Most Highest.
7 But ye shall die like men, * and fall like one of the princes.
8 Arise, O God, and judge thou the earth; * for thou shalt take all nations to thine inheritance.

**Psalm** **83**. *Deus,* *quis* *similis?*
HOLD not thy tongue, O God, keep not still silence: * refrain not thyself, O God.
2 For lo, thine enemies make a murmuring; * and they that hate thee have lift up their head.
3 They have imagined craftily against thy people, * and taken counsel against thy secret ones.
4 They have said, Come, and let us root them out, that they be no more a people, * and that the name of Israel may be no more in remembrance.
5 For they have cast their heads together with one consent, * and are confederate against thee:
6 The tabernacles of the Edomites, and the Ishmaelites; * the Moabites, and Hagarenes;
7 Gebal, and Ammon, and Amalek; * the Philistines, with them that dwell at Tyre.
8 Assyria also is joined with them; * they have holpen the children of Lot.
9 But do thou to them as unto the Midianites; * unto Sisera, and

unto     Jabin     at     the     brook     of     Kishon;
10 Who perished at Endor, * and became as the dung of the earth.
11 Make them and their princes like Oreb and Zeeb; * yea, make
all     their     princes     like     as     Zebah     and     Zalmunna;
12 Who say, Let us take to ourselves * the houses of God in
possession.
13 O my God, make them like unto the whirling dust, * and as the
stubble          before          the          wind;
14 Like as the fire that burneth up the forest, * and as the flame
that          consumeth          the          mountains;
15 Pursue them even so with thy tempest, * and make them afraid
with                    thy                    storm.
16 Make their faces ashamed, O LORD, * that they may seek thy
Name.
17 Let them be confounded and vexed ever more and more; * let
them     be     put     to     shame,     and     perish.
18 And they shall know that thou, whose Name is JEHOVAH, * art
only the Most Highest over all the earth.

**Psalm**          **84**.          *Quam*          *dilecta!*
O HOW amiable are thy dwellings, * thou LORD of hosts!
2 My soul hath a desire and longing to enter into the courts of the
LORD; * my heart and my flesh rejoice in the living God.
3 Yea, the sparrow hath found her an house, and the swallow a
nest, where she may lay her young; * even thy altars, O LORD of
hosts,     my     King     and     my     God.
4 Blessed are they that dwell in thy house; * they will be alway
praising                                        thee.
5 Blessed is the man whose strength is in thee; * in whose heart are
thy                                        ways.
6 Who going through the vale of misery use it for a well; * and the
pools     are     filled     with     water.
7 They will go from strength to strength, * and unto the God of
gods     appeareth     every     one     of     them     in     Sion.
8 O LORD God of hosts, hear my prayer; * hearken, O God of
Jacob.
9 Behold, O God our defender, * and look upon the face of thine
anointed.
10 For one day in thy courts * is better than a thousand.

11 I had rather be a door-keeper in the house of my God, * than to dwell in the tents of ungodliness.
12 For the LORD God is a light and defense; * the LORD will give grace and worship; and no good thing shall he withhold from them that live a godly life.
13 O LORD God of hosts, * blessed is the man that putteth his trust in thee.

**Psalm 85.** *Benedixisti, Domine.*

LORD, thou art become gracious unto thy land; * thou hast turned away the captivity of Jacob.
2 Thou hast forgiven the offense of thy people, * and covered all their sins.
3 Thou hast taken away all thy displeasure, * and turned thyself from thy wrathful indignation.
4 Turn us then, O God our Savior, * and let thine anger cease from us.
5 Wilt thou be displeased at us for ever? * and wilt thou stretch out thy wrath from one generation to another?
6 Wilt thou not turn again, and quicken us, * that thy people may rejoice in thee?
7 Show us thy mercy, O LORD, * and grant us thy salvation.
8 I will hearken what the LORD God will say; * for he shall speak peace unto his people, and to his saints, that they turn not again unto foolishness.
9 For his salvation is nigh them that fear him; * that glory may dwell in our land.
10 Mercy and truth are met together: * righteousness and peace have kissed each other.
11 Truth shall flourish out of the earth, * and righteousness hath looked down from heaven.
12 Yea, the LORD shall show loving-kindness; * and our land shall give her increase.
13 Righteousness shall go before him, * and shall direct his going in the way.

**Psalm 86.** *Inclina, Domine.*

BOW down thine ear, O LORD, and hear me; * for I am poor, and in misery.

2 Preserve thou my soul, for I am holy: * my God, save thy servant that putteth his trust in thee.

3 Be merciful unto me, O Lord; * for I will call daily upon thee.

4 Comfort the soul of thy servant; * for unto thee, O Lord, do I lift up my soul.

5 For thou, Lord, art good and gracious, * and of great mercy unto all them that call upon thee.

6 Give ear, LORD, unto my prayer, * and ponder the voice of my humble desires.

7 In the time of my trouble I will call upon thee; * for thou hearest me.

8 Among the gods there is none like unto thee, O Lord; * there is not one that can do as thou doest.

9 All nations whom thou hast made shall come and worship thee, O Lord; * and shall glorify thy Name.

10 For thou art great, and doest wondrous things: * thou art God alone.

11 Teach me thy way, O LORD, and I will walk in thy truth: * O knit my heart unto thee, that I may fear thy Name.

12 I will thank thee, O Lord my God, with all my heart; * and will praise thy Name for evermore.

13 For great is thy mercy toward me; * and thou hast delivered my soul from the nethermost hell.

14 O God, the proud are risen against me; * and the congregations of violent men have sought after my soul, and have not set thee before their eyes.

15 But thou, O Lord God, art full of compassion and mercy, * long-suffering, plenteous in goodness and truth.

16 O turn thee then unto me, and have mercy upon me; * give thy strength unto thy servant, and help the son of thine handmaid.

17 Show some token upon me for good; that they who hate me may see it, and be ashamed, * because thou, LORD, hast holpen me, and comforted me.

**Psalm** **87.** *Fundamenta* *ejus.*

HER foundations are upon the holy hills: * the LORD loveth the gates of Sion more than all the dwellings of Jacob.

2 Very excellent things are spoken of thee, * thou city of God.

3 I will make mention of Egypt and Babylon, * among them that know                                                                 me.
4 Behold, Philistia also; and Tyre, with Ethiopia; * lo, in Sion were they                                                              born.
5 Yea, of Sion it shall be reported, this one and that one were born in   her;   *   and   the   Most   High   shall   stablish   her.
6 The LORD shall record it, when he writeth up the peoples; * lo, in        Sion        were        they        born.
7 The singers also and trumpeters shall make answer: * All my fresh springs are in thee.

**Psalm**          **88**.         *Domine,*           *Deus.*

O LORD God of my salvation, I have cried day and night before thee: * O let my prayer enter into thy presence, incline thine ear unto                         my                         calling;
2 For my soul is full of trouble, * and my life draweth nigh unto the                                                                grave.
3 I am counted as one of them that go down into the pit, * and I am even     as     a     man     that     hath     no     strength;
4 Cast off among the dead, like unto them that are slain, and lie in the grave, * who are out of remembrance, and are cut away from thy                                                               hand.
5 Thou hast laid me in the lowest pit, * in a place of darkness, and in                         the                         deep.
6 Thine indignation lieth hard upon me, * and thou hast vexed me with             all             thy             storms.
7 Thou hast put away mine acquaintance far from me, * and made me       to       be       abhorred       of       them.
8 I   am   so   fast   in   prison   *   that   I   cannot   get   forth.
9 My sight faileth for very trouble; * LORD, I have called daily upon thee, I have stretched forth my hands unto thee.
10 Dost thou show wonders among the dead? * or shall the dead rise       up       again,       and       praise       thee?
11 Shall thy loving-kindness be showed in the grave? * or thy faithfulness               in               destruction?
12 Shall thy wondrous works be known in the dark? * and thy righteousness   in   the   land   where   all   things   are   forgotten?
13 Unto thee have I cried, O LORD; * and early shall my prayer come                         before                         thee.

14 LORD, why abhorrest thou my soul, * and hidest thou thy face from                                                                          me?
15 I am in misery, and like unto him that is at the point to die; * even from my youth up, thy terrors have I suffered with a troubled mind.
16 Thy wrathful displeasure goeth over me, * and the fear of thee hath                              undone                              me.
17 They came round about me daily like water, * and compassed me              together              on              every              side.
18 My lovers and friends hast thou put away from me, * and hid mine acquaintance out of my sight.

**Psalm          89.**          *Misericordias          Domini.*
MY song shall be alway of the loving-kindness of the LORD; * with my mouth will I ever be showing thy truth from one generation                              to                              another.
2 For I have said, Mercy shall be set up for ever; * thy truth shalt thou              stablish              in              the              heavens.
3 I have made a covenant with my chosen; * I have sworn unto David                              my                              servant:
4 Thy seed will I stablish for ever, * and set up thy throne from one generation                              to                              another.
5 O LORD, the very heavens shall praise thy wondrous works; * and        thy        truth        in        the        congregation        of        the        saints.
6 For who is he among the clouds, * that shall be compared unto the                                                                          LORD?
7 And what is he among the gods, * that shall be like unto the LORD?
8 God is very greatly to be feared in the council of the saints, * and to be had in reverence of all them that are round about him.
9 O Lord God of hosts, who is like unto thee? * thy truth, most mighty        LORD,        is        on        every        side.
10 Thou rulest the raging of the sea; * thou stillest the waves thereof              when              they              arise.
11 Thou hast subdued Egypt, and destroyed it; * thou hast scattered        thine        enemies        abroad        with        thy        mighty        arm.
12 The heavens are thine, the earth also is thine; * thou hast laid the foundation of the round world, and all that therein is.
13 Thou hast made the north and the south; * Tabor and Hermon

shall rejoice in thy Name.
14 Thou hast a mighty arm; * strong is thy hand, and high is thy right hand.
15 Righteousness and equity are the habitation of thy seat; * mercy and truth shall go before thy face.
16 Blessed is the people, O LORD, that can rejoice in thee; * they shall walk in the light of thy countenance.
17 Their delight shall be daily in thy Name; * and in thy righteousness shall they make their boast.
18 For thou art the glory of their strength, * and in thy loving-kindness thou shalt lift up our horns.
19 For the LORD is our defense; * the Holy One of Israel is our King.
20 Thou spakest sometime in visions unto thy saints, and saidst, * I have laid help upon one that is mighty, I have exalted one chosen out of the people.
21 I have found David my servant; * with my holy oil have I anointed him.
22 My hand shall hold him fast, * and my arm shall strengthen him.
23 The enemy shall not be able to do him violence; * the son of wickedness shall not hurt him.
24 I will smite down his foes before his face, * and plague them that hate him.
25 My truth also and my mercy shall be with him; * and in my Name shall his horn be exalted.
26 I will set his dominion also in the sea, * and his right hand in the floods.
27 He shall call me, Thou art my Father, * my God, and my strong salvation.
28 And I will make him my firstborn, * higher than the kings of the earth.
29 My mercy will I keep for him for evermore, * and my covenant shall stand fast with him.
30 His seed also will I make to endure for ever, * and his throne as the days of heaven.
31 But if his children forsake my law, * and walk not in my judgments;
32 If they break my statutes, and keep not my commandments; * I

will visit their offenses with the rod, and their sin with scourges.
33 Nevertheless, my loving-kindness will I not utterly take from him, * nor suffer my truth to fail.
34 My covenant will I not break, nor alter the thing that is gone out of my lips: * I have sworn once by my holiness, that I will not fail David.
35 His seed shall endure for ever, * and his throne is like as the sun before me.
36 He shall stand fast for evermore as the moon, * and as the faithful witness in heaven.
37 But thou hast abhorred and forsaken thine anointed, * and art displeased at him.
38 Thou hast broken the covenant of thy servant, * and cast his crown to the ground.
39 Thou hast overthrown all his hedges, * and broken down his strongholds.
40 All they that go by spoil him, * and he is become a reproach to his neighbors.
41 Thou hast set up the right hand of his enemies, * and made all his adversaries to rejoice.
42 Thou hast taken away the edge of his sword, * and givest him not victory in the battle.
43 Thou hast put out his glory, * and cast his throne down to the ground.
44 The days of his youth hast thou shortened, * and covered him with dishonor.
45 LORD, how long wilt thou hide thyself? for ever? * and shall thy wrath burn like fire?
46 O remember how short my time is; * wherefore hast thou made all men for nought?
47 What man is he that liveth, and shall not see death? * and shall he deliver his soul from the power of the grave?
48 Lord, where are thy old loving-kindnesses, * which thou swarest unto David in thy truth?
49 Remember, Lord, the rebuke that thy servants have, * and how I do bear in my bosom the rebukes of many people;
50 Wherewith thine enemies have blasphemed thee, * and slandered the footsteps of thine anointed.
51 Praised be the LORD for evermore. * Amen, and Amen.

**Psalm**        **90.**        *Domine,*        *refugium.*

LORD, thou hast been our refuge, * from one generation to another.

2 Before the mountains were brought forth, or ever the earth and the world were made, * thou art God from everlasting, and world without             end.

3 Thou turnest man to destruction; * again thou sayest, Come again,      ye      children      of      men.

4 For a thousand years in thy sight are but as yesterday when it is past,    *    and    as    a    watch    in    the    night.

5 As soon as thou scatterest them they are even as a sleep; * and fade     away     suddenly     like     the     grass.

6 In the morning it is green, and groweth up; * but in the evening it is    cut    down,    dried    up,    and    withered.

7 For we consume away in thy displeasure, * and are afraid at thy wrathful             indignation.

8 Thou hast set our misdeeds before thee; * and our secret sins in the      light      of      thy      countenance.

9 For when thou art angry all our days are gone: * we bring our years    to    an    end,    as    it    were    a    tale    that    is    told.

10 The days of our age are threescore years and ten; and though men be so strong that they come to fourscore years, * yet is their strength then but labor and sorrow; so soon passeth it away, and we             are             gone.

11 But who regardeth the power of thy wrath? * or feareth aright thy             indignation?

12 So teach us to number our days, * that we may apply our hearts unto             wisdom.

13 Turn thee again, O LORD, at the last, * and be gracious unto thy servants.

14 O satisfy us with thy mercy, and that soon: * so shall we rejoice and    be    glad    all    the    days    of    our    life.

15 Comfort us again now after the time that thou hast plagued us; * and for the years wherein we have suffered adversity.

16 Show thy servants thy work, * and their children thy glory.

17 And the glorious majesty of the LORD our God be upon us: * prosper thou the work of our hands upon us; O prosper thou our handy-work.

**Psalm**        **91**.        *Qui*        *habitat*.

WHOSO dwelleth under the defense of the Most High, * shall abide under the shadow of the Almighty.

2 I will say unto the LORD, Thou art my hope, and my stronghold; * my God, in him will I trust.

3 For he shall deliver thee from the snare of the hunter, * and from the noisome pestilence.

4 He shall defend thee under his wings, and thou shalt be safe under his feathers; * his faithfulness and truth shall be thy shield and buckler.

5 Thou shalt not be afraid for any terror by night, * nor for the arrow that flieth by day;

6 For the pestilence that walketh in darkness, * nor for the sickness that destroyeth in the noon-day.

7 A thousand shall fall beside thee, and ten thousand at thy right hand; * but it shall not come nigh thee.

8 Yea, with thine eyes shalt thou behold, * and see the reward of the ungodly.

9 For thou, LORD, art my hope; * thou hast set thine house of defense very high.

10 There shall no evil happen unto thee, * neither shall any plague come nigh thy dwelling.

11 For he shall give his angels charge over thee, * to keep thee in all thy ways.

12 They shall bear thee in their hands, * that thou hurt not thy foot against a stone.

13 Thou shalt go upon the lion and adder: * the young lion and the dragon shalt thou tread under thy feet.

14 Because he hath set his love upon me, therefore will I deliver him; * I will set him up, because he hath known my Name.

15 He shall call upon me, and I will hear him; * yea, I am with him in trouble; I will deliver him, and bring him to honor.

16 With long life will I satisfy him, * and show him my salvation.

**Psalm**        **92**.        *Bonum*        *est*        *confiteri*.

IT is a good thing to give thanks unto the LORD, * and to sing praises unto thy Name, O Most Highest;

2 To tell of thy loving-kindness early in the morning, * and of thy truth in the night season;

134

3 Upon an instrument of ten strings, and upon the lute; * upon a loud instrument, and upon the harp.
4 For thou, LORD, hast made me glad through thy works; * and I will rejoice in giving praise for the operations of thy hands.
5 O LORD, how glorious are thy works! * thy thoughts are very deep.
6 An unwise man doth not well consider this, * and a fool doth not understand it.
7 When the ungodly are green as the grass, and when all the workers of wickedness do flourish, * then shall they be destroyed for ever; but thou, LORD, art the Most Highest for evermore.
8 For lo, thine enemies, O LORD, lo, thine enemies shall perish; * and all the workers of wickedness shall be destroyed.
9 But my horn shall be exalted like the horn of an unicorn; * for I am anointed with fresh oil.
10 Mine eye also shall see his lust of mine enemies, * and mine ear shall hear his desire of the wicked that arise up against me.
11 The righteous shall flourish like a palm-tree, * and shall spread abroad like a cedar in Lebanon.
12 Such as are planted in the house of the LORD, * shall flourish in the courts of the house of our God.
13 They also shall bring forth more fruit in their age, * and shall be fat and well-liking;
14 That they may show how true the LORD my strength is, * and that there is no unrighteousness in him.

**Psalm** **93**. *Dominus regnavit.*
THE LORD is King, and hath put on glorious apparel; * the LORD hath put on his apparel, and girded himself with strength.
2 He hath made the round world so sure, * that it cannot be moved.
3 Ever since the world began, hath thy seat been prepared: * thou art from everlasting.
4 The floods are risen, O LORD, the floods have lift up their voice; * the floods lift up their waves.
5 The waves of the sea are mighty, and rage horribly; * but yet the LORD, who dwelleth on high, is mightier.
6 Thy testimonies, O LORD, are very sure: * holiness becometh thine house for ever.

**Psalm**        **94.**        *Deus*        *ultionum.*

O LORD God, to whom vengeance belongeth, * thou God, to whom vengeance belongeth, show thyself.

2 Arise, thou Judge of the world, * and reward the proud after their deserving.

3 LORD, how long shall the ungodly, * how long shall the ungodly triumph?

4 How long shall all wicked doers speak so disdainfully, * and make such proud boasting?

5 They smite down thy people, O LORD, * and trouble thine heritage.

6 They murder the widow and the stranger, * and put the fatherless to death.

7 And yet they say, Tush, the LORD shall not see, * neither shall the God of Jacob regard it.

8 Take heed, ye unwise among the people: * O ye fools, when will ye understand?

9 He that planted the ear, shall he not hear? * or he that made the eye, shall he not see?

10 Or he that instructeth the heathen, * it is he that teacheth man knowledge; shall not he punish?

11 The LORD knoweth the thoughts of man, * that they are but vain.

12 Blessed is the man whom thou chastenest, O LORD, * and teachest him in thy law;

13 That thou mayest give him patience in time of adversity, * until the pit be digged up for the ungodly.

14 For the LORD will not fail his people; * neither will he forsake his inheritance;

15 Until righteousness turn again unto judgment: * all such as are true in heart shall follow it.

16 Who will rise up with me against the wicked? * or who will take my part against the evil doers?

17 If the LORD had not helped me, * it had not failed, but my soul had been put to silence.

18 But when I said, My foot hath slipped; * thy mercy, O LORD, held me up.

19 In the multitude of the sorrows that I had in my heart, * thy comforts have refreshed my soul.

20 Wilt thou have any thing to do with the throne of wickedness, *
which imagineth mischief as a law?
21 They gather them together against the soul of the righteous, *
and condemn the innocent blood.
22 But the LORD is my refuge, * and my God is the strength of my
confidence.
23 He shall recompense them their wickedness, and destroy them
in their own malice; * yea, the LORD our God shall destroy them.

**Psalm 95.** *Venite, exultemus.*
O COME, let us sing unto the LORD; * let us heartily rejoice in the
strength of our salvation.
2 Let us come before his presence with thanksgiving; * and show
ourselves glad in him with psalms.
3 For the LORD is a great God; * and a great King above all gods.
4 In his hand are all the corners of the earth; * and the strength of
the hills is his also.
5 The sea is his, and he made it; * and his hands prepared the dry
land.
6 O come, let us worship and fall down, * and kneel before the
LORD our Maker.
7 For he is the Lord our God; * and we are the people of his
pasture, and the sheep of his hand.
8 To-day if ye will hear his voice, harden not your hearts * as in
the provocation, and as in the day of temptation in the wilderness;
9 When your fathers tempted me, * proved me, and saw my works.
10 Forty years long was I grieved with this generation, and said, *
It is a people that do err in their hearts, for they have not known
my ways:
11 Unto whom I sware in my wrath, * that they should not enter
into my rest.

**Psalm 96.** *Cantate Domino.*
O SING unto the LORD a new song; * sing unto the LORD, all the
whole earth.
2 Sing unto the LORD, and praise his Name; * be telling of his
salvation from day to day.
3 Declare his honor unto the heathen, * and his wonders unto all
peoples.

4 For the LORD is great, and cannot worthily be praised;* he is more to be feared than all gods.
5 As for all the gods of the heathen, they are but idols; * but it is the LORD that made the heavens.
6 Glory and worship are before him; * power and honor are in his sanctuary.
7 Ascribe unto the LORD, O ye kindreds of the peoples, * ascribe unto the LORD worship and power.
8 Ascribe unto the LORD the honor due unto his Name; * bring presents, and come into his courts.
9 O worship the LORD in the beauty of holiness; * let the whole earth stand in awe of him.
10 Tell it out among the heathen, that the LORD is King, and that it is he who hath made the round world so fast that it cannot be moved; * and how that he shall judge the peoples righteously.
11 Let the heavens rejoice, and let the earth be glad; * let the sea make a noise, and all that therein is.
12 Let the field be joyful, and all that is in it; * then shall all the trees of the wood rejoice before the LORD.
13 For he cometh, for he cometh to judge the earth; * and with righteousness to judge the world, and the peoples with his truth.

**Psalm** **97**. *Dominus* *regnavit.*
THE LORD is King, the earth may be glad thereof; * yea, the multitude of the isles may be glad thereof.
2 Clouds and darkness are round about him: * righteousness and judgment are the habitation of his seat.
3 There shall go a fire before him, * and burn up his enemies on every side.
4 His lightnings gave shine unto the world: * the earth saw it, and was afraid.
5 The hills melted like wax at the presence of the LORD; * at the presence of the Lord of the whole earth.
6 The heavens have declared his righteousness, * and all the peoples have seen his glory.
7 Confounded be all they that worship carved images, and that delight in vain gods: * worship him, all ye gods.
8 Sion heard of it, and rejoiced; and the daughters of Judah were glad, * because of thy judgments, O LORD.

9 For thou, LORD, art higher than all that are in the earth: * thou art
exalted              far              above              all              gods.
10 O ye that love the LORD, see that ye hate the thing which is
evil: * the Lord preserveth the souls of his saints; he shall deliver
them        from        the        hand        of        the        ungodly.
11 There is sprung up a light for the righteous, * and joyful
gladness        for        such        as        are        true-hearted.
12 Rejoice in the LORD, ye righteous; * and give thanks for a
remembrance of his holiness.

**Psalm                    98.**              *Cantate*              *Domino.*
O SING unto the LORD a new song; * for he hath done marvelous
things.
2 With his own right hand, and with his holy arm, * hath he gotten
himself                          the                          victory.
3 The LORD declared his salvation; * his righteousness hath he
openly        showed        in        the        sight        of        the        heathen.
4 He hath remembered his mercy and truth toward the house of
Israel; * and all the ends of the world have seen the salvation of
our                                                                          God.
5 Show yourselves joyful unto the LORD, all ye lands; * sing,
rejoice,                    and                    give                    thanks.
6 Praise the LORD upon the harp; * sing to the harp with a psalm of
thanksgiving.
7 With trumpets also and shawms, * O show yourselves joyful
before        the        LORD,        the        King.
8 Let the sea make a noise, and all that therein is; * the round
world,        and        they        that        dwell        therein.
9 Let the floods clap their hands, and let the hills be joyful together
before the LORD; * for he is come to judge the earth.
10 With righteousness shall he judge the world, * and the peoples
with equity.

**Psalm                    99.**              *Dominus*              *regnavit.*
THE LORD is King, be the people never so impatient; * he sitteth
between        the        Cherubim,        be        the        earth        never        so        unquiet.
2 The LORD is great in Sion, * and high above all people.
3 They shall give thanks unto thy Name, * which is great,
wonderful,                              and                              holy.

4 The King's power loveth judgment; thou hast prepared equity, *
thou hast executed judgment and righteousness in Jacob.
5 O magnify the LORD our God, and fall down before his
footstool;         *         for        he        is        holy.
6 Moses and Aaron among his priests, and Samuel among such as
call upon his Name: * these called upon the LORD, and he heard
them.
7 He spake unto them out of the cloudy pillar; * for they kept his
testimonies,    and    the    law    that    he    gave    them.
8 Thou heardest them, O LORD our God; * thou forgavest them, O
God,    though    thou    didst    punish    their    wicked    doings.
9 O magnify the LORD our God, and worship him upon his holy
hill; * for the LORD our God is holy.

**Psalm**            **100.**            *Jubilate*            *Deo.*
O BE joyful in the LORD, all ye lands: * serve the LORD with
gladness,    and    come    before    his    presence    with    a    song.
2 Be ye sure that the LORD he is God; it is he that hath made us,
and not we ourselves; * we are his people, and the sheep of his
pasture.
3 O go your way into his gates with thanksgiving, and into his
courts with praise; * be thankful unto him, and speak good of his
Name.
4 For the LORD is gracious, his mercy is everlasting; * and his
truth endureth from generation to generation.

**Psalm**        **101.**        *Misericordiam*        *et*        *judicium.*
MY song shall be of mercy and judgment; * unto thee, O LORD,
will                                I                                sing.
2 O let me have understanding * in the way of godliness!
3 When wilt thou come unto me? * I will walk in my house with a
perfect                                                                heart.
4 I will take no wicked thing in hand; I hate the sins of
unfaithfulness;    *    there    shall    no    such    cleave    unto    me.
5 A froward heart shall depart from me; * I will not know a wicked
person.
6 Whoso privily slandereth his neighbor, * him will I destroy.
7 Whoso hath also a haughty look and a proud heart, * I will not
suffer                                                                him.

8 Mine eyes look upon such as are faithful in the land, * that they may dwell with me.
9 Whoso leadeth a godly life, * he shall be my servant.
10 There shall no deceitful person dwell in my house; * he that telleth lies shall not tarry in my sight.
11 I shall soon destroy all the ungodly that are in the land; * that I may root out all wicked doers from the city of the LORD.

**Psalm**     **102**.     *Domine,*     *exaudi.*

HEAR my prayer, O LORD, * and let my crying come unto thee.
2 Hide not thy face from me in the time of my trouble; * incline thine ear unto me when I call; O hear me, and that right soon.
3 For my days are consumed away like smoke, * and my bones are burnt up as it were a firebrand.
4 My heart is smitten down, and withered like grass; * so that I forget to eat my bread.
5 For the voice of my groaning, * my bones will scarce cleave to my flesh.
6 I am become like a pelican in the wilderness, * and like an owl that is in the desert.
7 I have watched, and am even as it were a sparrow, * that sitteth alone upon the housetop.
8 Mine enemies revile me all the day long; * and they that are mad upon me are sworn together against me.
9 For I have eaten ashes as it were bread, * and mingled my drink with weeping;
10 And that, because of thine indignation and wrath; * for thou hast taken me up, and cast me down.
11 My days are gone like a shadow, * and I am withered like grass.
12 But thou, O LORD, shalt endure for ever, * and thy remembrance throughout all generations.
13 Thou shalt arise, and have mercy upon Sion; * for it is time that thou have mercy upon her, yea, the time is come.
14 And why? thy servants think upon her stones, * and it pitieth them to see her in the dust.
15 The nations shall fear thy Name, O LORD; * and all the kings of the earth thy majesty;
16 When the LORD shall build up Sion, * and when his glory shall appear;

17 When he turneth him unto the prayer of the poor destitute, * and despiseth not their desire.
18 This shall be written for those that come after, * and the people which shall be born shall praise the LORD.
19 For he hath looked down from his sanctuary; * out of the heaven did the LORD behold the earth;
20 That he might hear the mournings of such as are in captivity, * and deliver them that are appointed unto death;
21 That they may declare the Name of the LORD in Sion, * and his worship at Jerusalem;
22 When the peoples are gathered together, * and the kingdoms also, to serve the LORD.
23 He brought down my strength in my journey, * and shortened my days.
24 But I said, O my God, take me not away in the midst of mine age; * as for thy years, they endure throughout all generations.
25 Thou, Lord, in the beginning hast laid the foundation of the earth, * and the heavens are the work of thy hands.
26 They shall perish, but thou shalt endure: * they all shall wax old as doth a garment;
27 And as a vesture shalt thou change them, and they shall be changed; * but thou art the same, and thy years shall not fail.
28 The children of thy servants shall continue, * and their seed shall stand fast in thy sight.

**Psalm 103.** *Benedic, anima mea.*
PRAISE the LORD, O my soul; * and all that is within me, praise his holy Name.
2 Praise the LORD, O my soul, * and forget not all his benefits:
3 Who forgiveth all thy sin, * and healeth all thine infirmities;
4 Who saveth thy life from destruction, * and crowneth thee with mercy and loving-kindness;
5 Who satisfieth thy mouth with good things, * making thee young and lusty as an eagle.
6 The LORD executeth righteousness and judgment * for all them that are oppressed with wrong.
7 He showed his ways unto Moses, * his works unto the children of Israel.
8 The LORD is full of compassion and mercy, * long suffering, and

of                          great                          goodness.
9 He will not alway be chiding; * neither keepeth he his anger for ever.
10 He hath not dealt with us after our sins; * nor rewarded us according                    to                    our                    wickednesses.
11 For look how high the heaven is in comparison of the earth; * so great is his mercy also toward them that fear him.
12 Look how wide also the east is from the west; * so far hath he set                    our                    sins                    from                    us.
13 Yea, like as a father pitieth his own children; * even so is the LORD          merciful          unto          them          that          fear          him.
14 For he knoweth whereof we are made; * he remembereth that we                          are                          but                          dust.
15 The days of man are but as grass; * for he flourisheth as a flower                    of                    the                    field.
16 For as soon as the wind goeth over it, it is gone; * and the place thereof          shall          know          it          no          more.
17 But the merciful goodness of the LORD endureth for ever and ever upon them that fear him; * and his righteousness upon children's                                                    children;
18 Even upon such as keep his covenant, * and think upon his commandments                    to                    do                    them.
19 The LORD hath prepared his seat in heaven, * and his kingdom ruleth                          over                          all.
20 O praise the LORD, ye angels of his, ye that excel in strength; * ye that fulfill his commandment, and hearken unto the voice of his word.
21 O praise the LORD, all ye his hosts; * ye servants of his that do his                                                              pleasure.
22 O speak good of the LORD, all ye works of his, in all places of his dominion: * praise thou the LORD, O my soul.

**Psalm          104**.          *Benedic,          anima          mea.*
PRAISE the LORD, O my soul: * O LORD my God, thou art become exceeding glorious; thou art clothed with majesty and honor.
2 Thou deckest thyself with light as it were with a garment, * and spreadest          out          the          heavens          like          a          curtain.
3 Who layeth the beams of his chambers in the waters, * and

maketh the clouds his chariot, and walketh upon the wings of the wind.

4 He maketh his angels winds, * and his ministers a flaming fire.

5 He laid the foundations of the earth, * that it never should move at any time.

6 Thou coveredst it with the deep like as with a garment; * the waters stand above the hills.

7 At thy rebuke they flee; * at the voice of thy thunder they haste away.

8 They go up as high as the hills, and down to the valleys beneath; * even unto the place which thou hast appointed for them.

9 Thou hast set them their bounds, which they shall not pass, * neither turn again to cover the earth.

10 He sendeth the springs into the rivers, * which run among the hills.

11 All beasts of the field drink thereof, * and the wild asses quench their thirst.

12 Beside them shall the fowls of the air have their habitation, * and sing among the branches.

13 He watereth the hills from above; * the earth is filled with the fruit of thy works.

14 He bringeth forth grass for the cattle, * and green herb for the service of men;

15 That he may bring food out of the earth, and wine that maketh glad the heart of man; * and oil to make him a cheerful countenance, and bread to strengthen man's heart.

16 The trees of the LORD also are full of sap; * even the cedars of Lebanon which he hath planted;

17 Wherein the birds make their nests; * and the fir trees are a dwelling for the stork.

18 The high hills are a refuge for the wild goats; * and so are the stony rocks for the conies.

19 He appointed the moon for certain seasons, * and the sun knoweth his going down.

20 Thou makest darkness that it may be night; * wherein all the beasts of the forest do move.

21 The lions, roaring after their prey, * do seek their meat from God.

22 The sun ariseth, and they get them away together, * and lay

them down in their dens.
23 Man goeth forth to his work, and to his labor, * until the evening.
24 O LORD, how manifold are thy works! * in wisdom hast thou made them all; the earth is full of thy riches.
25 So is the great and wide sea also; * wherein are things creeping innumerable, both small and great beasts.
26 There go the ships, and there is that leviathan, * whom thou hast made to take his pastime therein.
27 These wait all upon thee, * that thou mayest give them meat in due season.
28 When thou givest it them, they gather it; * and when thou openest thy hand, they are filled with good.
29 When thou hidest thy face, they are troubled: * when thou takest away their breath, they die, and are turned again to their dust.
30 When thou lettest thy breath go forth, they shall be made; * and thou shalt renew the face of the earth.
31 The glorious majesty of the LORD shall endure for ever; * the LORD shall rejoice in his works.
32 The earth shall tremble at the look of him; * if he do but touch the hills, they shall smoke.
33 I will sing unto the LORD as long as I live; * I will praise my God while I have my being.
34 And so shall my words please him: * my joy shall be in the LORD.
35 As for sinners, they shall be consumed out of the earth, * and the ungodly shall come to an end.
36 Praise thou the LORD, O my soul. * Praise the LORD.

**Psalm 105.** *Confitemini Domino.*
GIVE thanks unto the LORD, and call upon his Name; * tell the people what things he hath done.
2 O let your songs be of him, and praise him; * and let your talking be of all his wondrous works.
3 Rejoice in his holy Name; * let the heart of them rejoice that seek the LORD.
4 Seek the LORD and his strength; * seek his face evermore.
5 Remember the marvelous works that he hath done; * his

wonders, and the judgments of his mouth;

6 O ye seed of Abraham his servant, * ye children of Jacob his chosen.

7 He is the LORD our God; * his judgments are in all the world.

8 He hath been alway mindful of his covenant and promise, * that he made to a thousand generations;

9 Even the covenant that he made with Abraham; * and the oath that he sware unto Isaac;

10 And appointed the same unto Jacob for a law, * and to Israel for an everlasting testament;

11 Saying, Unto thee will I give the land of Canaan, * the lot of your inheritance:

12 When there were yet but a few of them, * and they strangers in the land;

13 What time as they went from one nation to another, * from one kingdom to another people;

14 He suffered no man to do them wrong, * but reproved even kings for their sakes;

15 Touch not mine anointed, * and do my prophets no harm.

16 Moreover, he called for a dearth upon the land, * and destroyed all the provision of bread.

17 But he had sent a man before them, * even Joseph, who was sold to be a bond-servant;

18 Whose feet they hurt in the stocks; * the iron entered into his soul;

19 Until the time came that his cause was known: * the word of the LORD tried him.

20 The king sent, and delivered him; * the prince of the people let him go free.

21 He made him lord also of his house, * and ruler of all his substance;

22 That he might inform his princes after his will, * and teach his senators wisdom.

23 Israel also came into Egypt, * and Jacob was a stranger in the land of Ham.

24 And he increased his people exceedingly, * and made them stronger than their enemies;

25 Whose heart turned so, that they hated his people, * and dealt untruly with his servants.

26 Then sent he Moses his servant, * and Aaron whom he had chosen.

27 And these showed his tokens among them, * and wonders in the land of Ham.

28 He sent darkness, and it was dark; * and they were not obedient unto his word.

29 He turned their waters into blood, * and slew their fish.

30 Their land brought forth frogs; * yea, even in their kings' chambers.

31 He spake the word, and there came all manner of flies, * and lice in all their quarters.

32 He gave them hailstones for rain; * and flames of fire in their land.

33 He smote their vines also and fig-trees; * and destroyed the trees that were in their coasts.

34 He spake the word, and the grasshoppers came, and caterpillars innumerable, * and did eat up all the grass in their land, and devoured the fruit of their ground.

35 He smote all the firstborn in their land; * even the chief of all their strength.

36 He brought them forth also with silver and gold; * there was not one feeble person among their tribes.

37 Egypt was glad at their departing; * for they were afraid of them.

38 He spread out a cloud to be a covering, * and fire to give light in the night season.

39 At their desire he brought quails; * and he filled them with the bread of heaven.

40 He opened the rock of stone, and the waters flowed out, * so that rivers ran in the dry places.

41 For why? he remembered his holy promise; * and Abraham his servant.

42 And he brought forth his people with joy, * and his chosen with gladness;

43 And gave them the lands of the heathen; * and they took the labors of the people in possession;

44 That they might keep his statutes, * and observe his laws.

**Psalm**      **106.**      *Confitemini*      *Domino.*

O GIVE thanks unto the LORD; for he is gracious, * and his mercy endureth for ever.

2 Who can express the noble acts of the LORD, * or show forth all his praise?

3 Blessed are they that alway keep judgment, * and do righteousness.

4 Remember me, O LORD, according to the favor that thou bearest unto thy people; * O visit me with thy salvation;

5 That I may see the felicity of thy chosen, * and rejoice in the gladness of thy people, and give thanks with thine inheritance.

6 We have sinned with our fathers; * we have done amiss, and dealt wickedly.

7 Our fathers regarded not thy wonders in Egypt, neither kept they thy great goodness in remembrance; * but were disobedient at the sea, even at the Red Sea.

8 Nevertheless, he helped them for his Name's sake, * that he might make his power to be known.

9 He rebuked the Red Sea also, and it was dried up; * so he led them through the deep, as through a wilderness.

10 And he saved them from the adversary's hand, * and delivered them from the hand of the enemy.

11 As for those that troubled them, the waters overwhelmed them; * there was not one of them left.

12 Then believed they his words, * and sang praise unto him.

13 But within a while they forgat his works, * and would not abide his counsel.

14 But lust came upon them in the wilderness, * and they tempted God in the desert.

15 And he gave them their desire, * and sent leanness withal into their soul.

16 They angered Moses also in the tents, * and Aaron the saint of the LORD.

17 So the earth opened, and swallowed up Dathan, * and covered the congregation of Abiram.

18 And the fire was kindled in their company; * the flame burnt up the ungodly.

19 They made a calf in Horeb, * and worshipped the molten image.

20 Thus they turned their glory * into the similitude of a calf that

eateth                                                                        hay.

21 And they forgat God their Savior, * who had done so great
things                              in                              Egypt;

22 Wondrous works in the land of Ham; * and fearful things by the
Red                                                                          Sea.

23 So he said he would have destroyed them, had not Moses his
chosen stood before him in the gap, * to turn away his wrathful
indignation,        lest        he        should        destroy        them.

24 Yea, they thought scorn of that pleasant land, * and gave no
credence                    unto                    his                    word;

25 But murmured in their tents, * and hearkened not unto the voice
of                              the                              LORD.

26 Then lift he up his hand against them, * to overthrow them in
the                                                                  wilderness;

27 To cast out their seed among the nations, * and to scatter them
in                              the                              lands.

28 They joined themselves unto Baal-peor, * and ate the offerings
of                              the                              dead.

29 Thus they provoked him to anger with their own inventions; *
and        the        plague        was        great        among        them.

30 Then stood up Phinehas, and interposed; * and so the plague
ceased.

31 And that was counted unto him for righteousness, * among all
posterities                    for                    evermore.

32 They angered him also at the waters of strife, * so that he
punished            Moses            for            their            sakes;

33 Because they provoked his spirit, * so that he spake unadvisedly
with                              his                              lips.

34 Neither destroyed they the heathen, * as the LORD commanded
them;

35 But were mingled among the heathen, * and learned their
works.

36 Insomuch that they worshipped their idols, which became a
snare unto them; * yea, they offered their sons and their daughters
unto                                                                  devils;

37 And shed innocent blood, even the blood of their sons and of
their daughters, * whom they offered unto the idols of Canaan; and
the        land        was        defiled        with        blood.

38 Thus were they stained with their own works, * and went a

whoring with their own inventions.

39 Therefore was the wrath of the LORD kindled against his people, * insomuch that he abhorred his own inheritance.

40 And he gave them over into the hand of the heathen; * and they that hated them were lords over them.

41 Their enemies oppressed them, * and had them in subjection.

42 Many a time did he deliver them; * but they rebelled against him with their own inventions, and were brought down in their wickedness.

43 Nevertheless, when he saw their adversity, * he heard their complaint.

44 He thought upon his covenant, and pitied them, according unto the multitude of his mercies; * yea, he made all those that led them away captive to pity them.

45 Deliver us, O LORD our God, and gather us from among the heathen; * that we may give thanks unto thy holy Name, and make our boast of thy praise.

46 Blessed be the LORD God of Israel, from everlasting, and world without end; * And let all the people say, Amen.


**Psalm 107.** *Confitemini Domino.*

O GIVE thanks unto the LORD, for he is gracious, * and his mercy endureth for ever.

2 Let them give thanks whom the LORD hath redeemed, * and delivered from the hand of the enemy;

3 And gathered them out of the lands, from the east, and from the west; * from the north, and from the south.

4 They went astray in the wilderness out of the way, * and found no city to dwell in.

5 Hungry and thirsty, * their soul fainted in them.

6 So they cried unto the LORD in their trouble, * and he delivered them from their distress.

7 He led them forth by the right way, * that they might go to the city where they dwelt.

8 O that men would therefore praise the LORD for his goodness; * and declare the wonders that he doeth for the children of men!

9 For he satisfieth the empty soul, * and filleth the hungry soul with goodness.

10 Such as sit in darkness, and in the shadow of death, * being fast

bound in misery and iron;

11 Because they rebelled against the words of the Lord, * and lightly regarded the counsel of the Most Highest;

12 He also brought down their heart through heaviness: * they fell down, and there was none to help them.

13 So when they cried unto the LORD in their trouble, * he delivered them out of their distress.

14 For he brought them out of darkness, and out of the shadow of death, * and brake their bonds in sunder.

15 O that men would therefore praise the LORD for his goodness; * and declare the wonders that he doeth for the children of men !

16 For he hath broken the gates of brass, * and smitten the bars of iron in sunder.

17 Foolish men are plagued for their offense, * and because of their wickedness.

18 Their soul abhorred all manner of meat, * and they were even hard at death's door.

19 So when they cried unto the LORD in their trouble, * he delivered them out of their distress.

20 He sent his word, and healed them; * and they were saved from their destruction.

21 O that men would therefore praise the LORD for his goodness; * and declare the wonders that he doeth for the children of men!

22 That they would offer unto him the sacrifice of thanksgiving, * and tell out his works with gladness!

23 They that go down to the sea in ships, * and occupy their business in great waters;

24 These men see the works of the LORD, * and his wonders in the deep.

25 For at his word the stormy wind ariseth, * which lifteth up the waves thereof.

26 They are carried up to the heaven, and down again to the deep; * their soul melteth away because of the trouble.

27 They reel to and fro, and stagger like a drunken man, * and are at their wit's end.

28 So when they cry unto the LORD in their trouble, * he delivereth them out of their distress.

29 For he maketh the storm to cease, * so that the waves thereof are still.

30 Then are they glad, because they are at rest; * and so he bringeth them unto the haven where they would be.
31 O that men would therefore praise the LORD for his goodness; * and declare the wonders that he doeth for the children of men!
32 That they would exalt him also in the congregation of the people, * and praise him in the seat of the elders!
33 He turneth the floods into a wilderness, * and drieth up the water-springs.
34 A fruitful land maketh he barren, * for the wickedness of them that dwell therein.
35 Again, he maketh the wilderness a standing water, * and water-springs of a dry ground.
36 And there he setteth the hungry, * that they may build them a city to dwell in;
37 That they may sow their land, and plant vineyards, * to yield them fruits of increase.
38 He blesseth them, so that they multiply exceedingly; * and suffereth not their cattle to decrease.
39 And again, when they are minished and brought low * through oppression, through any plague or trouble;
40 Though he suffer them to be evil entreated through tyrants, * and let them wander out of the way in the wilderness;
41 Yet helpeth he the poor out of misery, * and maketh him households like a flock of sheep.
42 The righteous will consider this, and rejoice; * and the mouth of all wickedness shall be stopped.
43 Whoso is wise, will ponder these things; * and they shall understand the loving-kindness of the LORD.

**Psalm 108.** *Paratum cor meum.*
O GOD, my heart is ready, my heart is ready; * I will sing, and give praise with the best member that I have.
2 Awake, thou lute and harp; * I myself will awake right early.
3 I will give thanks unto thee, O LORD, among the peoples; * I will sing praises unto thee among the nations.
4 For thy mercy is greater than the heavens, * and thy truth reacheth unto the clouds.
5 Set up thyself, O God, above the heavens, * and thy glory above all the earth;

152

6 That thy beloved may be delivered: * let thy right hand save them, and hear thou me.

7 God hath spoken in his holiness; * I will rejoice therefore, and divide Shechem, and mete out the valley of Succoth.

8 Gilead is mine, and Manasseh is mine; * Ephraim also is the strength of my head; Judah is my lawgiver;

9 Moab is my wash-pot; over Edom will I cast out my shoe; * upon Philistia will I triumph.

10 Who will lead me into the strong city? * and who will bring me into Edom?

11 Hast not thou forsaken us, O God? * and wilt not thou, O God, go forth with our hosts?

12 O help us against the enemy: * for vain is the help of man.

13 Through God we shall do great acts; * and it is he that shall tread down our enemies.

**Psalm** **109**. *Deus,* *laudem.*

HOLD not thy tongue, O God of my praise; * for the mouth of the ungodly, yea, the mouth of the deceitful is opened upon me.

2 And they have spoken against me with false tongues; * they compassed me about also with words of hatred, and fought against me without a cause.

3 For the love that I had unto them, lo, they take now my contrary part; * but I give myself unto prayer.

4 Thus have they rewarded me evil for good, * and hatred for my good will.

5 Set thou an ungodly man to be ruler over him, * and let an adversary stand at his right hand.

6 When sentence is given upon him, let him be condemned; * and let his prayer be turned into sin.

7 Let his days be few; * and let another take his office.

8 Let his children be fatherless, * and his wife a widow.

9 Let his children be vagabonds, and beg their bread; * let them seek it also out of desolate places.

10 Let the extortioner consume all that he hath; * and let the stranger spoil his labor.

11 Let there be no man to pity him, * nor to have compassion upon his fatherless children.

12 Let his posterity be destroyed; * and in the next generation let

his     name     be     clean     put     out.

13 Let the wickedness of his fathers be had in remembrance in the sight of the LORD; * and let not the sin of his mother be done away.

14 Let them alway be before the LORD, * that he may root out the memorial    of    them    from    off    the    earth;

15 And that, because his mind was not to do good; * but persecuted the poor helpless man, that he might slay him that was vexed    at    the    heart.

16 His delight was in cursing, and it shall happen unto him; * he loved not blessing, therefore shall it be far from him.

17 He clothed himself with cursing like as with a raiment, * and it shall come into his bowels like water, and like oil into his bones.

18 Let it be unto him as the cloak that he hath upon him, * and as the    girdle    that    he    is    alway    girded    withal.

19 Let it thus happen from the LORD unto mine enemies, * and to those    that    speak    evil    against    my    soul.

20 But deal thou with me, O LORD God, according unto thy Name; *    for    sweet    is    thy    mercy.

21 O deliver me, for I am helpless and poor, * and my heart is wounded    within    me.

22 I go hence like the shadow that departeth, * and am driven away as    the    grasshopper.

23 My knees are weak through fasting; * my flesh is dried up for want    of    fatness.

24 I am become also a reproach unto them: * they that look upon me    shake    their    heads.

25 Help me, O LORD my God; * O save me according to thy mercy;

26 And they shall know how that this is thy hand, * and that thou, LORD,    hast    done    it.

27 Though they curse, yet bless thou; * and let them be confounded that rise up against me; but let thy servant rejoice.

28 Let mine adversaries be clothed with shame; * and let them cover themselves with their own confusion, as with a cloak.

29 As for me, I will give great thanks unto the LORD with my mouth,    *    and    praise    him    among    the    multitude;

30 For he shall stand at the right hand of the poor, * to save his soul from unrighteous judges.

**Psalm**       **110.**       *Dixit*       *Dominus.*

THE LORD said unto my Lord, * Sit thou on my right hand, until I make thine enemies thy footstool.

2 The LORD shall send the rod of thy power out of Sion: * be thou ruler, even in the midst among thine enemies.

3 In the day of thy power shall thy people offer themselves willingly with an holy worship: * thy young men come to thee as dew from the womb of the morning.

4 The LORD sware, and will not repent, * Thou art a Priest for ever after the order of Melchizedek.

5 The Lord upon thy right hand * shall wound even kings in the day of his wrath.

6 He shall judge among the heathen; * he shall fill the places with the dead bodies, and smite in sunder the heads over divers countries.

7 He shall drink of the brook in the way; * therefore shall he lift up his head.

**Psalm**       **111.**       *Confitebor*       *tibi.*

I WILL give thanks unto the LORD with my whole heart, * secretly among the faithful, and in the congregation.

2 The works of the LORD are great, * sought out of all them that have pleasure therein.

3 His work is worthy to be praised and had in honor, * and his righteousness endureth for ever.

4 The merciful and gracious LORD hath so done his marvelous works, * that they ought to be had in remembrance.

5 He hath given meat unto them that fear him; * he shall ever be mindful of his covenant.

6 He hath showed his people the power of his works, * that he may give them the heritage of the heathen.

7 The works of his hands are verity and judgment; * all his commandments are true.

8 They stand fast for ever and ever, * and are done in truth and equity.

9 He sent redemption unto his people; * he hath commanded his covenant for ever; holy and reverend is his Name.

10 The fear of the LORD is the beginning of wisdom; * a good

understanding have all they that do thereafter; his praise endureth for ever.

**Psalm 112.** *Beatus vir.*

BLESSED is the man that feareth the LORD; * he hath great delight in his commandments.

2 His seed shall be mighty upon earth; * the generation of the faithful shall be blessed.

3 Riches and plenteousness shall be in his house; * and his righteousness endureth for ever.

4 Unto the godly there ariseth up light in the darkness; * he is merciful, loving, and righteous.

5 A good man is merciful, and lendeth; * and will guide his words with discretion.

6 For he shall never be moved: * and the righteous shall be had in everlasting remembrance.

7 He will not be afraid of any evil tidings; * for his heart standeth fast, and believeth in the LORD.

8 His heart is stablished, and will not shrink, * until he see his desire upon his enemies.

9 He hath dispersed abroad, and given to the poor. * and his righteousness remaineth for ever; his horn shall be exalted with honor.

10 The ungodly shall see it, and it shall grieve him; * he shall gnash with his teeth, and consume away; the desire of the ungodly shall perish.

**Psalm 113.** *Laudate, pueri.*

PRAISE the LORD, ye servants; * O praise the Name of the LORD.

2 Blessed be the Name of the LORD * from this time forth for evermore.

3 The LORD's Name is praised * from the rising up of the sun unto the going down of the same.

4 The LORD is high above all nations, * and his glory above the heavens.

5 Who is like unto the LORD our God, that hath his dwelling so high, * and yet humbleth himself to behold the things that are in heaven and earth!

6 He taketh up the simple out of the dust, * and lifteth the poor out

of                          the                          mire;
7 That he may set him with the princes, * even with the princes of his                                                    people.
8 He maketh the barren woman to keep house, * and to be a joyful mother of children.

**Psalm          114.          *In          exitu          Israel.***
WHEN Israel came out of Egypt, * and the house of Jacob from among                  the                  strange                  people,
2 Judah was his sanctuary, * and Israel his dominion.
3 The sea saw that, and fled; * Jordan was driven back.
4 The mountains skipped like rams, * and the little hills like young sheep.
5 What aileth thee, O thou sea, that thou fleddest? * and thou Jordan,          that          thou          wast          driven          back?
6 Ye mountains, that ye skipped like rams? * and ye little hills, like young                                                    sheep?
7 Tremble, thou earth, at the presence of the Lord: * at the presence          of          the          God          of          Jacob;
8 Who turned the hard rock into a standing water, ': and the flint-stone into a springing well.

**Psalm          115.          *Non          nobis,          Domine.***
NOT unto us, O LORD, not unto us, but unto thy Name give the praise; * for thy loving mercy, and for thy truth's sake.
2 Wherefore shall the heathen say, * Where is now their God?
3 As for our God, he is in heaven: * he hath done whatsoever pleased                                                    him.
4 Their idols are silver and gold, * even the work of men's hands.
5 They have mouths, and speak not; * eyes have they, and see not.
6 They have ears, and hear not; * noses have they, and smell not.
7 They have hands, and handle not; feet have they, and walk not; * neither          speak          they          through          their          throat.
8 They that make them are like unto them; * and so are all such as put          their          trust          in          them.
9 But thou, house of Israel, trust thou in the LORD; * he is their helper                          and                          defender.
10 Ye house of Aaron, put your trust in the LORD; * he is their helper                          and                          defender.

11 Ye that fear the LORD, put your trust in the LORD; * he is their
helper                                    and                           defender.
12 The LORD hath been mindful of us, and he shall bless us; *
even he shall bless the house of Israel, he shall bless the house of
Aaron.
13 He shall bless them that fear the LORD, * both small and great.
14 The LORD shall increase you more and more, * you and your
children.
15 Ye are the blessed of the LORD, * who made heaven and earth.
16 All the whole heavens are the LORD's; * the earth hath he
given            to           the         children          of          men.
17 The dead praise not thee, O LORD, * neither all they that go
down                                    into                            silence.
18 But we will praise the LORD, * from this time forth for
evermore. Praise the LORD.

**Psalm**            **116.**                *Dilexi,*            *quoniam.*
MY delight is in the LORD; * because he hath heard the voice of
my                                                                    prayer;
2 Because he hath inclined his ear unto me; * therefore will I call
upon        him        as        long        as        I        live.
3 The snares of death compassed me round about, * and the pains
of            hell           gat          hold          upon          me.
4 I found trouble and heaviness; then called I upon the Name of the
LORD;      *      O      LORD,      I      beseech      thee,      deliver      my      soul.
5 Gracious is the LORD, and righteous; * yea, our God is merciful.
6 The LORD preserveth the simple: * I was in misery, and he
helped                                                                    me.
7 Turn again then unto thy rest, O my soul; * for the LORD hath
rewarded                                                                thee.
8 And why? thou hast delivered my soul from death, * mine eyes
from        tears,        and        my        feet        from        falling.
9 I will walk before the LORD * in the land of the living.
10 I believed, and therefore will I speak; but I was sore troubled: *
I        said        in        my        haste,        All        men        are        liars.
11 What reward shall I give unto the LORD * for all the benefits
that          he          hath          done          unto          me?
12 I will receive the cup of salvation, * and call upon the Name of
the                                                                    LORD.

13 I will pay my vows now in the presence of all his people: *
right dear in the sight of the LORD is the death of his saints.
14 Behold, O LORD, how that I am thy servant; * I am thy servant,
and the son of thine handmaid; thou hast broken my bonds in
sunder.
15 I will offer to thee the sacrifice of thanksgiving, * and will call
upon      the      Name      of      the      LORD.
16 I will pay my vows unto the LORD, in the sight of all his people,
* in the courts of the LORD's house; even in the midst of thee, O
Jerusalem. Praise the LORD.

**Psalm**          **117.**          *Laudate*          *Dominum.*
O PRAISE the LORD, all ye nations; * praise him, all ye peoples.
2 For his merciful kindness is ever more and more toward us; *
and the truth of the LORD endureth for ever. Praise the LORD.

**Psalm**          **118.**          *Confitemini*          *Domino.*
O GIVE thanks unto the LORD, for he is gracious; * because his
mercy          endureth          for          ever.
2 Let Israel now confess that he is gracious, * and that his mercy
endureth          for          ever.
3 Let the house of Aaron now confess, * that his mercy endureth
for          ever.
4 Yea, let them now that fear the LORD confess, * that his mercy
endureth          for          ever.
5 I called upon the LORD in trouble; * and the LORD heard me at
large.
6 The LORD is on my side; * I will not fear what man doeth unto
me.
7 The LORD taketh my part with them that help me; * therefore
shall      I      see      my      desire      upon      mine      enemies.
8 It is better to trust in the LORD, * than to put any confidence in
man.
9 It is better to trust in the LORD, * than to put any confidence in
princes.
10 All nations compassed me round about; * but in the Name of
the          LORD          will          I          destroy          them.
11 They kept me in on every side, they kept me in, I say, on every
side; * but in the Name of the LORD will I destroy them.

12 They came about me like bees, and are extinct even as the fire among the thorns; * for in the Name of the LORD I will destroy them.
13 Thou hast thrust sore at me, that I might fall; * but the LORD was                          my                          help.
14 The LORD is my strength, and my song; * and is become my salvation.
15 The voice of joy and health is in the dwellings of the righteous; * the right hand of the LORD bringeth mighty things to pass.
16 The right hand of the LORD hath the preeminence; * the right hand    of    the    LORD    bringeth    mighty    things    to    pass.
17 I shall not die, but live, * and declare the works of the LORD.
18 The LORD hath chastened and corrected me; * but he hath not given              me              over              unto              death.
19 Open me the gates of righteousness, * that I may go into them, and          give          thanks          unto          the          LORD.
20 This is the gate of the LORD, * the righteous shall enter into it.
21 I will thank thee; for thou hast heard me, * and art become my salvation.
22 The same stone which the builders refused, * is become the headstone              in              the              corner.
23 This is the LORD's doing, * and it is marvelous in our eyes.
24 This is the day which the LORD hath made; * we will rejoice and              be              glad              in              it.
25 Help me now, O LORD: * O LORD, send us now prosperity.
26 Blessed be he that cometh in the Name of the LORD: * we have wished you good luck, we that are of the house of the .
27 God is the Lord, who hath showed us light: * bind the sacrifice with    cords,    yea,    even    unto    the    horns    of    the    altar.
28 Thou art my God, and I will thank thee; * thou art my God, and I              will              praise              thee.
29 O give thanks unto the LORD; for he is gracious, * and his mercy endureth for ever.

**Psalm          119.          I.          *Beati          immaculati.*
BLESSED are those that are undefiled in the way, and walk in the law              of              the              LORD.
2 Blessed are they that keep his testimonies, * and seek him with their              whole              heart;

160

3 Even they who do no wickedness, * and walk in his ways.
4 Thou hast charged * that we shall diligently keep thy commandments.
5 O that my ways were made so direct, * that I might keep thy statutes!
6 So shall I not be confounded, * while I have respect unto all thy commandments.
7 I will thank thee with an unfeigned heart, * when I shall have learned the judgments of thy righteousness.
8 I will keep thy statutes; * O forsake me not utterly.

II.                    *In*                    *quo*                    *corrigit?*
WHEREWITHAL shall a young man cleanse his way? * even by ruling himself after thy word.
10 With my whole heart have I sought thee; * O let me not go wrong out of thy commandments.
11 Thy word have I hid within my heart, * that I should not sin against thee.
12 Blessed art thou, O LORD; * O teach me thy statutes.
13 With my lips have I been telling * of all the judgments of thy mouth.
14 I have had as great delight in the way of thy testimonies, * as in all manner of riches.
15 I will talk of thy commandments, * and have respect unto thy ways.
16 My delight shall be in thy statutes, * and I will not forget thy word.

III.                    *Retribue*                    *servo*                    *tuo.*
O DO well unto thy servant; * that I may live, and keep thy word.
18 Open thou mine eyes; * that I may see the wondrous things of thy law.
19 I am a stranger upon earth; * O hide not thy commandments from me.
20 My soul breaketh out for the very fervent desire * that it hath alway unto thy judgments.
21 Thou hast rebuked the proud; * and cursed are they that do err from thy commandments.
22 O turn from me shame and rebuke; * for I have kept thy

testimonies.

23 Princes also did sit and speak against me; * but thy servant is occupied in thy statutes.

24 For thy testimonies are my delight, * and my counsellors.

IV. *Adhaesit* *pavimento.*

MY soul cleaveth to the dust; * O quicken thou me, according to thy word.

26 I have acknowledged my ways, and thou heardest me: * O teach me thy statutes.

27 Make me to understand the way of thy commandments; * and so shall I talk of thy wondrous works.

28 My soul melteth away for very heaviness; * comfort thou me according unto thy word.

29 Take from me the way of lying, * and cause thou me to make much of thy law.

30 I have chosen the way of truth, * and thy judgments have I laid before me.

31 I have stuck unto thy testimonies; * O LORD, confound me not.

32 I will run the way of thy commandments, * when thou hast set my heart at liberty.

V. *Legem* *pone.*

TEACH me, O LORD, the way of thy statutes, * and I shall keep it unto the end.

34 Give me understanding, and I shall keep thy law; * yea, I shall keep it with my whole heart.

35 Make me to go in the path of thy commandments; * for therein is my desire.

36 Incline my heart unto thy testimonies, * and not to covetousness.

37 O turn away mine eyes, lest they behold vanity; * and quicken thou me in thy way.

38 O stablish thy word in thy servant, * that I may fear thee.

39 Take away the rebuke that I am afraid of; * for thy judgments are good.

40 Behold, my delight is in thy commandments; * O quicken me in thy righteousness.

VI.                    *Et           veniat          super           me.*
LET thy loving mercy come also unto me, O LORD, * even thy
salvation,          according          unto          thy          word.
42 So shall I make answer unto my blasphemers; * for my trust is
in                        thy                        word.
43 O take not the word of thy truth utterly out of my mouth; * for
my          hope          is          in          thy          judgments.
44 So shall I alway keep thy law; * yea, for ever and ever.
45 And I will walk at liberty; * for I seek thy commandments.
46 I will speak of thy testimonies also, even before kings, * and
will                    not                    be                    ashamed.
47 And my delight shall be in thy commandments, * which I have
loved.
48 My hands also will I lift up unto thy commandments, which I
have loved; * and my study shall be in thy statutes.

VII.              *Memor          esto          verbi          tui.*
O THINK upon thy servant, as concerning thy word, * wherein
thou      hast      caused      me      to      put      my      trust.
50 The same is my comfort in my trouble; * for thy word hath
quickened                                                        me.
51 The proud have had me exceedingly in derision; * yet have I
not            shrinked            from            thy            law.
52 For I remembered thine everlasting judgments, O LORD, * and
received                                                        comfort.
53 I am horribly afraid, * for the ungodly that forsake thy law.
54 Thy statutes have been my songs, * in the house of my
pilgrimage.
55 I have thought upon thy Name, O LORD, in the night season, *
and            have            kept            thy            law.
56 This I had, * because I kept thy commandments.

VIII.            *Portio          mea,          Domine.*
THOU art my portion, O LORD; * I have promised to keep thy law.
58 I made my humble petition in thy presence with my whole
heart; * O be merciful unto me, according to thy word.
59 I called mine own ways to remembrance, * and turned my feet
unto                        thy                        testimonies.
60 I made haste, and prolonged not the time, * to keep thy

commandments.

61 The snares of the ungodly have compassed me about; * but I have not forgotten thy law.

62 At midnight I will rise to give thanks unto thee, * because of thy righteous judgments.

63 I am a companion of all them that fear thee, * and keep thy commandments.

64 The earth, O LORD, is full of thy mercy: * O teach me thy statutes.

IX. *Bonitatem* *fecisti.*

O LORD, thou hast dealt graciously with thy servant, * according unto thy word.

66 O teach me true understanding and knowledge; * for I have believed thy commandments.

67 Before I was troubled, I went wrong; * but now have I kept thy word.

68 Thou art good and gracious; * O teach me thy statutes.

69 The proud have imagined a lie against me; * but I will keep thy commandments with my whole heart.

70 Their heart is as fat as brawn; * but my delight hath been in thy law.

71 It is good for me that I have been in trouble; * that I may learn thy statutes.

72 The law of thy mouth is dearer unto me * than thousands of gold and silver.

X. *Manus* *tuae* *fecerunt* *me.*

THY hands have made me and fashioned me: * O give me understanding, that I may learn thy commandments.

74 They that fear thee will be glad when they see me; * because I have put my trust in thy word.

75 I know, O LORD, that thy judgments are right, * and that thou of very faithfulness hast caused me to be troubled.

76 O let thy merciful kindness be my comfort, * according to thy word unto thy servant.

77 O let thy loving mercies come unto me, that I may live; * for thy law is my delight.

78 Let the proud be confounded, for they go wickedly about to

destroy me; * but I will be occupied in thy commandments.
79 Let such as fear thee, and have known thy testimonies, * be turned unto me.
80 O let my heart be sound in thy statutes, * that I be not ashamed.

XI.                    *Defecit*              *anima*              *mea.*
MY soul hath longed for thy salvation, * and I have a good hope because of thy word.
82 Mine eyes long sore for thy word; * saying, O when wilt thou comfort me?
83 For I am become like a bottle in the smoke; * yet do I not forget thy statutes.
84 How many are the days of thy servant? * when wilt thou be avenged of them that persecute me?
85 The proud have digged pits for me, * which are not after thy law.
86 All thy commandments are true: * they persecute me falsely; O be thou my help.
87 They had almost made an end of me upon earth; * but I forsook not thy commandments.
88 O quicken me after thy loving-kindness; * and so shall I keep the testimonies of thy mouth.

XII.                   *In*              *aeternum,*              *Domine.*
O LORD, thy word * endureth for ever in heaven.
90 Thy truth also remaineth from one generation to another; * thou hast laid the foundation of the earth, and it abideth.
91 They continue this day according to thine ordinance; * for all things serve thee.
92 If my delight had not been in thy law, * I should have perished in my trouble.
93 I will never forget thy commandments; * for with them thou hast quickened me.
94 I am thine: O save me, * for I have sought thy commandments.
95 The ungodly laid wait for me, to destroy me; * but I will consider thy testimonies.
96 I see that all things come to an end; * but thy commandment is exceeding broad.

XIII.                    *Quomodo*                    *dilexi!*
LORD, what love have I unto thy law! * all the day long is my
study                           in                           it.
98 Thou, through thy commandments, hast made me wiser than
mine      enemies;      *      for      they      are      ever      with      me.
99 I have more understanding than my teachers; * for thy
testimonies                    are                    my                    study.
100 I am wiser than the aged; * because I keep thy
commandments.
101 I have refrained my feet from every evil way, * that I may
keep                           thy                           word.
102 I have not shrunk from thy judgments; * for thou teachest me.
103 O how sweet are thy words unto my throat; * yea, sweeter than
honey                    unto                    my                    mouth!
104 Through thy commandments I get understanding: * therefore I
hate all evil ways.


XIV.                    *Lucerna*                    *pedibus*                    *meis.*
THY word is a lantern unto my feet, * and a light unto my paths.
106 I have sworn, and am steadfastly purposed, * to keep thy
righteous                                                    judgments.
107 I am troubled above measure: * quicken me, O LORD,
according                    to                    thy                    word.
108 Let the free-will offerings of my mouth please thee, O LORD;
*          and          teach          me          thy          judgments.
109 My soul is alway in my hand; * yet do I not forget thy law.
110 The ungodly have laid a snare for me; * but yet I swerved not
from                           thy                           commandments.
111 Thy testimonies have I claimed as mine heritage for ever; *
and      why?      they      are      the      very      joy      of      my      heart.
112 I have applied my heart to fulfill thy statutes alway, * even
unto the end.


XV.                    *Iniquos*                    *odio*                    *habui.*
I HATE them that imagine evil things; * but thy law do I love.
114 Thou art my defense and shield; * and my trust is in thy word.
115 Away from me, ye wicked; * I will keep the commandments
of                           my                           God.
116 O stablish me according to thy word, that I may live; * and let

me not be disappointed of my hope.
117 Hold thou me up, and I shall be safe; * yea, my delight shall be ever in thy statutes.
118 Thou hast trodden down all them that depart from thy statutes; * for they imagine but deceit.
119 Thou puttest away all the ungodly of the earth like dross; * therefore I love thy testimonies.
120 My flesh trembleth for fear of thee; * and I am afraid of thy judgments.

XVI.                          *Feci*                        *judicium.*
I DEAL with the thing that is lawful and right; * O give me not over unto mine oppressors.
122 Make thou thy servant to delight in that which is good, * that the proud do me no wrong.
123 Mine eyes are wasted away with looking for thy health, * and for the word of thy righteousness.
124 O deal with thy servant according unto thy loving mercy, * and teach me thy statutes.
125 I am thy servant; O grant me understanding, * that I may know thy testimonies.
126 It is time for thee, LORD, to lay to thine hand; * for they have destroyed thy law.
127 For I love thy commandments * above gold and precious stones.
128 Therefore hold I straight all thy commandments; * and all false ways I utterly abhor.

XVII.                                                     *Mirabilia.*
THY testimonies are wonderful; * therefore doth my soul keep them.
130 When thy word goeth forth, * it giveth light and understanding unto the simple.
131 I opened my mouth, and drew in my breath; * for my delight was in thy commandments.
132 O look thou upon me, and be merciful unto me, * as thou usest to do unto those that love thy Name.
133 Order my steps in thy word; * and so shall no wickedness have dominion over me.

134 O deliver me from the wrongful dealings of men; * and so shall I keep thy commandments.
135 Show the light of thy countenance upon thy servant, * and teach me thy statutes.
136 Mine eyes gush out with water, * because men keep not thy law.

XVIII. *Justus es, Domine.*
RIGHTEOUS art thou, O LORD; * and true are thy judgments.
138 The testimonies that thou hast commanded * are exceeding righteous and true.
139 My zeal hath even consumed me; * because mine enemies have forgotten thy words.
140 Thy word is tried to the uttermost, * and thy servant loveth it.
141 I am small and of no reputation; * yet do I not forget thy commandments.
142 Thy righteousness is an everlasting righteousness, * and thy law is the truth.
143 Trouble and heaviness have taken hold upon me; * yet is my delight in thy commandments.
144 The righteousness of thy testimonies is everlasting: * O grant me understanding, and I shall live.

XIX. *Clamavi in toto corde meo.*
I CALL with my whole heart; * hear me, O LORD; I will keep thy statutes.
146 Yea, even unto thee do I call; * help me, and I shall keep thy testimonies.
147 Early in the morning do I cry unto thee; * for in thy word is my trust.
148 Mine eyes prevent the night watches; * that I might be occupied in thy word.
149 Hear my voice, O LORD, according unto thy lovingkindness; * quicken me, according to thy judgments.
150 They draw nigh that of malice persecute me, * and are far from thy law.
151 Be thou nigh at hand, O LORD; * for all thy commandments are true.

152 As concerning thy testimonies, I have known long since, * that thou hast grounded them for ever.

XX. *Vide* *humilitatem.*
O CONSIDER mine adversity, and deliver me, * for I do not forget thy law.
154 Avenge thou my cause, and deliver me; * quicken me according to thy word.
155 Health is far from the ungodly; * for they regard not thy statutes.
156 Great is thy mercy, O LORD; * quicken me, as thou art wont.
157 Many there are that trouble me, and persecute me; * yet do I not swerve from thy testimonies.
158 It grieveth me when I see the transgressors; * because they keep not thy law.
159 Consider, O LORD, how I love thy commandments; * O quicken me, according to thy loving-kindness.
160 Thy word is true from everlasting; * all the judgments of thy righteousness endure for evermore.

XXI. *Principes* *persecuti* *sunt.*
PRINCES have persecuted me without a cause; * but my heart standeth in awe of thy word.
162 I am as glad of thy word, * as one that findeth great spoils.
163 As for lies, I hate and abhor them; * but thy law do I love.
164 Seven times a day do I praise thee; * because of thy righteous judgments.
165 Great is the peace that they have who love thy law; * and they have none occasion of stumbling.
166 LORD, I have looked for thy saving health, * and done after thy commandments.
167 My soul hath kept thy testimonies, * and loved them exceedingly.
168 I have kept thy commandments and testimonies; * for all my ways are before thee.

XXII. *Appropinquet* *deprecatio.*
LET my complaint come before thee, O LORD; * give me understanding according to thy word.

170 Let my supplication come before thee; * deliver me according to thy word.

171 My lips shall speak of thy praise, * when thou hast taught me thy statutes.

172 Yea, my tongue shall sing of thy word; * for all thy commandments are righteous.

173 Let thine hand help me; * for I have chosen thy commandments.

174 I have longed for thy saving health, O LORD; * and in thy law is my delight.

175 O let my soul live, and it shall praise thee; * and thy judgments shall help me.

176 I have gone astray like a sheep that is lost; * O seek thy servant, for I do not forget thy commandments.


**Psalm**       **120.**       *Ad*       *Dominum.*

WHEN I was in trouble, I called upon the LORD, * and he heard me.

2 Deliver my soul, O LORD, from lying lips, * and from a deceitful tongue.

3 What reward shall be given or done unto thee, thou false tongue? * even mighty and sharp arrows, with hot burning coals.

4 Woe is me, that I am constrained to dwell with Meshech, * and to have my habitation among the tents of Kedar!

5 My soul hath long dwelt among them * that are enemies unto peace.

6 I labor for peace; but when I speak unto them thereof, * they make them ready to battle.


**Psalm**       **121.**       *Levavi*       *oculos.*

I WILL lift up mine eyes unto the hills; * from whence cometh my help?

2 My help cometh even from the LORD, * who hath made heaven and earth.

3 He will not suffer thy foot to be moved; * and he that keepeth thee will not sleep.

4 Behold, he that keepeth Israel * shall neither slumber nor sleep.

5 The LORD himself is thy keeper; * the LORD is thy defense upon thy right hand;

6 So that the sun shall not burn thee by day, * neither the moon by night.

7 The LORD shall preserve thee from all evil; * yea, it is even he that shall keep thy soul.

8 The LORD shall preserve thy going out, and thy coming in, * from this time forth for evermore.


**Psalm 122.** *Laetatus sum.*

I WAS glad when they said unto me, * We will go into the house of the LORD.

2 Our feet shall stand in thy gates, * O Jerusalem.

3 Jerusalem is built as a city * that is at unity in itself.

4 For thither the tribes go up, even the tribes of the LORD, * to testify unto Israel, to give thanks unto the Name of the LORD.

5 For there is the seat of judgment, * even the seat of the house of David.

6 O pray for the peace of Jerusalem; * they shall prosper that love thee.

7 Peace be within thy walls, * and plenteousness within thy palaces.

8 For my brethren and companions' sakes, * I will wish thee prosperity.

9 Yea, because of the house of the LORD our God, * I will seek to do thee good.


**Psalm 123.** *Ad te levavi oculos meos.*

UNTO thee lift I up mine eyes, * O thou that dwellest in the heavens.

2 Behold, even as the eyes of servants look unto the hand of their masters, and as the eyes of a maiden unto the hand of her mistress, * even so our eyes wait upon the LORD our God, until he have mercy upon us.

3 Have mercy upon us, O LORD, have mercy upon us; * for we are utterly despised.

4 Our soul is filled with the scornful reproof of the wealthy, * and with the despitefulness of the proud.


**Psalm 124.** *Nisi quia Dominus.*

IF the LORD himself had not been on our side, now may Israel say;

* if the LORD himself had not been on our side, when men rose up against                                                                us;
2 They had swallowed us up alive; * when they were so wrathfully displeased                          at                          us.
3 Yea, the waters had drowned us, * and the stream had gone over our                                                                soul.
4 The deep waters of the proud * had gone even over our soul.
5 But praised be the LORD, * who hath not given us over for a prey unto                          their                          teeth.
6 Our soul is escaped even as a bird out of the snare of the fowler; * the snare is broken, and we are delivered.
7 Our help standeth in the Name of the LORD, * who hath made heaven and earth.

**Psalm**                          **125.**                          *Qui*                          *confidunt.*
THEY that put their trust in the LORD shall be even as the mount Sion, * which may not be removed, but standeth fast for ever.
2 The hills stand about Jerusalem; * even so standeth the LORD round about his people, from this time forth for evermore.
3 For the scepter of the ungodly shall not abide upon the lot of the righteous; * lest the righteous put their hand unto wickedness.
4 Do well, O LORD, * unto those that are good and true of heart.
5 As for such as turn back unto their own wickedness, * the LORD shall lead them forth with the evil doers; but peace shall be upon Israel.

**Psalm**                          **126.**                          *In*                          *convertendo.*
WHEN the LORD turned again the captivity of Sion, then were we like                 unto                 them                 that                 dream.
2 Then was our mouth filled with laughter, * and our tongue with joy.
3 Then said they among the heathen, * The LORD hath done great things                                                                for                                                                them.
4 Yea, the LORD hath done great things for us already; * whereof we                                                                rejoice.
5 Turn our captivity, O LORD, * as the rivers in the south.
6 They that sow in tears * shall reap in joy.
7 He that now goeth on his way weeping, and beareth forth good

seed, * shall doubtless come again with joy, and bring his sheaves with him.

**Psalm** **127.** *Nisi* *Dominus.*
EXCEPT the LORD build the house, * their labor is but lost that build it.
2 Except the LORD keep the city, * the watchman waketh but in vain.
3 It is but lost labor that ye haste to rise up early, and so late take rest, and eat the bread of carefulness; * for so he giveth his beloved sleep.
4 Lo, children, and the fruit of the womb, * are an heritage and gift that cometh of the LORD.
5 Like as the arrows in the hand of the giant, * even so are the young children.
6 Happy is the man that hath his quiver full of them; * they shall not be ashamed when they speak with their enemies in the gate.

**Psalm** **128.** *Beati* *omnes.*
BLESSED are all they that fear the LORD, * and walk in his ways.
2 For thou shalt eat the labors of thine hands: * O well is thee, and happy shalt thou be.
3 Thy wife shall be as the fruitful vine * upon the walls of thine house;
4 Thy children like the olive-branches * round about thy table.
5 Lo, thus shall the man be blessed * that feareth the LORD.
6 The LORD from out of Sion shall so bless thee, * that thou shalt see Jerusalem in prosperity all thy life long;
7 Yea, that thou shalt see thy children's children, * and peace upon Israel.

**Psalm** **129.** *Saepe* *expugnaverunt.*
MANY a time have they fought against me from my youth up, * may Israel now say;
2 Yea, many a time have they vexed me from my youth up; * but they have not prevailed against me.
3 The plowers plowed upon my back, * and made long furrows.
4 But the righteous LORD * hath hewn the snares of the ungodly in pieces.

5 Let them be confounded and turned backward, * as many as have evil will at Sion.
6 Let them be even as the grass upon the housetops, * which withereth afore it be grown up;
7 Whereof the mower filleth not his hand, * neither he that bindeth up the sheaves his bosom.
8 So that they who go by say not so much as, The LORD prosper you; * we wish you good luck in the Name of the LORD.

**Psalm 130.** *De profundis.*

OUT of the deep have I called unto thee, O LORD; * Lord, hear my voice.
2 O let thine ears consider well * the voice of my complaint.
3 If thou, LORD, wilt be extreme to mark what is done amiss, * O Lord, who may abide it?
4 For there is mercy with thee; * therefore shalt thou be feared.
5 I look for the LORD; my soul doth wait for him; * in his word is my trust.
6 My soul fleeth unto the Lord before the morning watch; * I say, before the morning watch.
7 O Israel, trust in the LORD; for with the LORD there is mercy, * and with him is plenteous redemption.
8 And he shall redeem Israel * from all his sins.

**Psalm 131.** *Domine, non est.*

LORD, I am not high-minded; * I have no proud looks.
2 I do not exercise myself in great matters * which are too high for me.
3 But I refrain my soul, and keep it low, like as a child that is weaned from his mother: * yea, my soul is even as a weaned child.
4 O Israel, trust in the LORD * from this time forth for evermore.

**Psalm 132.** *Memento, Domine.*

LORD, remember David, * and all his trouble:
2 How he sware unto the LORD, * and vowed a vow unto the Almighty God of Jacob:
3 I will not come within the tabernacle of mine house, * nor climb up into my bed;
4 I will not suffer mine eyes to sleep, nor mine eyelids to slumber;

* neither the temples of my head to take any rest;
5 Until I find out a place for the temple of the LORD; * an
habitation for the Mighty God of Jacob.
6 Lo, we heard of the same at Ephratah, * and found it in the wood.
7 We will go into his tabernacle, * and fall low on our knees before
his                                                                footstool.
8 Arise, O LORD, into thy resting-place; * thou, and the ark of thy
strength.
9 Let thy priests be clothed with righteousness; * and let thy saints
sing                        with                        joyfulness.
10 For thy servant David's sake, * turn not away the face of thine
anointed.
11 The LORD hath made a faithful oath unto David, * and he shall
not                shrink                from                it:
12 Of the fruit of thy body * shall I set upon thy throne.
13 If thy children will keep my covenant, and my testimonies that I
shall teach them; * their children also shall sit upon thy throne for
evermore.
14 For the LORD hath chosen Sion to be an habitation for himself;
*        he        hath        longed        for        her.
15 This shall be my rest for ever: * here will I dwell, for I have a
delight                                                        therein.
16 I will bless her victuals with increase, * and will satisfy her
poor                        with                        bread.
17 I will deck her priests with health, * and her saints shall rejoice
and                                                                sing.
18 There shall I make the horn of David to flourish: * I have
ordained        a        lantern        for        mine        anointed.
19 As for his enemies, I shall clothe them with shame; * but upon
himself shall his crown flourish.

**Psalm        133**.        *Ecce,        quam        bonum!*
BEHOLD, how good and joyful a thing it is, * for brethren to
dwell                together                in                unity!
2 It is like the precious oil upon the head, that ran down unto the
beard, * even unto Aaron's beard, and went down to the skirts of
his                                                                clothing.
3 Like as the dew of Hermon, * which fell upon the hill of Sion.

4 For there the LORD promised his blessing, * and life for evermore.

## Psalm 134. *Ecce nunc.*

BEHOLD now, praise the LORD, * all ye servants of the LORD;
2 Ye that by night stand in the house of the LORD, * even in the courts of the house of our God.
3 Lift up your hands in the sanctuary, * and praise the LORD.
4 The LORD that made heaven and earth * give thee blessing out of Sion.

## Psalm 135. *Laudate Nomen.*

O PRAISE the LORD, laud ye the Name of the LORD; * praise it, O ye servants of the LORD;
2 Ye that stand in the house of the LORD, * in the courts of the house of our God.
3 O praise the LORD, for the LORD is gracious; * O sing praises unto his Name, for it is lovely.
4 For why? the LORD hath chosen Jacob unto himself, * and Israel for his own possession.
5 For I know that the LORD is great, * and that our Lord is above all gods.
6 Whatsoever the LORD pleased, that did he in heaven, and in earth; * and in the sea, and in all deep places.
7 He bringeth forth the clouds from the ends of the world, * and sendeth forth lightnings with the rain, bringing the winds out of his treasuries.
8 He smote the firstborn of Egypt, * both of man and beast.
9 He hath sent tokens and wonders into the midst of thee, O thou land of Egypt; * upon Pharaoh, and all his servants.
10 He smote divers nations, * and slew mighty kings:
11 Sihon, king of the Amorites; and Og, the king of Bashan; * and all the kingdoms of Canaan;
12 And gave their land to be an heritage, * even an heritage unto Israel his people.
13 Thy Name, O LORD, endureth for ever; * so doth thy memorial, O LORD, from one generation to another.
14 For the LORD will avenge his people, * and be gracious unto his servants.

15 As for the images of the heathen, they are but silver and gold; * the work of men's hands.

16 They have mouths, and speak not; * eyes have they, but they see not.

17 They have ears, and yet they hear not; * neither is there any breath in their mouths.

18 They that make them are like unto them; * and so are all they that put their trust in them.

19 Praise the LORD, ye house of Israel; * praise the LORD, ye house of Aaron.

20 Praise the LORD, ye house of Levi; * ye that fear the LORD, praise the LORD.

21 Praised be the LORD out of Sion, * who dwelleth at Jerusalem.

**Psalm** **136**. *Confitemini.*

O GIVE thanks unto the LORD, for he is gracious: * and his mercy endureth for ever.

2 O give thanks unto the God of all gods: * for his mercy endureth for ever.

3 O thank the Lord of all lords: * for his mercy endureth for ever.

4 Who only doeth great wonders: * for his mercy endureth for ever.

5 Who by his excellent wisdom made the heavens: for his mercy endureth for ever.

6 Who laid out the earth above the waters: * for his mercy endureth for ever.

7 Who hath made great lights: * for his mercy endureth for ever:

8 The sun to rule the day: * for his mercy endureth for ever;

9 The moon and the stars to govern the night: * for his mercy endureth for ever.

10 Who smote Egypt, with their firstborn: * for his mercy endureth for ever;

11 And brought out Israel from among them: * for his mercy endureth for ever;

12 With a mighty hand and stretched-out arm: * for his mercy endureth for ever.

13 Who divided the Red Sea in two parts: * for his mercy endureth for ever;

14 And made Israel to go through the midst of it: * for his mercy

endureth                    for                           ever.
15 But as for Pharaoh and his host, he overthrew them in the Red
Sea:      *      for      his      mercy      endureth      for      ever.
16 Who led his people through the wilderness: * for his mercy
endureth                    for                           ever.
17 Who smote great kings: * for his mercy endureth for ever;
18 Yea, and slew mighty kings: * for his mercy endureth for ever:
19 Sihon, king of the Amorites: * for his mercy endureth for ever;
20 And Og, the king of Bashan: * for his mercy endureth for ever;
21 And gave away their land for an heritage: * for his mercy
endureth                    for                           ever;
22 Even for an heritage unto Israel his servant: * for his mercy
endureth                    for                           ever.
23 Who remembered us when we were in trouble: * for his mercy
endureth                    for                           ever;
24 And hath delivered us from our enemies: * for his mercy
endureth                    for                           ever.
25 Who giveth food to all flesh: * for his mercy endureth for ever.
26 O give thanks unto the God of heaven: * for his mercy endureth
for                                                        ever.
27 O give thanks unto the Lord of lords: * for his mercy endureth
for ever.

**Psalm          137.          *Super          flumina.***
BY the waters of Babylon we sat down and wept, * when we
remembered            thee,            O            Sion.
2 As for our harps, we hanged them up * upon the trees that are
therein.
3 For they that led us away captive, required of us then a song, and
melody in our heaviness: * Sing us one of the songs of Sion.
4 How shall we sing the LORD's song * in a strange land?
5 If I forget thee, O Jerusalem, * let my right hand forget her
cunning.
6 If I do not remember thee, let my tongue cleave to the roof of my
mouth; * yea, if I prefer not Jerusalem above my chief joy.
7 Remember the children of Edom, O LORD, in the day of
Jerusalem; * how they said, Down with it, down with it, even to
the                                                        ground.
8 O daughter of Babylon, wasted with misery; * yea, happy shall

he be that rewardeth thee as thou hast served us.
9 Blessed shall he be that taketh thy children, * and throweth them against the stones.

**Psalm        138.**        *Confitebor        tibi.*
I WILL give thanks unto thee, O Lord, with my whole heart; *
even before the gods will I sing praise unto thee.
2 I will worship toward thy holy temple, and praise thy Name, because of thy loving-kindness and truth; * for thou hast magnified thy Name, and thy word, above all things.
3 When I called upon thee, thou heardest me; * and enduedst my soul with much strength.
4 All the kings of the earth shall praise thee, O LORD; * for they have heard the words of thy mouth.
5 Yea, they shall sing of the ways of the LORD, * that great is the glory of the LORD.
6 For though the LORD be high, yet hath he respect unto the lowly; * as for the proud, he beholdeth them afar off.
7 Though I walk in the midst of trouble, yet shalt thou refresh me; * thou shalt stretch forth thy hand upon the furiousness of mine enemies, and thy right hand shall save me.
8 The LORD shall make good his loving-kindness toward me; * yea, thy mercy, O LORD, endureth for ever; despise not then the works of thine own hands.

**Psalm        139.**        *Domine,        probasti.*
O LORD, thou hast searched me out, and known me. * Thou knowest my down-sitting, and mine uprising; thou understandest my thoughts long before.
2 Thou art about my path, and about my bed; * and art acquainted with all my ways.
3 For lo, there is not a word in my tongue, * but thou, O LORD, knowest it altogether.
4 Thou hast beset me behind and before, * and laid thine hand upon me.
5 Such knowledge is too wonderful and excellent for me; * I cannot attain unto it.
6 Whither shall I go then from thy Spirit? * or whither shall I go then from thy presence?

179

7 If I climb up into heaven, thou art there; * if I go down to hell, thou art there also.

8 If I take the wings of the morning, * and remain in the uttermost parts of the sea;

9 Even there also shall thy hand lead me, * and thy right hand shall hold me.

10 If I say, Peradventure the darkness shall cover me; * then shall my night be turned to day.

11 Yea, the darkness is no darkness with thee, but the night is as clear as the day; * the darkness and light to thee are both alike.

12 For my reins are thine; * thou hast covered me in my mother's womb.

13 I will give thanks unto thee, for I am fearfully and wonderfully made: * marvelous are thy works, and that my soul knoweth right well.

14 My bones are not hid from thee, * though I be made secretly, and fashioned beneath in the earth.

15 Thine eyes did see my substance, yet being imperfect; * and in thy book were all my members written;

16 Which day by day were fashioned, * when as yet there was none of them.

17 How dear are thy counsels unto me, O God; * O how great is the sum of them!

18 If I tell them, they are more in number than the sand: * when I wake up, I am present with thee.

19 Wilt thou not slay the wicked, O God? * Depart from me, ye blood-thirsty men.

20 For they speak unrighteously against thee; * and thine enemies take thy Name in vain.

21 Do not I hate them, O LORD, that hate thee? * and am not I grieved with those that rise up against thee?

22 Yea, I hate them right sore; * even as though they were mine enemies.

23 Try me, O God, and seek the ground of my heart; * prove me, and examine my thoughts.

24 Look well if there be any way of wickedness in me; * and lead me in the way everlasting.

**Psalm                140.**              *Eripe             me,             Domine.*

DELIVER me, O LORD, from the evil man; * and preserve me from              the              wicked              man;

2 Who imagine mischief in their hearts, * and stir up strife all the day                                                                                long.

3 They have sharpened their tongues like a serpent; * adder's poison              is              under              their              lips.

4 Keep me, O LORD, from the hands of the ungodly; * preserve me from the wicked men, who are purposed to overthrow my goings.

5 The proud have laid a snare for me, and spread a net abroad with cords;        *        yea,        and        set        traps        in        my        way.

6 I said unto the LORD, Thou art my God, * hear the voice of my prayers,                                O                                LORD.

7 O LORD God, thou strength of my health; * thou hast covered my head              in              the              day              of              battle.

8 Let not the ungodly have his desire, O LORD; * let not his mischievous    imagination    prosper,    lest    they    be    too    proud.

9 Let the mischief of their own lips fall upon the head of them * that                compass                me                about.

10 Let hot burning coals fall upon them; * let them be cast into the fire,    and    into    the    pit,    that    they    never    rise    up    again.

11 A man full of words shall not prosper upon the earth: * evil shall    hunt    the    wicked    person    to    overthrow    him.

12 Sure I am that the LORD will avenge the poor, * and maintain the                cause                of                the                helpless.

13 The righteous also shall give thanks unto thy Name; * and the just        shall        continue        in        thy        sight.

**Psalm                141.**              *Domine,             clamavi.*

LORD, I call upon thee; haste thee unto me, * and consider my voice,        when        I        cry        unto        thee.

2 Let my prayer be set forth in thy sight as the incense; * and let the    lifting    up    of    my    hands    be    an    evening    sacrifice.

3 Set a watch, O LORD, before my mouth, * and keep the door of my                                                                                lips.

4 O let not mine heart be inclined to any evil thing; * let me not be occupied in ungodly works with the men that work wickedness, neither    let    me    eat    of    such    things    as    please    them.

5 Let the righteous rather smite me friendly, and reprove me; *

yea, let not my head refuse their precious balms.

6 As for the ungodly, * I will pray yet against their wickedness.

7 Let their judges be overthrown in stony places, * that they may hear my words; for they are sweet.

8 Our bones lie scattered before the pit, * like as when one breaketh and heweth wood upon the earth.

9 But mine eyes look unto thee, O LORD God; * in thee is my trust; O cast not out my soul.

10 Keep me from the snare that they have laid for me, * and from the traps of the wicked doers.

11 Let the ungodly fall into their own nets together, * and let me ever escape them.

**Psalm 142.** *Voce mea ad Dominum.*

I CRIED unto the LORD with my voice; * yea, even unto the LORD did I make my supplication.

2 I poured out my complaints before him, * and showed him of my trouble.

3 When my spirit was in heaviness, thou knewest my path; * in the way wherein I walked, have they privily laid a snare for me.

4 I looked also upon my right hand, * and saw there was no man that would know me.

5 I had no place to flee unto, * and no man cared for my soul.

6 I cried unto thee, O LORD, and said, * Thou art my hope, and my portion in the land of the living.

7 Consider my complaint; * for I am brought very low.

8 O deliver me from my persecutors; * for they are too strong for me.

9 Bring my soul out of prison, that I may give thanks unto thy Name; * which thing if thou wilt grant me, then shall the righteous resort unto my company.

**Psalm 143.** *Domine, exaudi.*

HEAR my prayer, O LORD, and consider my desire; * hearken unto me for thy truth and righteousness' sake.

2 And enter not into judgment with thy servant; * for in thy sight shall no man living be justified.

3 For the enemy hath persecuted my soul; he hath smitten my life down to the ground; * he hath laid me in the darkness, as the men

that have been long dead.
4 Therefore is my spirit vexed within me, * and my heart within me is desolate.
5 Yet do I remember the time past; I muse upon all thy works; * yea, I exercise myself in the works of thy hands.
6 I stretch forth my hands unto thee; * my soul gaspeth unto thee as a thirsty land.
7 Hear me, O LORD, and that soon; for my spirit waxeth faint: * hide not thy face from me, lest I be like unto them that go down into the pit.
8 O let me hear thy loving-kindness betimes in the morning; for in thee is my trust: * show thou me the way that I should walk in; for I lift up my soul unto thee.
9 Deliver me, O LORD, from mine enemies; * for I flee unto thee to hide me.
10 Teach me to do the thing that pleaseth thee; for thou art my God: * let thy loving Spirit lead me forth into the land of righteousness.
11 Quicken me, O LORD, for thy Name's sake; * and for thy righteousness' sake bring my soul out of trouble.
12 And of thy goodness slay mine enemies, * and destroy all them that vex my soul; for I am thy servant.

**Psalm 144.** *Benedictus Dominus.*
BLESSED be the LORD my strength, * who teacheth my hands to war, and my fingers to fight:
2 My hope and my fortress, my castle and deliverer, my defender in whom I trust; * who subdueth my people that is under me.
3 LORD, what is man, that thou hast such respect unto him? * or the son of man, that thou so regardest him?
4 Man is like a thing of nought; * his time passeth away like a shadow.
5 Bow thy heavens, O LORD, and come down; * touch the mountains, and they shall smoke.
6 Cast forth thy lightning, and tear them; * shoot out thine arrows, and consume them.
7 Send down thine hand from above; * deliver me, and take me out of the great waters, from the hand of strangers;
8 Whose mouth talketh of vanity, * and their right hand is a right

hand                        of                      wickedness.
9 I will sing a new song unto thee, O God; * and sing praises unto
thee         upon          a         ten-stringed        lute.
10 Thou hast given victory unto kings, * and hast delivered David
thy    servant    from    the    peril    of    the    sword.
11 Save me, and deliver me from the hand of strangers, * whose
mouth talketh of vanity, and their right hand is a right hand of
iniquity:
12 That our sons may grow up as the young plants, * and that our
daughters may be as the polished corners of the temple;
13 That our garners may be full and plenteous with all manner of
store; * that our sheep may bring forth thousands, and ten
thousands            in            our            fields;
14 That our oxen may be strong to labor; that there be no decay, *
no leading into captivity, and no complaining in our streets.
15 Happy are the people that are in such a case; * yea, blessed are
the people who have the LORD for their God.

**Psalm          145.**          *Exaltabo          te,          Deus.*
I WILL magnify thee, O God, my King; * and I will praise thy
Name          for          ever          and          ever.
2 Every day will I give thanks unto thee; * and praise thy Name for
ever                        and                        ever.
3 Great is the LORD, and marvelous worthy to be praised; * there is
no          end          of          his          greatness.
4 One generation shall praise thy works unto another, * and declare
thy                                                    power.
5 As for me, I will be talking of thy worship, * thy glory, thy
praise,          and          wondrous          works;
6 So that men shall speak of the might of thy marvelous acts; * and
I    will    also    tell    of    thy    greatness.
7 The memorial of thine abundant kindness shall be showed; * and
men     shall     sing     of     thy     righteousness.
8 The LORD is gracious and merciful; * long-suffering, and of
great                                                  goodness.
9 The LORD is loving unto every man; * and his mercy is over all
his                                                    works.
10 All thy works praise thee, O LORD; * and thy saints give thanks
unto                                                    thee.

11 They show the glory of thy kingdom, * and talk of thy power;

12 That thy power, thy glory, and mightiness of thy kingdom, * might be known unto men.

13 Thy kingdom is an everlasting kingdom, * and thy dominion endureth throughout all ages.

14 The LORD upholdeth all such as fall, * and lifteth up all those that are down.

15 The eyes of all wait upon thee, O Lord; * and thou givest them their meat in due season.

16 Thou openest thine hand, * and fillest all things living with plenteousness.

17 The LORD is righteous in all his ways, * and holy in all his works.

18 The LORD is nigh unto all them that call upon him; * yea, all such as call upon him faithfully.

19 He will fulfill the desire of them that fear him; * he also will hear their cry, and will help them.

20 The LORD preserveth all them that love him; * but scattereth abroad all the ungodly.

21 My mouth shall speak the praise of the LORD; * and let all flesh give thanks unto his holy Name for ever and ever.

**Psalm 146.** *Lauda, anima mea.*

PRAISE the LORD, O my soul: while I live, will I praise the LORD; * yea, as long as I have any being, I will sing praises unto my God.

2 O put not your trust in princes, nor in any child of man; * for there is no help in them.

3 For when the breath of man goeth forth, he shall turn again to his earth, * and then all his thoughts perish.

4 Blessed is he that hath the God of Jacob for his help, * and whose hope is in the LORD his God:

5 Who made heaven and earth, the sea, and all that therein is; * who keepeth his promise for ever;

6 Who helpeth them to right that suffer wrong; * who feedeth the hungry.

7 The LORD looseth men out of prison; * the LORD giveth sight to the blind.

8 The LORD helpeth them that are fallen; * the LORD careth for the righteous.

9 The LORD careth for the strangers; he defendeth the fatherless and widow: * as for the way of the ungodly, he turneth it upside down.

10 The LORD thy God, O Sion, shall be King for evermore, * and throughout all generations.

**Psalm** **147**. *Laudate* *Dominum.*

PRAISE the LORD, for it is a good thing to sing praises unto our God; * yea, a joyful and pleasant thing it is to be thankful.

2 The LORD doth build up Jerusalem, * and gather together the outcasts of Israel.

3 He healeth those that are broken in heart, * and giveth medicine to heal their sickness.

4 He telleth the number of the stars, * and calleth them all by their names.

5 Great is our Lord, and great is his power; * yea, and his wisdom is infinite.

6 The LORD setteth up the meek, * and bringeth the ungodly down to the ground.

7 O sing unto the LORD with thanksgiving; * sing praises upon the harp unto our God:

8 Who covereth the heaven with clouds, and prepareth rain for the earth; * and maketh the grass to grow upon the mountains, and herb for the use of men;

9 Who giveth fodder unto the cattle, * and feedeth the young ravens that call upon him.

10 He hath no pleasure in the strength of an horse; * neither delighteth he in any man's legs.

11 But the LORD's delight is in them that fear him, * and put their trust in his mercy.

12 Praise the LORD, O Jerusalem; * praise thy God, O Sion.

13 For he hath made fast the bars of thy gates, * and hath blessed thy children within thee.

14 He maketh peace in thy borders, * and filleth thee with the flour of wheat.

15 He sendeth forth his commandment upon earth, * and his word runneth very swiftly.

16 He giveth snow like wool, * and scattereth the hoarfrost like ashes.

17 He casteth forth his ice like morsels: * who is able to abide his

frost?

18 He sendeth out his word, and melteth them: * he bloweth with his wind, and the waters flow.

19 He showeth his word unto Jacob, * his statutes and ordinances unto Israel.

20 He hath not dealt so with any nation; * neither have the heathen knowledge of his laws.


**Psalm**          **148.**         *Laudate*        *Dominum.*

O PRAISE the LORD from the heavens: * praise him in the heights.

2 Praise him, all ye angels of his: * praise him, all his host.

3 Praise him, sun and moon: * praise him, all ye stars and light.

4 Praise him, all ye heavens, * and ye waters that are above the heavens.

5 Let them praise the Name of the LORD: * for he spake the word, and they were made; he commanded, and they were created.

6 He hath made them fast for ever and ever: * he hath given them a law which shall not be broken.

7 Praise the LORD from the earth, * ye dragons and all deeps;

8 Fire and hail, snow and vapors, * wind and storm, fulfilling his word;

9 Mountains and all hills; * fruitful trees and all cedars;

10 Beasts and all cattle; * creeping things and flying fowls;

11 Kings of the earth, and all peoples; * princes, and all judges of the world;

12 Young men and maidens, old men and children, praise the Name of the LORD: * for his Name only is excellent, and his praise above heaven and earth.

13 He shall exalt the horn of his people: all his saints shall praise him; * even the children of Israel, even the people that serveth him.


**Psalm**          **149.**         *Cantate*        *Domino.*

O SING unto the LORD a new song; * let the congregation of saints praise him.

2 Let Israel rejoice in him that made him, * and let the children of Sion be joyful in their King.

3 Let them praise his Name in the dance: * let them sing praises unto him with tabret and harp.

4 For the LORD hath pleasure in his people, * and helpeth the meek-hearted.

5 Let the saints be joyful with glory; * let them rejoice in their beds.

6 Let the praises of God be in their mouth; * and a two-edged sword in their hands;

7 To be avenged of the nations, * and to rebuke the peoples;

8 To bind their kings in chains, * and their nobles with links of iron;

9 To execute judgment upon them; as it is written, * Such honor have all his saints.

## Psalm 150. *Laudate Dominum.*

O PRAISE God in his sanctuary: * praise him in the firmament of his power.

2 Praise him in his noble acts: * praise him according to his excellent greatness.

3 Praise him in the sound of the trumpet: * praise him upon the lute and harp.

4 Praise him in the timbrels and dances: * praise him upon the strings and pipe.

5 Praise him upon the well-tuned cymbals: * praise him upon the loud cymbals.

6 Let every thing that hath breath * praise the LORD.

# Lectionary

**Week of 1 Advent** *(November 30 is St. Andrew's Day)*
*Sunday*          *Psalms 146, 1477\*111,112,113*
Isa. 1:1-9                    2 Pet. 3:1-10                    Mt 25:1-13
Amos 1:1-5, 13--2:8   1Thess. 5:1-11          Lk 21:5-19

*Monday*          *Psalms 1,2,3\*4,7*
Isa. 1:10-20                  1 Thess. 1:1-10          Luke 20:1-8
Amos 2:6-16                 2 Pet. 1:1-11              Mt. 21:1-11

*Tuesday*          *Psalms 5,6\*10,11*
Isa. 1:21-31                  1 Thess. 2:1-12          Lk 20:9-18
Amos 3:1-11                 2 Pet. 1:12-21            Mt21:12-22

*Wednesday*     *Psalms 119.1-24\*12,13,14*
Isa. 2:1-11                    1 Thess. 2:13-20        Lk 20:19-26
Amos 3:12--4:5           2 Pet. 3:1-10              Mt.21:23-32

*Thursday*        *Psalms 18,1-20\*18,21-50*
Isa. 2:12-22                  1 Thess. 3:1-13          Lk 20:27-40
Amos 4:6-13                 2 Pet. 3:11-18            Mt 21:33-46

*Friday*           *Psalms 16,17\*22*
Isa. 3:8-15                    1 Thess. 4:1-12          Lk 20:41--21:4
Amos 5:1-17                 Jude 1-16                   Mt 22:1-14

*Saturday*        *Psalms 20,21.1-13\*110, 116, 117*
Isa. 4:2-6                      1 Thess. 4:13-18        Lk 21:5-19
Amos 5:18-27               Jude 17-25                Mt 22:15-22

**Week of 2 Advent**
*Sunday*          *148, 149,150\*114, 115*
Isa. 5:1-7                      2 Pet. 3:11-18          Lk 7:28-35

189

| Amos 6:1-14 | 2 Thess. 1:5-12 | Lk 1:57-67 |

*Monday*      *25\*9, 15*
| Isa. 5:8-12, 18-23 | 1 Thess. 5:1-11 | Lk 21:20-28 |
| Amos 7:1-9 | Rev. 1:1-8 | Mt 22:23-33 |

*Tuesday*      *26, 28\*36, 39*
| Isa. 5:13-17, 24-25 | 1 Thess. 5:12-28 | Lk 21:29-38 |
| Amos 7:10-17 | Rev. 1:9-16 | Mt 22:34-46 |

*Wednesday*      *38\*119.25-48*
| Isa. 6:1-13 | 2 Thess. 1:1-12 | Jn 7:53--8:11 |
| Amos 8:1-14 | Rev. 1:17--2:7 | .Mt 23:1-12 |

*Thursday*      *37.1-18\*37.19-42*
| Isa. 7:1-9 | 2 Thess. 2:1-12 | Lk 22:1-13 |
| Amos 9:1-10 | Rev. 2:8-17 | Mt 23:13-26 |

*Friday*      *31\*35*
| Isa. 7:10-25 | 2 Thess. 2:13–3:5 | Lk 22:14-30 |
| Haggai 1:1-15 | Rev. 2:18-29 | Mt 23:27-39 |

*Saturday*      *30, 32\*42, 43*
| Isa. 8:1-15 | 2 Thess. 3:6-18 | Lk 22:31-38 |
| Haggai 2:1-9 | Rev. 3:1-6 | Mt 24:1-14 |

## Week of 3 Advent
*Sunday*      *63, 98\*103*
| Isa. 13:6-13 | Heb. 12:18-29 | Jn 3:22-30 |
| Amos 9:11-15 | 2 Thess. 2:1-3, 13-17 | Jn 5:30-47 |

*Monday*      *41, 52\*44*
| Isa. 8:16--9:1 | 2 Pet. 1:1-11 | Lk 22:39-53 |
| Zech. 1:7-17 | Rev. 3:7-13 | Mt 24:15-31 |

*Tuesday*      *45\*47, 48*
| Isa. 9:1-7 | 2 Pet. 1:12-21 | Lk 22:54-69 |
| Zech. 2:1-13 | Rev. 3:14-22 | Mt 24:32-44 |

| *Wednesday* | *119.44-72*49, 53* | |
|---|---|---|
| Isa. 9:8-17 | 2 Pet. 2:1-10a | Mark 1:1-8 |
| Zech. 3:1-10 | Rev. 4:1-8 | Mt 24:45-51 |

| *Thursday* | *50*33* | |
|---|---|---|
| Isa. 9:18--10:4 | 2 Pet. 2:10b-16 | Mt 3:1-12 |
| Zech. 4:1-14 | Rev. 4:9-5:5 | Mt 25:1-13 |

| *Friday* | *40, 54*51* | |
|---|---|---|
| Isa. 10:5-19 | 2 Pet. 2:17-22 | Mt 11:2-15 |
| Zech. 7:8--8:8 | Rev. 5:6-14 | Mt 25:14-30 |

| *Saturday* | *55*138, 139* | |
|---|---|---|
| Isa. 10:20-27 | Jude 17-25 | Lk 3:1-9 |
| Zech. 8:9-17 | Rev. 6:1-17 | Mt 25:31-46 |

**Week of 4 Advent** *(December 21 is St. Thomas' Day)*

| *Sunday* | *24, 29*8, 84* | |
|---|---|---|
| Isa. 42:1-12 | Eph. 6:10-20 | Jn 3:16-21 |
| Gen. 3:8-15 | Rev. 12:1-10 | Jn 3:16-21 |

| *Monday* | *61, 62*1112, 115* | |
|---|---|---|
| Isa. 11:1-9 | Rev. 20:1-10 | Jn 5:30-47 |
| Zeph. 3:14-20 | Titus 1:1-16 | Lk 1:1-25 |

| *Tuesday* | *66, 67*116, 117* | |
|---|---|---|
| Isa 11:10-16 | Rev. 20:11--21:8 | Lk 1:5-25 |
| 1 Samuel 2:1b-10 | Titus 2:1-10 | Lk 1:26-38 |

| *Wednesday* | *72*111,113* | |
|---|---|---|
| Isa. 28:9-22 | Rev. 21:9-21 | Lk 1:26-38 |
| 2 Samuel 7:1-17 | Titus 2:11–3:8a | Lk 1:39-56 |

| *Thursday* | *80*146, 147* | |
|---|---|---|
| Isa. 29:13-24 | Rev. 21:22--22:5 | Lk 1:39-56 |
| 2 Samuel 7:18-29 | Gal. 3:1-14 | Lk 1:57-66 |

| *Friday* | *93, 96*148, 150* | |
|---|---|---|
| Isa. 33:17-22 | Rev. 22:6-11, 18-20 | Lk 1:57-66 |
| Baruch 4:21-29 | Gal 3:15-22 | Mt 1:1-17 |

*Dec 24*        *45, 46*
Isa. 35:1-10          Rev. 22:12-17, 21      Lk 1:67-80
Baruch 4:36--5:9      Gal. 3:23--4:7         Mt 1:18-25


*Christmas Eve*       *89.1-29*
Isa. 59:15b-21        Phil. 2:5-11


**Christmas Day and Following**  *(Dec 26 St. Stephen; 27 St. John;*
*28 Holy Innocents')*
*Christmas Day*       *2, 85\*110, 132*
Zech. 2:10-13        Heb 1:1-12            Jn 1:1-18
Micah 4:1-5: 5:2-4   1 John 4:7-16         Jn 3:31-36


*Dec. 26: St. Stephen*   *28, 30\*118*
2 Chron. 24:17-22    Acts 6:1-7            Mt 23:34-39
Wisdom 4:7-15        Acts 7:59-8:8         Mt 23:34-39


*Dec. 27: St. John*    *97, 98\*145*
Proverbs 8:22-30     1 John 1:1-9          John 13:20-35
Isaiah 44:1-8        1 John 5:1-12         Jn 21:19b-24


*Dec. 28: Holy Innocents*    *2, 26\*19, 126*
Isaiah 49:13-23      Rev. 21:1-7           Mt 18:1-14
Isaiah 54:1-13       Rev. 14:1-5           Mk 10:13-16


*First Sunday after Christmas 93, 96\*34*
Isa. 62:6-7, 10-12    Heb. 2:10-18         Mt 1:18-25
1 Samuel 1:1-2, 7b-28  Col. 1:9-20         Lk 2:22-40


*Dec. 29*      *18.1-20\*18.21-50*
Isa. 12:1-6          Rev. 1:1-8            Jn 7:37-52
2 Samuel 23:13-17b   2 John 1-13           Jn 2:1-11


*Dec. 30*      *20, 21\*23, 27*
Isa. 25:1-9          Rev. 1:9-20           Jn 7:53--8:11
1 Kings 17:17-24     3 John 1-15           Jn 4:46-54


192

*Dec. 31*        *46, 48*
Isa. 26:1-9           2 Cor. 5:16--6:2       Jn 8:12-19
1 Kings 3:5-14      James 4:13-17: 5:7-11   Jn 5:1-15

*Eve of Holy Name*     *90*
Isa. 65:15b-25      Rev. 21:1-6

*Holy Name*     *103\*148*
Gen. 17:1-12a, 15-16    Col. 2:6-12        Jn 16:23b-30
Isa. 62:1-5, 10-12      Rev. 19:11-16       Mt 1:18-25

*Second Sunday after Christmas*     *66, 67\*145*
Ecclus. 3:3-9, 14-17   1 John 2:12-17       Jn 6:41-47
Wisdom 7:3-14       Col. 3:12-17        Jn 6:41-47

*Jan. 2*          *34\*33*
Gen. 12:1-7        Heb. 11:1-12    Jn 6:35-41, 48-51
1 Kings 19:1-8     Eph. 4:1-16         Jn 6:1-14

*Jan. 3*          *68\*72*
Gen. 28:10-22      Heb. 11:13-22      Jn 10:7-17
1 Kings 19:9-18     Eph. 4:17-32       Jn 6:15-27

*Jan. 4*          *85, 87\*89.1-29*
Exod. 3:1-12       Heb. 11:23-31      Jn 14:6-14
Joshua 3:14--4:7    Eph. 5:1-20    Jn 9:1-12, 35-38

*Jan. 5*          *2, 110*
Joshua 1:1-9       Heb. 11:32--12:2     Jn 15:1-16
Jonah 2:2-9        Eph. 6:10-20   Jn 11:17-27, 38-44

*Eve of Epiphany*     *29, 98*
Isa. 66:18-23       Rom. 15:7-13

## The Epiphany and Following
*Epiphany*     *46, 97\*96, 100*
Isa. 52:7-10       Rev. 21:22-27      Mt 12:14-21
Isa. 49:1-7        Rev. 21:22-27      Mt 12-14-21

*Jan. 7*          *103\*114, 115*
Isa. 52:3-6          Rev. 2:1-7                    Jn 2:1-11
Deut. 8:1-3          Col. 1:1-14          Jn 6:30-33, 48-51

*Jan 8*          *117, 118\*112, 113*
Isa. 59:15-21          Rev. 2:8-17                    Jn 4:46-54
Exod. 17:1-7          Col. 1:15-23                    Jn 7:37-52

*Jan. 9*          *121, 122, 123\*131, 132*
Isa. 63:1-5          Rev. 2:18-29                    Jn 5:1-15
Isa. 45:14-19          Col. 1:24--2:7                    Jn 8:12-19

*Jan. 10*          *138, 139\*147*
Isa. 65:1-9          Rev. 3:1-6                    Jn 6:1-14
Jer. 23:1-8          Col. 2:8-23                    Jn 10:7-17

*Jan. 11*          *148, 150\*91, 92*
Isa. 65:13-16          Rev. 3:7-13                    Jn 6:15-27
Isa. 55:3-9          Col. 3:1-17                    Jn 14:6-14

*Jan. 12*          *98, 99, 100*
Isa. 66:1-2, 22-23          Rev. 3:14-22          Jn 9:1-12, 35-38
Gen. 49:1-2, 8-12          Col. 3:18--4:6                    Jn 15:1-16

*Eve of 1 Epiphany*          *104*
Isa. 61:1-9          Gal. 3:23-29, 4:4-7

## Week of 1 Epiphany
*Sunday*          *146, 147\*111, 112, 113*
Isa. 40:1-11          Heb, 1:1-12 Jn 1:1-7, 19-20, 29-34
Gen. 1:1--2:3          Eph. 1:3-14                    Jn 1:29-34

*Monday*          *1, 2, 3\*4, 7*
Isa. 40:12-23          Eph. 1:1-14                    Mk 1:1-13
Gen. 2:4-9-25          Heb 1:1-14                    Jn 1:1-18

*Tuesday*          *5, 6\*10, 11*
Isa. 40:25-31          Eph. 1:15-23                    Mk 1:14-28

194

| Gen. 3:1-24 | Heb. 2:1-10 | Jn 1:19-28 |
| --- | --- | --- |

*Wednesday*   *119.1-24\*12, 13, 14*

| Isa. 41:1-16 | Eph. 2:1-10 | Mk 1:29-45 |
| --- | --- | --- |
| Gen 4:1-16 | Heb. 2:11-18 | Jn 1:29-42 |

*Thursday*   *18.1-20\*18.21-50*

| Isa. 41:17-29 | Eph. 2:11-22 | Mk 2:1-12 |
| --- | --- | --- |
| Gen 4:17-26 | Heb. 3:1-11 | Jn 1:43-51 |

*Friday*   *16, 17\*22*

| Isa. 42:(1-9)10-17 | Eph. 3:1-13 | Mk 2:13-22 |
| --- | --- | --- |
| Gen. 6:1-8 | Heb. 3:12-19 | Jn 2:1-12 |

*Saturday*   *20, 21\*110, 116, 117*

| Isa. 43:1-13 | Eph. 3:14-21 | Mk 2:23--3:6 |
| --- | --- | --- |
| Gen. 6:9-22 | Heb. 4:1-13 | Jn 2:13-22 |

**Week of 2 Epiphany**  *(Jan 18 Confession of St. Peter)*
*Sunday*   *148, 149, 150\*114, 115*

| Isa. 43:14--44:5 | Heb. 6:17--7:10 | Jn 4:27-42 |
| --- | --- | --- |
| Gen. 7:1-10, 17-23 | Eph. 4:1-16 | Mk 3:7-19 |

*Monday*   *25\*9, 15*

| Isa. 44:6-8, 21-23 | Eph. 4:1-16 | Mk 3:7-19a |
| --- | --- | --- |
| Gen. 8:6-22 | Heb. 4:14--5:6 | Jn 2:23--3:15 |

*Tuesday*   *26, 28\*36, 39*

| Isa. 44:9-20 | Eph. 4:17-32 | Mk 3:19b-35 |
| --- | --- | --- |
| Gen. 9:1-17 | Heb. 5:7-14 | Jn 3:16-21 |

*Wednesday*   *38\*119.25-48*

| Isa. 44:24--45:7 | Eph. 5:1-14 | Mk 4:1-20 |
| --- | --- | --- |
| Gen. 9:18-29 | Heb. 6:1-12 | Jn 3:22-36 |

*Thursday*   *37.1-18\*37.19-42*

| Isa. 45:5-17 | Eph. 5:15-33 | Mk 4:21-34 |
| --- | --- | --- |
| Gen. 11:1-9 | Heb. 6:13-20 | Jn 4:1-15 |

*Friday*      *31\*35*
Isa. 45:18-25      Eph. 6:1-9      Mk 4:35-41
Gen. 11:27--12:8      Heb. 7:1-17      Jn 4:16-26

*Saturday*      *30, 32\*42, 43*
Isa. 46:1-13      Eph. 6:10-24      Mk 5:1-20
Gen. 12:9--13:1      Heb. 7:18-28      Jn 4:27-42

**Week of 3 Epiphany** *(Jan 25 Conversion of St. Paul)*
*Sunday*      *63, 98\*103*
Isa. 47:1-15      Heb. 10:19-31      Jn 5:2-18
Gen. 13:2-18      Gal. 2:1-10      Mk 7:31-37

*Monday*      *41, 52\*44*
Isa. 48:1-11      Gal. 1:1-17      Mk 5:21-43
Gen. 14:(1-7)8-24      Heb. 8:1-13      Jn 4:43-54

*Tuesday*      *45\*47, 48*
Isa. 48:12-21      Gal. 1:18--2:10      Mk 6:1-13
Gen. 15:1-11, 17-21      Heb. 9:1-14      Jn 5:1-18

*Wednesday*      *119.42-72\*49, 53*
Isa. 49:1-12      Gal. 2:11-21      Mk 6:13-29
Gen. 16:1-14      Heb. 9:15-28      Jn 5:19-29

*Thursday*      *50\*118*
Isa. 49:13-23      Gal. 3:1-14      Mk 6:30-46
Gen. 16:15--17:14      Heb. 10:1-10      Jn 5:30-47

*Friday*      *40, 54\*51*
Isa. 50:1-11      Gal:3:15-22      Mk 6:47-56
Gen. 17:15-27      Heb. 10:11-25      Jn 6:1-15

*Saturday*      *55\*138, 139*
Isa. 51:1-8      Gal. 3:23-29      Mk 7:1-23
Gen. 18:1-16      Heb. 10:26-39      Jn 6:16-27

**Week of 4 Epiphany** *(Feb 2 The Presentation)*
*Sunday*     24, 29*8, 84

| | | |
|---|---|---|
| Isa. 51:9-16 | Heb. 11:8-16 | Jn 7:14-31 |
| Gen. 18:16-33 | Gal. 5:13-25 | Mk 8:22-30 |

*Monday*     56-58*64-65

| | | |
|---|---|---|
| Isa. 51:17-23 | Gal. 4:1-11 | Mk 7:24-37 |
| Gen. 19:1-29 | Heb. 11:1-12 | Jn 6:27-40 |

*Tuesday*     61-62*68

| | | |
|---|---|---|
| Isa. 52:1-12 | Gal. 4:12-20 | Mk 8:1-10 |
| Gen. 21:1-21 | Heb. 11:13-22 | Jn 6:41-51 |

*Wednesday*     72*119.73-96

| | | |
|---|---|---|
| Isa. 54:1-10(11-17) | Gal. 4:21-31 | Mk 8:11-26 |
| Gen. 22:1-18 | Heb. 11:23-31 | Jn 6:52-59 |

*Thursday*     70-71*74

| | | |
|---|---|---|
| Isa. 55:1-13 | Gal. 5:1-15 | Mk 8:27--9:1 |
| Gen. 23:1-20 | Heb. 11:32-12:2 | Jn 6:60-71 |

*Friday*     69*73

| | | |
|---|---|---|
| Isa. 56:1-8 | Gal. 5:16-24 | Mk 9:2-13 |
| Gen. 24:1-27 | Heb. 12:3-11 | Jn 7:1-13 |

*Saturday*     75-76*23, 27

| | | |
|---|---|---|
| Isa. 57:3-13 | Gal. 5:25--6:10 | Mk 9:14-29 |
| Gen. 24:28-38, 49-51 | Heb. 12:12-29 | Jn 7:14-36 |

**Week of 5 Epiphany**
*Sunday*     93, 96*34

| | | |
|---|---|---|
| Isa. 57:14-21 | Heb. 12:1-6 | Jn 7:37-46 |
| Gen. 24:50-67 | 2 Tim. 2:14-21 | Mk 10:13-22 |

*Monday*     80*77, 79

| | | |
|---|---|---|
| Isa. 58:1-12 | Gal. 6:11-18 | Mk 9:30-41 |
| Gen. 25:19-34 | Heb. 13:1-16 | Jn 7:37-52 |

*Tuesday*        *78.1-39*78.40-72*
Isa. 59:1-15a        2 Tim. 1:1-14        Mk 9:42-50
Gen. 26:1-6, 12-33        Heb. 13:17-25        Jn 7:53--8:11

*Wednesday*        *119.97-120*81-82*
Isa. 59:15b-21        2 Tim. 1:15--2:13        Mk 10:1-16
Gen. 27:1-29        Rom. 12:1-8        Jn 8:12-20

*Thursday*        *146-147*85-86*
Isa. 60:1-17        2 Tim. 2:14-26        Mk 10:17-31
Gen. 27:30-45        Rom. 12:9-21        Jn 8:21-32

*Friday 88*91-92*
Isa. 61:1-9        2 Tim. 3:1-17        Mk 10:32-45
Gen. 27:46--28:4, 10-22  Rom. 13:1-14        Jn 8:33-47

*Saturday*        *87, 90*136*
Isa. 61:10--62:5        2 Tim. 4:1-8        Mk 10:46-52
Gen. 29:1-20        Rom. 14:1-23        Jn 8:47-59

**Week of 6 Epiphany**
*Sunday*        *66-67*19, 46*
Isa. 62:6-12        1 John 2:3-11        Jn 8:12-19
Gen. 29:20-35        1 Tim. 3:14–4:10        Mk 10:23-31

*Monday*        *89.1-18*89.19-52*
Isa. 63:1-6        1 Tim. 1:1-17        Mk 11:1-11
Gen. 30:1-24        1 John 1:1-10        Jn 9:1-17

*Tuesday*        *97, 99-100*94-95*
Isa. 63:7-14        1 Tim. 1:18–2:8        Mk 11:12-26
Gen. 31:1-24        1 John 2:1-11        Jn 9:18-41

*Wednesday*        *101, 109*119.121-144*
Isa. 63:15--64:9        1 Tim. 3:1-16        Mk 11:27--12:12
Gen. 31:25-50        1 John 2:12-17        Jn 10:1-18

*Thursday*        *105.1-22*105.23-45*
Isa. 65:1-12        1 Tim. 4:1-16        Mk 12:13-27

Gen. 32:3-21            1 John 2:18-29            Jn 10:19-30

*Friday*            *102\*107.1-32*
Isa. 65:17-25          1 Tim. 5:17-25                    Mk 12:28-34
Gen. 32:22--33:17      1 John 3:1-10            Jn 10:31-42

*Saturday*          *107.33-43, 108\*33*
Isa. 66:1-6            1 Tim. 6:6-21            Mk 12:35-44
Gen. 35:1-20          1 John 3:11-18                    Jn 11:1-16

**Week of 7 Epiphany** *(Feb 24 St. Matthias)*
*Sunday*            *118\*145*
Isa. 66:7-14          1 John 3:4-10            Jn 10:7-16
Prov. 1:20-33        2 Cor. 5:11-21          Mk 10:35-45

*Monday*            *106.1-18\*106.19-48*
Ruth 1:1-14          2 Cor. 1:1-11                    Mt 5:1-12
Prov. 3:11-20        1 John 3:18--4:6        Jn 11:17-29

*Tuesday*          *120-123\*124-127*
Ruth 1:15-22        2 Cor. 1:12-22                    Mt 5:13-20
Prov. 4:1-27          1 John 4:7-21            Jn 11:30-44

*Wednesday*        *119.145-176\*128-130*
Ruth 2:1-13          2 Cor. 1:23--2:17              Mt 5:21-26
Prov. 6:1-19          1 John 5:1-12            Jn 11:45-54


*Thursday*          *131-133\*134-135*
Ruth 2:14-23        2 Cor. 3:1-18                    Mt 5:27-37
Prov. 7:1-27          1 John 5:13-21          Jn 11:55--12:8

*Friday*            *140, 142\*141, 143*
Ruth 3:1-18          2 Cor. 4:1-12                    Mt 5:38-48
Prov. 8:1-21          Philemon 1-25            Jn 12:9-19

*Saturday*          *137, 144\*104*
Ruth 4:1-17          2 Cor. 4:13--5:10              Mt 6:1-16
Prov. 8:22-36        2 Tim. 1:1-14            Jn 12:20-26

199

**Week of 8 Epiphany**

*Sunday*         *146-147\*111-113*
Deut. 6:1-9          2 Tim. 4:1-8          Jn 12:1-8
Prov. 9:1-12         2 Cor. 9:6b-15       Mk 10:46-52


*Monday*         *1-3\*4, 7*
Deut. 4:9-14         2 Cor. 10:1-18       Mt 6:7-15
Prov. 10:1-12        2 Tim. 1:15–2:13     Jn 12:27-36a


*Tuesday*        *5-6\*10-11*
Deut. 4:15-24        2 Cor. 11:1-21a      Mt 6:16-23
Prov. 15:16-33           2 Tim. 2:14-26                      Jn
12:36b-50


*Wednesday*      *119.1-24\*12-14*
Deut. 4:23-31        2 Cor. 11:21b-33     Mt 6:24-34
Prov. 17:1-20        2 Tim. 3:1-17        Jn 13:1-20


*Thursday*       *18.1-20\*18.21-50*
Deut. 4:32-40        2 Cor. 12:1-10       Mt 7:1-12
Prov. 21:30--22:6    2 Tim. 4:1-8         Jn 13:21-30


*Friday*         *16-17\*22*
Deut. 5:1-22         2 Cor. 12:11-21      Mt 7:13-21
Prov. 23:19-21, 29–24:2  2 Tim. 4:9-22    Jn 13:31-38


*Saturday*       *20-21\*110, 116, 117*
Deut. 5:22-33        2 Cor. 13:1-14       Mt 7:22-29
Prov. 25:15-28           Phil. 1:1-11              Jn 18:1-14


**Week of Last Epiphany**  *(Mar 19 St. Joseph)*
*Sunday*         *148-150\*114-115*
Deut. 6:1-9          Heb. 12:18-29        Jn 12:24-32
Ecclus. 48:1-11      2 Cor. 3:7-18        Lk 9:18-27


*Monday*         *25\*9, 15*
Deut. 6:10-15        Heb. 1:1-14          Jn 1:1-18
Prov. 27:1-6, 10-12  Phil. 2:1-13         Jn 18:15-18, 25-27

| *Tuesday* | 26, 28*36, 39 | |
|---|---|---|
| Deut. 6:16-25 | Heb. 2:1-10 | Jn 1:19-28 |
| Prov. 30:1-4, 24-33 | Phil. 3:1-11 | Jn 18:28-38 |

| *Ash Wednesday* | 95, 32, 143*102, 130 | |
|---|---|---|
| Jonah 3:1--4:11 | Heb. 12:1-14 | Lk 18:9-14 |
| Amos 5:6-15 | Heb. 12:1-14 | Lk 18:9-14 |

| *Thursday* | 37.1-18*37.19-42 | |
|---|---|---|
| Deut. 7:6-11 | Titus 1:1-16 | Jn 1:29-34 |
| Hab. 3:1-18 | Phil. 3:12-21 | Jn 17:1-8 |

| *Friday* | 95, 31*35 | |
|---|---|---|
| Deut. 7:12-16 | Titus 2:1-15 | Jn 1:35-42 |
| Ezek. 18:1-4, 25-32 | Phil. 4:1-9 | Jn 17:9-19 |

| *Saturday* | 30, 32*42-43 | |
|---|---|---|
| Deut. 7:17-26 | Titus 3:1-15 | Jn 1:43-51 |
| Ezek. 39:21-29 | Phil. 4:10-20 | Jn 17:20-26 |

**Week of 1 Lent** (*Mar 25 The Annunciation*)

| *Sunday* | 63, 98*103 | |
|---|---|---|
| Deut. 8:1-10 | 1 Cor. 1:17-31 | Mk 2:18-22 |
| Dan. 9:3-10 | Heb. 2:10-18 | Jn 12:44-50 |

| *Monday* | 41, 52*44 | |
|---|---|---|
| Deut. 8:11-20 | Heb. 2:11-18 | Jn 2:1-12 |
| Gen. 37:1-11 | 1 Cor. 1:1-19 | Mk 1:1-13 |

| *Tuesday* | 45*47-48 | |
|---|---|---|
| Deut. 9:4-12 | Heb. 3:1-11 | Jn 2:13-22 |
| Gen. 37:12-24 | 1 Cor. 1:20-31 | Mk 1:14-28 |

| *Wednesday* | 119.49-72*49, 53 | |
|---|---|---|
| Deut. 9:13-21 | Heb. 3:12-19 | Jn 2:23--3:15 |
| Gen. 37:25-36 | 1 Cor. 2:1-13 | Mk 1:29-45 |

| *Thursday* | 50*19, 46 | |
|---|---|---|

| | | |
|---|---|---|
| Deut. 9:23--10:5 | Heb. 4:1-10 | Jn 3:16-21 |
| Gen. 39:1-23 | 1 Cor. 2:14--3:15 | Mk 2:1-12 |

*Friday*      *95, 40, 54\*51*
| | | |
|---|---|---|
| Deut. 10:12-22 | Heb. 4:11-16 | Jn 3:22-36 |
| Gen. 40:1-23 | 1 Cor. 3:16-23 | Mk 2:13-22 |

*Saturday*      *55\*138-139*
| | | |
|---|---|---|
| Deut. 11:18-28 | Heb. 5:1-10 | Jn 4:1-26 |
| Gen. 41:1-13 | 1 Cor. 4:1-7 | Mk 2:23–3:6 |

## Week of 2 Lent
*Sunday*      *24, 29\*8, 84*
| | | |
|---|---|---|
| Jer. 1:1-10 | 1 Cor. 3:11-23 | Mk 3:31--4:9 |
| Gen. 41:14-45 | Rom. 6:3-14 | Jn 5:19-24 |

*Monday*      *56-58\*64-65*
| | | |
|---|---|---|
| Jer. 1:11-19 | Rom. 1:1-15 | Jn 4:27-42 |
| Gen. 41:46-57 | 1 Cor. 4:8-21 | Mk 3:7-19a |

*Tuesday*      *61-62\*68*
| | | |
|---|---|---|
| Jer. 2:1-13 | Rom. 1:16-25 | Jn 4:43-54 |
| Gen. 42:1-17 | 1 Cor. 5:1-8 | Mk 3:19b-35 |

*Wednesday*      *72\*119.73-96*
| | | |
|---|---|---|
| Jer. 3:6-18 | Rom. 1:28--2:11 | Jn 5:1-18 |
| Gen. 42:18-28 | 1 Cor. 5:9--6:8 | Mk 4:1-20 |

*Thursday*      *70-71\*74*
| | | |
|---|---|---|
| Jer. 4:9-10, 19-28 | Rom. 2:12-24 | Jn 5:19-29 |
| Gen. 42:29-38 | 1 Cor. 6:12-20 | Mk 4:21-34 |

*Friday 95, 69\*73*
| | | |
|---|---|---|
| Jer. 5:1-9 | Rom. 2:25--3:18 | Jn 5:30-47 |
| Gen. 43:1-15 | 1 Cor. 7:1-9 | Mk 4:35-41 |

*Saturday*      *75-76\*23, 27*
| | | |
|---|---|---|
| Jer. 5:20-31 | Rom. 3:19-31 | Jn 7:1-13 |

| | | |
|---|---|---|
| Gen. 43:16-34 | 1 Cor. 7:10-24 | Mk 5:1-20 |

## Week of 3 Lent
*Sunday*      *93, 96\*34*

| | | |
|---|---|---|
| Jer. 6:9-15 | 1 Cor. 6:12-20 | Mk 5:1-20 |
| Gen. 44:1-17 | Rom. 8:1-10 | Jn 5:25-29 |

*Monday*      *80\*77, 79*

| | | |
|---|---|---|
| Jer. 7:1-15 | Rom. 4:1-12 | Jn 7:14-36 |
| Gen. 44:18-34 | 1 Cor. 7:25-31 | Mk 5:21-43 |

*Tuesday*      *78.1-39\*78.40-72*

| | | |
|---|---|---|
| Jer. 7:21-34 | Rom. 4:13-25 | Jn 7:37-52 |
| Gen. 45:1-15 | 1 Cor. 7:32-40 | Mk 6:1-13 |

*Wednesday*      *119.97-120\*81-82*

| | | |
|---|---|---|
| Jer. 8:18--9:6 | Rom. 5:1-11 | Jn 8:12-20 |
| Gen. 45:16-28 | 1 Cor. 8:1-13 | Mk 6:13-29 |

*Thursday*

| | | |
|---|---|---|
| Jer. 10:11-24 | Rom. 5:12-21 | Jn 8:21-32 |
| Gen. 46:1-7, 28-34 | 1 Cor. 9:1-15 | Mk 6:30-46 |

*Friday*      *95, 88\*91-92*

| | | |
|---|---|---|
| Jer. 11:1-8, 14-20 | Rom. 6:1-11 | Jn 8:33-47 |
| Gen. 47:1-26 | 1 Cor. 9:16-27 | Mk 6:47-56 |

*Saturday*      *87, 90\*136*

| | | |
|---|---|---|
| Jer. 13:1-11 | Rom. 6:12-23 | Jn 8:47-59 |
| Gen. 47:27--48:7 | 1 Cor. 10:1-13 | Mk 7:1-23 |

## Week of 4 Lent
*Sunday*      *66-67\*19, 46*

| | | |
|---|---|---|
| Jer. 14:1-9, 17-22 | Gal. 4:21--5:1 | Mk 8:11-21 |
| Gen. 48:8-22 | Rom. 8:11-25 | Jn 6:27-40 |

*Monday*      *89.1-18\*89.19-52*

| | | |
|---|---|---|
| Jer. 16:10-21 | Rom. 7:1-12 | Jn 6:1-15 |

Gen. 49:1-28            1 Cor. 10:14--11:1      Mk 7:24-37

*Tuesday            97, 99-100\*94*
Jer. 17:19-27            Rom. 7:13-25            Jn 6:16-27
Gen. 49:29--50:14       1 Cor. 11:17-34         Mk 8:1-10

*Wednesday        101, 109\*119.121-144*
Jer. 18:1-11            Rom. 8:1-11             Jn 6:27-40
Gen. 50:15-26          1 Cor. 12:1-11          Mk 8:11-26

*Thursday           69\*73*
Jer. 22:13-23           Rom. 8:12-27            Jn 6:41-51
Exod. 1:6-22           1 Cor. 12:12-26         Mk 8:27--9:1

*Friday            95, 102\*107.1-32*
Jer. 23:1-8            Rom. 8:28-39            Jn 6:52-59
Exod. 2:1-22           1 Cor. 12:27--13:3      Mk 9:2-13

*Saturday        107.33-43, 108\*33*
Jer. 23:9-15            Rom. 9:1-18             Jn 6:60-71
Exod. 2:23--3:15       1 Cor. 13:1-13          Mk 9:14-29


## Week of 5 Lent
*Sunday            118\*145*
Jer. 23:16-32           1 Cor. 9:19-27          Mk 8:31--9:1
Exod. 3:16--4:12       Rom. 12:1-21            Jn 8:46-59

*Monday            31\*35*
Jer. 24:1-10            Rom. 9:19-33            Jn 9:1-17
Exod. 4:10-31          1 Cor. 14:1-19          Mk 9:30-41

*Tuesday         120-123\*124-127*
Jer. 25:8-17            Rom. 10:1-13            Jn 9:18-41
Exod. 5:1--6:1    1 Cor. 14:20-33a, 39-40      Mk 9:42-50

*Wednesday      119:145-176\*128-130*
Jer. 25:30-38           Rom. 10:14-21           Jn 10:1-18
Exod. 7:8-24           2 Cor. 2:14--3:6        Mk 10:1-16

*Thursday*        *131-133\*140, 142*
Jer. 26:1-16              Rom. 11:1-12                Jn 10:19-42
Exod. 7:25--8:19        2 Cor. 3:7-18              Mk 10:17-31


*Friday*          95, 22\*141, 143
Jer. 29:1, 4-13          Rom. 11:13-24            Jn 11:1-27. *or* 12:1-10
Exod. 9:13-35            2 Cor. 4:1-12            Mk 10:32-45


*Saturday*        *137, 144\*42-43*
Jer. 31:27-34            Rom. 11:25-36            Jn 11:28-44
*or* 12:37-50
Exod. 10:21--11:8        2 Cor. 4:13-18            Mk 10:46-52


**Holy Week**
*Palm Sunday   24, 29\*103*
Zech. 9:9-12              1 Tim. 6:12-16                Lk 19:41-48
Zech. 12:9-11, 13:1, 7-9      Php 2:5-11      Mt 21:12-17


*Monday*          *51\*69.1-23*
Jer. 12:1-16              Phil. 3:1-14              Jn 12:9-19
Lam. 1:1-2, 6-12        2 Cor. 1:1-7            Mk 11:12-25
*Tuesday*        *6, 12\*94*
Jer. 15:10-21            Phil. 3:15-21            Jn 12:20-26
Lam. 1:17-22            2 Cor. 1:8-22            Mk 11:27-33


*Wednesday   55\*74*
Jer. 17:5-10, 14-17    Phil. 4:1-13              Jn 12:27-36
Lam. 2:1-9              2 Cor. 1:23--2:11        Mk 12:1-11


*Maundy Thursday   102\*142-143*
Jer. 20:7-11            1 Cor. 10:14-17          Jn 17:1-26
Lam. 2:10-18            1 Cor. 11:22-32          Mk 14:12-25


*Good Friday   95,, 22\*40, 54*
Wisdom 1:16--2:1, 12-22   1 Peter 1:10-20   Jn13:36-38
Lam. 3:1-9, 19-33        1 Peter 1:10-20          Jn 19:1-37


*Holy Saturday   95, 88\*27*

| Job 19:21-27a | Heb. 4:1-16 | Mt 27:57-66 |
| Lam. 3:37-58 | Rom. 8:1-11 | Jn 19:38-42 |

## Easter Week
*Easter Day*     *148-150\*113-114*
| Exod. 12:1-14 | Romans 6:3-11 | Jn 1:1-18 |
| Isa. 51:9-11 | 1 Cor 5:6b-8 | Lk 24:13-35 |
*or* John 20:19-23

*Monday*       *93, 98\*66*
| Jonah 2:1-9 | Acts 2:14, 22-32\* | Jn 14:1-14 |
| Exod. 12:14-27 | 1 Cor. 15:1-11 | Mk 16:1-8 |

*Tuesday*      *103\*111, 114*
| Isa. 30:18-21 | Acts 2:36-47 | Jn 14:15-31 |
| Exod. 12:28-39 | 1 Cor. 15:12-28 | Mk 16:9-20 |

*Wednesday*    *97, 99\*115*
| Micah 7:7-15 | Acts 3:1-10 | Jn 15:1-11 |
| Exod. 12:40-51 | 1 Cor. 15:(29)30-41 | Mt 28:1-16 |

*Thursday*     *146-147\*148-149*
| Ezek. 37:1-14 | Acts 3:11-26 | Jn 15:12-27 |
| Exod. 13:3-10 | 1 Cor. 15:41-50 | Mt 28:16-20 |

*Friday*       *136\*118*
| Dan. 12:1-4, 13 | Acts 4:1-12 | Jn 16:1-15 |
| Exod. 13:1-2, 11-16 | 1 Cor. 15:51-58 | Lk 24:1-12 |

*Saturday*     *145\*104*
| Isa. 25:1-9 | Acts 4:13-31 | Jn 16:16-33 |
| Exod 13:17--14:4 | 2 Cor. 4:16–5:10 | Mk 12:18-27 |

## Week of 2 Easter *(April 25 St. Mark)*
*Sunday*       *146-147\*111-113*
| Isa. 43:8-13 | 1 Pet. 2:2-10 | Jn 14:1-7 |
| Exod. 14:5-22 | 1 John 1:1-7 | Jn 20:19-31 |

*Monday*       *1-3\*4, 7*

| | | |
|---|---|---|
| Dan. 1:1-21 | 1 John 1:1-10 | Jn 17:1-11 |
| Exod. 14:21-31 | 1 Pet. 1:1-12 | Jn 14:1-17 |

*Tuesday*         *5-6\*10-11*

| | | |
|---|---|---|
| Dan. 2:1-16 | 1 John 2:1-11 | Jn 17:12-19 |
| Exodus. 15:1-21 | 1 Peter 1:13-25 | Jn 14:18-31 |

*Wednesday*    *119.1-24\*12-14*

| | | |
|---|---|---|
| Dan. 2:17-30 | 1 John 2:12-17 | Jn 17:20-26 |
| Exod. 15:22--16:10 | 1 Peter 2:1-10 | Jn 15:1-11 |

*Thursday*     *18.1-20\*18.21-50*

| | | |
|---|---|---|
| Dan. 2:31-49 | 1 John 2:18-29 | Lk 3:1-14 |
| Exodus 16:10-21 | 1 Peter 2:11-25 | Jn 15:12-27 |

*Friday*        *16-17\*134-135*

| | | |
|---|---|---|
| Dan. 3:1-18 | 1 John 3:1-10 | Lk 3:15-22 |
| Exodus 16:22-36 | 1 Peter 3:13--4:6 | Jn 16:1-15 |


*Saturday*    *20-21\*110, 116-117*

| | | |
|---|---|---|
| Dan. 3:19-30 | 1 John 3:11-18 | Lk 4:1-13 |
| Exodus 17:1-16 | 1 Peter 4:7-19 | Jn 16:16-33 |

**Week of 3 Easter**  *(May 2 SS Philip and James)*
*Sunday*     *148-150\*114-115*

| | | |
|---|---|---|
| Dan. 4:1-18 | 1 Peter 4:7-11 | Jn 21:15-25 |
| Exodus 18:1-12 | 1 John 2:7-17 | Mk 16:9-20 |

*Monday*     *25\*9, 15*

| | | |
|---|---|---|
| Dan. 4:19-27 | 1 John 3:19--4:6 | Lk 4:14-30 |
| Exodus 18:13-27 | 1 Peter 5:1-14  Mt (1:1-17): 3:1-6 | |

*Tuesday*    *26, 28\*36, 39*

| | | |
|---|---|---|
| Dan. 4:28-37 | 1 John 4:7-21 | Lk 4:31-37 |
| Exodus 19:1-16 | Col. 1:1-14 | Mt 3:7-12 |

*Wednesday*   *38\*119.25-48*

| | | |
|---|---|---|
| Dan. 5:1-12 | 1 John 5:1-12 | Lk 4:38-44 |

Exodus 19:16-25     Col. 1:15-23          Mt 3:13-17


*Thursday*     *37.1-18\*37.19-42*
Dan. 5:13-30         1 John 5:13-21         Lk 5:1-11
Exod. 20:1-21        Col. 1:24--2:7         Mt 4:1-11


*Friday*       *105.1-22\*105.23-45*
Dan. 6:1-15          2 John 1-13            Lk 5:12-26
Exod. 24:1-18        Col. 2:8-23            Mt 4:12-17


*Saturday*     *30, 32\*42-43*
Dan. 6:16-28         3 John 1-15            Lk 5:27-39
Exod. 25:1-22        Col. 3:1-17            Mt 4:18-25


## Week of 4 Easter
*Sunday*       *63, 98\*103*
Wisdom 1:1-15        1 Pet. 5:1-11          Mt 7:15-29
Exod. 28:1-4, 30-38  1 John 2:18-29         Mk 6:30-44


*Monday*       *41, 52\*44*
Wisdom 1:16--2:11, 21-24    Col. 1:1-14     Lk 6:1-11
Exod. 32:1-20        Col. 3:18--4:6(7-18)   Mt 5:1-10


*Tuesday*      *45\*47-48*
Wisdom 3:1-9         Col. 1:15-23           Lk 6:12-26
Exod. 32:21-34       1 Thess. 1:1-10        Mt 5:11-16


*Wednesday*    *119.49-72\*49, 53*
Wisdom 4:16--5:8     Col. 1:24--2:7         Lk 6:27-38
Exod. 33:1-23        1 Thess. 2:1-12        Mt 5:17-20


*Thursday*     *50\*114-115*
Wisdom 5:9-23        Col. 2:8-23            Lk 6:39-49
Exod. 34:1-17        1 Thess. 2:13-20       Mt 5:21-26


*Friday*       *40, 54\*51*
Wisdom 6:12-23       Col. 3:1-11            Lk 7:1-17
Exod. 34:18-35       1 Thess. 3:1-13        Mt 5:27-37

*Saturday*　　　*55\*138-139*
Wisdom 7:1-14　　　Col. 3:12-17　　　Lk 7:18-35
Exod. 40:18-38　　　1 Thess. 4:1-12　　Mt. 5:38-48

**Week of 5 Easter**
*Sunday*　　　*24, 29\*8, 84*
Wisdom 7:22--8:1　　2 Thess. 2:13-17　　　Mt 7:7-14
Lev. 8:1-13, 30-36　　Heb. 12:1-14　　　Lk 4:16-30

*Monday*　　　*56-58\*64-65*
Wisdom 9:1, 7-18　　Col. (3:18--4:1)2-18　Lk 7:36-50
Lev. 16:1-9　　　　1 Thess 4:13-18　　Lk 4:16-30

*Tuesday*　　　*61-62\*68*
Wisdom 10:1-4(5-12)13-21　Rom. 12:1-21　Lk 8:1-15
Lev. 16:20-34　　　1 Thess. 5:1-11　　Mt 6:7-15

*Wednesday*　　*72\*119.73-96*
Wisdom 13:1-9　　　Rom. 13:1-14　　Lk 8:16-25
Lev. 19:1-18　　　1 Thess. 5:12-28　　Mt 6:19-24

*Thursday*　　　*70-71\*74*
Wisdom 14:27--15:3　Rom. 14:1-12　　Lk 8:26-39
Lev. 19:26-37　　　2 Thess. 1:1-12　　Mt 6:25-34

*Friday*　　　*106.1-18\*106.19-48*
Wisdom 16:15--17:1　Rom. 14:13-23　　Lk 8:40-56
Lev. 23:1-22　　　2 Thess. 2:1-17　　Mt 7:1-12

*Saturday*　　　*75-76\*23, 27*
Wisdom 19:1-8, 18-22　Rom. 15:1-13　　Lk 9:1-17
Lev. 23:23-44　　　2 Thess. 3:1-18　　Mt 7:13-21

**Week of 6 Easter**
*Sunday*　　　*93, 96\*34*
Ecclus. 43:1-12, 27-32　1 Tim. 3:14—4:5　Mt 13:24-34a
Lev. 25:1-17　　　James 1:2-8, 16-18　Lk 12:13-21

*Monday*          *80\*77, 79*
Deut. 8:1-10          James 1:1-15          Lk 9:18-27
Lev. 25:35-55          Col. 1:9-14          Mt 13:1-16

*Tuesday*          *78.1-39\*78.40-72*
Deut. 8:11-20          James 1:16-27          Lk 11:1-13
Lev. 26:1-20          1 Tim. 2:1-6          Mt 13:18-23

*Wednesday*          *119.97-120\*68.1-20*
Baruch 3:24-37          James 5:13-18          Lk 12:22-31
Lev. 26:27-42          Eph. 1:1-10          Mt. 22:41-46

*Ascension Day*          *8, 47\*24, 96*
Ezek. 1:14, 24-28b          Heb. 2:5-18          Mt 28:16-20
Dan. 7:9-14          Heb. 2:5-18          Mt 28:16-20


*Friday*          *85-86\*91-92*
Ezek. 1:28--3:3          Heb. 4:14--5:6          Lk 9:28-36
1 Sam. 2:1-10          Eph. 2:1-10          Mt 7:22-27

*Saturday*          *87, 90\*136*
Ezek. 3:4-17          Heb. 5:7-14          Lk 9:37-50
Num. 11:16-17, 24-29  Eph. 2:11-22          Mt 7:28--8:4

**Week of 7 Easter** *(May 31 The Visitation)*
*Sunday*          *66-67\*19, 46*
Ezek. 3:16-27          Eph. 2:1-10     Mt 10:24-33, 40-42
Exod. 3:1-12          Heb. 12:18-29          Lk 10:17-24

*Monday*          *89.1-18\*89.19-52*
Ezek. 4:1-17          Heb. 6:1-12          Lk 9:51-62
Joshua 1:1-9          Eph. 3:1-13          Mt 8:5-17

*Tuesday*          *97, 99-100\*94*
Ezek. 7:10-15, 23b-27  Heb. 6:13-20          Lk 10:1-17
1 Sam. 16:1-13a          Eph. 3:14-21          Mt 8:18-27

*Wednesday*          *101, 109\*119.121-144*

| | | |
|---|---|---|
| Ezek. 11:14-25 | Heb. 7:1-17 | Lk 10:17-24 |
| Isa. 4:2-6 | Eph. 4:1-16 | Mt 8:28-34 |

*Thursday*     *105.1-22\*105.23-45*
| | | |
|---|---|---|
| Ezek. 18:1-4, 19-32 | Heb. 7:18-28 | Lk 10:25-37 |
| Zech. 4:1-14 | Eph. 4:17-32 | Mt 9:1-8 |

*Friday*     *102\*107.1-32*
| | | |
|---|---|---|
| Ezek. 34:17-31 | Heb. 8:1-13 | Lk 10:38-42 |
| Jer. 31:27-34 | Eph. 5:1-20 | Mt 9:9-17 |

*Saturday*     *107.33-43, 108\*33*
| | | |
|---|---|---|
| Ezek. 43:1-12 | Heb. 9:1-14 | Lk 11:14-23 |
| Ezek. 36:22-27 | Eph. 6:10-24 | Mt 9:18-26 |

*The Day of Pentecost*     *118\*145*
| | | |
|---|---|---|
| Isa. 11:1-9 | 1 Cor. 2:1-13 | Jn 14:21-29 |
| Deut. 16:9-12 | Acts 4:18-21, 23-33 | Jn 4:19-26 |

*Trinity Sunday*     *146-147\*111-113*
| | | |
|---|---|---|
| Ecclus. 43:1-12(27-33) | Eph. 4:1-16 | Jn 1:1-18 |
| Job 38:1-11, 42:1-5 | Rev. 19:4-16 | Jn 1:29-34 |

**Proper 1** *Week of the Sunday May 8-14*
*Monday*     *106.1-18\*106.19-48*
| | | |
|---|---|---|
| Isa. 63:7-14 | 2 Tim. 1:1-14 | Lk 11:24-36 |
| Ezekiel 33:1-11 | 1 John 1:1-10 | Mt 9:27-34 |

*Tuesday*     *120-123\*124-127*
| | | |
|---|---|---|
| Isa. 63:15-64:9 | 2 Tim. 1:15-2:13 | Lk 11:37-42 |
| Ezek. 33:21-33 | 1 John 2:1-11 | Mt 9:35-10:4 |

*Wednesday*     *119.145-176\*128-130*
| | | |
|---|---|---|
| Isa. 65:1-12 | 2 Tim. 2:14-26 | Lk 11:53-12:12 |
| Ezek. 34:1-16 | 1 John 2:12-17 | Mt 10:5-15 |

*Thursday*     *131-133\*134-135*
| | | |
|---|---|---|
| Isa. 65:17-25 | 2 Tim. 3:1-17 | Lk 12:13-31 |

Ezek. 37:21b-28     1 John 2:18-29     Mt 10:16-23

*Friday*     *140, 142\*141, 143*
Isa. 66:1-6     2 Tim. 4:1-18     Lk 12:32-48
Ezek. 39:21-29     1 John 3:1-10     Mt 10:24-33

*Saturday*     *137, 144\*104*
Isa. 66:7-14     2 Tim. 4:9-22     Lk 12:49-59
Ezek. 47:1-12     1 John 3:11-18     Mt 10:34-42

**Proper 2** *May 15-21*
*Monday*     *1-3\*4, 7*
Ruth 1:1-18     1 Tim. 1:1-17     Lk 13:1-9
Prov. 3:11-20     1 John 3:18-4:6     Mt 11:1-6

*Tuesday*     *5-6\*10-11*
Ruth 1:19-2:13     1 Tim. 1:18-2:8     Lk 13:10-17
Prov. 4:1-27     1 John 4:7-21     Mt 11:7-15

*Wednesday*     *119.1-24\*12-14*
Ruth 2:14-23     1 Tim. 3:1-16     Lk 13:18-30
Prov. 6:1-19     1 John 5:1-12     Mt 11:16-24

*Thursday*     *18.1-20\*18.21-50*
Ruth 3:1-18     1 Tim. 4:1-16     Lk 13:31-35
Prov. 7:1-27     1 John 5:13-21     Mt 11:25-30

*Friday*     *16-17\*22*
Ruth 4:1-17     1 Tim. 5:17-25     Lk 14:1-11
Prov. 8:1-21     2 John 1-13     Mt 12:1-14

*Saturday*     *20-21\*110, 116-117*
Deut. 1:1-8     1 Tim. 6:6-21     Lk14:12-24
Prov. 8:22-36     3 John 1-15     Mt 12:15-21

**Proper 3** *May 22-28*
*Sunday*     *148-150\*114-115*
Deut. 4:1-9     Rev. 7:1-4, 9-17     Mt 12:33-45
Prov. 9:1-12     Acts 8:14-25     Lk10:25-28,38-42

*Monday*        25*9, 15
Deut. 4:9-14            2 Cor. 1:1-11            Lk 14:25-35
Prov. 10:1-12           1 Tim. 1:1-17           Mt 12:22-32

*Tuesday*       26, 28*36, 39
Deut. 4:15-24           2 Cor. 1:12-22          Lk 15:1-10
Prov. 15:16-33          1 Tim. 1:18-2:8         Mt 12:33-42

*Wednesday*     38*119.25-48
Deut. 4:25-31           2 Cor. 1:23-2:17        Lk 15:1-2, 11-32
Prov. 17:1-20           1 Tim. 3:1-16           Mt 12:43-50


*Thursday*      37.1-18*37.19-42
Deut. 4:32-40           2 Cor. 3:1-18           Lk 16:1-9
Prov. 21:30-22:6        1 Tim. 4:1-16           Mt. 13:24-30

*Friday*        31*35
Deut. 5:1-22            2 Cor. 4:1-12           Lk 16:10-18
Prov. 23:19-21,29-24:2  1 Tim. 5:17-25          Mt. 13:31-35

*Saturday*      30, 32*42-43
Deut. 5:22-33           2 Cor. 4:13-5:10        Lk 16:19-31
Prov. 25:15-28          1 Tim. 6:6-21           Mt 13:36-43

**Proper 4** *May 28-June 4   (May 31 The Visitation)*
*Sunday*        63, 98*103
Deut. 11:1-12           Rev. 10:1-11            Mt. 13:44-58
Eccles. 1:1-11          Acts 8:26-40            Lk 11:1-13

*Monday*        41, 52*44
Deut. 11:13-19          2 Cor 5:11-6:2          Lk 17:1-10
Eccles. 2:1-15          Gal. 1:1-17             Mt 13:44-52

*Tuesday*       45*47-48
Deut. 12:1-12           2 Cor. 6:3-7:1          Lk 17:11-19
Eccles. 2:16-26         Gal. 1:18-2:10          Mt 13:53-58

213

*Wednesday*    119.49-72*49, 53
Deut. 13:1-11          2 Cor. 7:2-16          Lk 17:20-37
Eccles. 3:1-15         Gal. 2:11-21           Mt 14:1-12

*Thursday*    50*8, 84
Deut. 16:18-20, 17:14-20  2 Cor. 8:1-16                    Lk 18:1-8
Eccles. 3:16-4:3       Gal. 3:1-14            Mt 14:13-21

*Friday*    40, 54*51
Deut. 26:1-11          2 Cor. 8:16-24         Lk 18:9-14
Eccles. 5:1-7          Gal. 3:15-22           Mt 14:22-36


*Saturday*    55*138-139
Deut. 29:2-15          2 Cor. 9:1-15          Lk 18:15-30
Eccles. 5:8-20         Gal. 3:23-4:11         Mt 15:1-20

**Proper 5** *June 5-11  (June 11 St.Barnabas)*
*Sunday*    24, 29*8, 84
Deut. 29:16-29         Rev. 12:1-12           Mt. 15:29-39
Eccles. 6:1-12         Acts 10:9-23           Lk 12:32-40

*Monday*    56-58*64-65
Deut. 30:1-10          2 Cor. 10:1-18         Lk 18:31-43
Eccles. 7:1-14         Gal. 4:12-20           Mt 15:21-28

*Tuesday*    61-62*68
Deut. 30:11-20         2 Cor. 11:1-21a        Lk 19:1-10
Eccles. 8:14-9:10      Gal. 4:21-31           Matt. 15:29-39

*Wednesday*    72*119.73-96
Deut. 31:30-32:14      2 Cor. 11:21b-33       Lk 19:11-27
Eccles. 9:11-18        Gal. 5:1-15            Mt 16:1-12

*Thursday*    70-71*74
Ecclus. 44:19-45:5     2 Cor. 12:1-10         Lk 19:28-40
Eccles. 11:1-8         Gal. 5:16-24           Mt. 16:13-20

*Friday*    69*73

| Ecclus. 45:6-16 | 2 Cor. 12:11-21 | Lk 19:41-48 |
| Eccles. 11:9-12:14 | Gal. 5:25-6:10 | Mt. 16:21-28 |

*Saturday*      *75-76\*23, 27*
| Ecclus. 46:1-10 | 2 Cor. 13:1-14 | Lk 20:1-8 |
| Num. 3:1-13 | Gal. 6:11-18 | Mt. 17:1-13 |

**Proper 6**    *June 12-18*
*Sunday*      *93, 96\*34*
| Ecclus. 46:11-20 | Rev. 15:1-8 | Mt. 18:1-14 |
| Num. 6:22-27 | Acts 13:1-12 | Lk 12:41-48 |

*Monday*      *80\*77, 79*
| 1 Samuel 1:1-20 | Acts 1:1-14 | Lk 20:9-19 |
| Num. 9:15-23,10:29-36 | Rom. 1:1-15 | Mt. 17:14-21 |

*Tuesday*      *78.1-39\*78.40-72*
| 1 Samuel 1:21-2:11 | Acts 1:15-26 | Lk 20:19-26 |
| Num. 11:1-23 | Rom. 1:16-25 | Mt 17:22-27 |

*Wednesday*    *119.97-120\*81-82*
| 1 Samuel 2:12-26 | Acts 2:1-21 | Lk 20:27-40 |
| Num. 11:24-33(34-35) | Rom. 1:28-2:11 | Mt. 18:1-9 |

*Thursday*      *34\*85-86*
| 1 Samuel 2:27-36 | Acts 2:22-36 | Lk 20:41-21:4 |
| Num. 12:1-16 | Rom. 2:12-24 | Mt. 18:10-20 |

*Friday*      *88\*91-92*
| 1 Samuel 3:1-21 | Acts 2:37-47 | Lk 21:5-19 |
| Num. 13:1-3,21-30 | Rom. 2:25-3:8 | Mt. 18:21-35 |

*Saturday*      *87, 90\*136*
| 1 Samuel 4:1b-11 | Acts 4:32-5:11 | Lk 21:20-28 |
| Num. 13:31-14:25 | Rom. 3:9-20 | Mt. 19:1-12 |

**Proper 7** *June 19-25   (June 24 Nativity of John the Baptist)*
*Sunday*      *66-67\*19, 46*
| 1 Samuel 4:12-22 | James 1:1-18 | Mt 19:23-30 |

| | | |
|---|---|---|
| Num. 14:26-45 | Acts 15:1-12 | Lk 12:49-56 |

*Monday*     *89.1-18\*89.19-52*
| | | |
|---|---|---|
| 1 Samuel 5:1-12 | Acts 5:12-26 | Lk 21:29-36 |
| Num. 16:1-19 | Rom. 3:21-31 | Mt. 19:13-22 |

*Tuesday*     *97, 99-100\*94*
| | | |
|---|---|---|
| 1 Samuel 6:1-16 | Acts 5:27-42 | Lk 21:37-22:13 |
| Num. 16:20-35 | Rom. 4:1-12 | Mt. 19:23-30 |

*Wednesday*     *101, 109\*119.121-144*
| | | |
|---|---|---|
| 1 Samuel 7:2-17 | Acts 6:1-15 | Lk 22:14-23 |
| Num. 16:36-50 | Rom. 4:13-25 | Mt. 20:1-16 |

*Thursday*     *105.1-22\*105.23-45*
| | | |
|---|---|---|
| 1 Samuel 8:1-22 | Acts 6:15-7:16 | Lk 22:24-30 |
| Num. 17:1-11 | Rom. 5:1-11 | Mt. 20:17-28 |

*Friday*     *102\*107.1-32*
| | | |
|---|---|---|
| 1 Samuel 9:1-14 | Acts 7:17-29 | Lk 22:31-38 |
| Num. 20:1-13 | Rom. 5:12-21 | Mt. 20:29-34 |

*Saturday*     *107.33-43, 108\*33*
| | | |
|---|---|---|
| 1 Samuel 9:15-10:1 | Acts 7:30-43 | Lk 22:39-51 |
| Num. 20:14-29 | Rom. 6:1-11 | Mt. 21:1-11 |

**Proper 8**  *June 26-July 2*  *(June 29 SS Peter and Paul)*
*Sunday*     *118\*145*
| | | |
|---|---|---|
| 1 Samuel 10:1-16 | Rom. 4:13-25 | Mt. 21:23-32 |
| Num. 21:4-9,21-35 | Acts 17:12-34 | Lk 13:10-17 |

*Monday*     *106.1-18\*106.19-48*
| | | |
|---|---|---|
| 1 Samuel 10:17-27 | Acts 7:44-8:1a | Lk 22:52-62 |
| Num. 22:1-21 | Rom. 6:12-23 | Mt. 21:12-22 |

*Tuesday*     *120-123\*1124-127*
| | | |
|---|---|---|
| 1 Samuel 11:1-15 | Acts 8:1-13 | Lk 22:63-71 |
| Num. 22:21-38 | Rom. 7:1-12 | Mt. 21:23-32 |

*Wednesday*     *119.145-176\*128-130*
1 Samuel 12:1-6,16-25   Acts 8:14-25          Lk 23:1-12
Num. 22:41-23:12        Rom. 7:13-25          Mt. 21:33-46

*Thursday*     *131-133\*134-135*
1 Samuel 13:5-18        Acts 8:26-40          Lk 23:13-25
Num. 23:11-26           Rom. 8:1-11           Mt. 22:1-14


*Friday*     *140, 142\*141, 143*
1 Samuel 13:19-14:15    Acts 9:1-9            Lk 23:26-31
Num. 24:1-13            Rom. 8:12-17          Mt 22:15-22

*Saturday*     *137, 144\*104*
1 Samuel 14:16-30       Acts 9:10-19a         Lk 23:32-43
Num. 24:12-25           Rom. 8:18-25          Mt 22:23-40

**Proper 9** *July 3-9*
*Sunday* *146-147\*111-113*
1 Samuel 14:36-45       Rom. 5:1-11           Mt. 22:1-14
Num. 27:12-23           Acts 19:11-20         Mk 1:14-20

*Monday*     *1-3\*4, 7*
1 Samuel 15:1-3,7-23    Acts 9:19b-31         Lk 23:44-56a
Num. 32:1-6,16-27       Rom. 8:26-30          Mt. 23:1-12

*Tuesday*     *5-6\*10-11*
1 Samuel 15:24-35    Acts 9:32-43    Lk 23:56b-24:11
Num. 35:1-3,9-15,30-34     Rom. 8:31-3  Mt. 23:13-26

*Wednesday*     *119.1-24\*12-14*
1 Samuel 16:1-13        Acts 10:1-16          Lk 24:12-35
Deut. 1:1-18            Rom. 9:1-18           Mt. 23:27-39

*Thursday*     *18.1-20\*18.21-50*
1 Samuel 16:14-17:11  Acts 10:17-33           Lk 24:36-53
Deut. 3:18-28           Rom. 9:19-33          Mt. 24:1-14

*Friday*       *16-17\*22*
1 Samuel 17:17-30    Acts 10:34-48       Mk 1:1-13
Deut. 31:7-13,24-32:4 Rom 10:1-13       Mt. 24:15-3

*Saturday*      *20-21\*110, 116-117*
1 Samuel 17:31-49    Acts 11:1-18       Mk 1:14-28
Deut. 34:1-12       Rom. 10:14-21     Mt. 24:32-51


**Proper 10** *July 10-16*
*Sunday*       *148-150\*114-115*
1 Samuel 17:50-18:4     Rom. 10:4-17    Mt. 23:29-39
Joshua 1:1-18       Acts 21:3-15       Mk 1:21-27

*Monday*      *25\*9, 15*
1 Samuel 18:5-16,27b-30     Acts 11:19-30 Mk 1:29-45
Joshua 2:1-14       Rom. 11:1-12       Mt. 25:1-13

*Tuesday*      *26, 28\*36, 39*
1 Samuel 19:1-18    Acts 12:1-17       Mk 2:1-12
Joshua 2:15-24     Rom. 11:13-24     Mt. 25:14-30

*Wednesday*    *38\*119.25-48*
1 Samuel 20:1-23    Acts 12:18-25     Mk 2:13-22
Joshua 3:1-13       Rom. 11:25-36     Mt. 25:31-46

*Thursday*    *37.1-18\*37.19-42*
1 Samuel 20:24-42    Acts 13:1-12      Mk 2:23-3:6
Joshua 3:14-4:7      Rom. 12:1-8       Mt. 26:1-16

*Friday*       *31\*35*
1 Samuel 21:1-15    Acts 13:13-25     Mk 3:7-19a
Joshua 4:19-5:1,10-15   Rom. 12:9-21     Mt. 26:17-25

*Saturday*      *30, 32\*42-43*
1 Samuel 22:1-23    Acts 13:26-43     Mk 3:19b-35
Joshua 6:1-14       Rom. 13:1-7       Mt. 26:26-35


**Proper 11** *July 17-23 (July 22 St Mary Magadlene; 25 St. James)*

*Sunday*          *63, 98\*103*
1 Samuel 23:7-18      Rom. 11:33-12:2      Mt. 25:14-30
Joshua 6:15-27        Acts 22:30-23:11     Mk 2:1-12

*Monday*          *41, 53\*44*
1 Samuel 24:1-22      Acts 13:44-52        Mk 4:1-20
Joshua 7:1-13         Rom. 13:8-14         Mt. 26:36-46

*Tuesday*         *45\*47-48*
1 Samuel 25:1-22      Acts 14:1-18         Mk 4:21-34
Joshua 8:1-22         Rom. 14:1-12         Mt. 26:47-56

*Wednesday*       *119.49-72\*49, 53*
1 Samuel 25:23-44     Acts 14:19-28        Mk 4:35-41
Joshua 8:30-35        Rom. 14:13-23        Mt. 26:57-68

*Thursday*        *50\*66-67*
1 Samuel 28:3-20      Acts 15:1-11         Mk 5:1-20
Joshua 9:3-21         Rom. 15:1-13         Mt. 26:69-75

*Friday*          *40, 54\*51*
1 Samuel 31:1-13      Acts 15:12-21        Mk 5:21-43
Joshua 9:22-10:15     Rom. 15:14-24        Mt. 27:1-10

*Saturday*        *55\*138-139*
2 Samuel 1:1-16       Acts 15:22-35        Mk 6:1-13
Joshua 23:1-16        Rom. 15:25-33        Mt. 27:11-23

**Proper 12** *July 24-30*
*Sunday*          *24, 29\*8, 84*
2 Samuel 1:17-27      Rom. 12:9-21         Mt. 25:31-46
Joshua 24:1-15        Acts 28:23-31        Mk 2:23-28

*Monday*          *56-58\*64-65*
2 Samuel 2:1-11       Acts 15:36-16:5      Mk 6:14-29
Joshua 24:16-33       Rom. 16:1-16         Mt. 27:24-31

*Tuesday*         *61-62\*68*
2 Samuel 3:6-21       Acts 16:6-15         Mk 6:30-46

| | | |
|---|---|---|
| Judges 2:1-5,11-23 | Rom. 16:17-27 | Mt. 27:32-44 |

*Wednesday*     *72\*119.73-96*
| | | |
|---|---|---|
| 2 Samuel 3:22-39 | Acts 16:16-24 | Mk 6:47-56 |
| Judges 3:12-30 | Acts 1:1-14 | Mt. 27:45-54 |

*Thursday*     *70-71\*74*
| | | |
|---|---|---|
| 2 Samuel 4:1-12 | Acts 16:25-40 | Mk 7:1-23 |
| Judges 4:4-23 | Acts 1:15-26 | Mt. 27:55-66 |

*Friday*     *69\*73*
| | | |
|---|---|---|
| 2 Samuel 5:1-12 | Acts 17:1-15 | Mk 7:24-37 |
| Judges 5:1-18 | Acts 2:1-21 | Mt. 28:1-10 |

*Saturday*     *75-76\*23, 27*
| | | |
|---|---|---|
| 2 Samuel 5:22-6:11 | Acts 17:16-34 | Mk 8:1-10 |
| Judges 5:19-31 | Acts 2:22-36 | Mt. 28:11-20 |

**Proper 13** *July 31-August 5*
*Sunday*     *93, 96\*34*
| | | |
|---|---|---|
| 2 Samuel 6:12-23 | Rom. 4:7-12 | Jn 1:43-51 |
| Judges 6:1-24 | 2 Cor. 9:6-15 | Mk 3:20-30 |

*Monday*     *80\*77, 79*
| | | |
|---|---|---|
| 2 Samuel 7:1-17 | Acts 18:1-11 | Mk 8:11-21 |
| Judges 6:25-40 | Acts 2:37-47 | Jn 1:1-18 |

*Tuesday*     *78.1-39\*78.40-72*
| | | |
|---|---|---|
| 2 Samuel 7:18-29 | Acts 18:12-28 | Mk 8:22-33 |
| Judges 7:1-18 | Acts 3:1-11 | Jn 1:19-28 |

*Wednesday*     *119.97-120\*81-82*
| | | |
|---|---|---|
| 2 Samuel 9:1-13 | Acts 19:1-10 | Mk 8:34-9:1 |
| Judges 7:19-8:12 | Acts 3:12-26 | Jn 1:29-42 |

*Thursday*     *145\*85-86*
| | | |
|---|---|---|
| 2 Samuel 11:1-27 | Acts 19:11-20 | Mk 9:2-13 |
| Judges 8:22-35 | Acts 4:1-12 | Jn 1:43-51 |

*Friday*　　　　88*91-92
2 Samuel 12:1-14　　Acts 19:21-41　　Mk 9:14-29
Judges 9:1-16,19-21　Acts 4:13-31　　Jn 2:1-12


*Saturday*　　　87, 90*136
2 Samuel 12:15-31　　Acts 20:1-16　　Mk 9:30-41
Judges 9:22-25,50-57　Acts 4:32-5:11　　Jn 2:13-25

**Proper 14** *August 6-13 (Aug 6 The Transfiguration)*
*Sunday*　　　　66-67*19, 46
2 Samuel 13:1-22　　Rom. 15:1-13　　Jn 3:22-36
Judges 11:1-11,29-40　2 Cor. 11:21b-31　Mk 4:35-41

*Monday*　　　89.1-18*89.19-52
2 Samuel 13:23-39　　Acts 20:17-38　　Mk 9:42-50
Judges 12:1-7　　　Acts 5:12-26　　Jn 3:1-21

*Tuesday*　　　97. 99*94
2 Samuel 14:1-20　　Acts 21:1-14　　Mk 10:1-16
Judges 13:1-15　　　Acts 5:27-42　　Jn 3:22-36

*Wednesday*　　101, 109*119.121-144
2 Samuel 14:21-33　　Acts 21:15-26　　Mk 10:17-31
Judges 13:15-24　　　Acts 6:1-15　　Jn 4:1-26

*Thursday*　　　105.1-22*105.23-45
2 Samuel 15:1-18　　Acts 21:27-36　　Mk 10:32-45
Judges 14:1-19　　　Acts 6:15-7:16　　Jn 4:27-42

*Friday*　　　　102*107.1-32
2 Samuel 15:19-37　　Acts 21:37-22:16　Mk 10:46-52
Judges 14:20-15:20　Acts 7:17-29　　Jn 4:43-54

*Saturday*　　　107.33-43, 108*33
2 Samuel 16:1-23　　Acts 22:17-29　　Mk 11:1-11
Judges 16:1-14　　　Acts 7:30-43　　Jn 5:1-18

**Proper 15**  *August 14-20  (Aug 15 St. Mary the Virgin)*
*Sunday*        *118\*145*
2 Samuel 17:1-23      Gal. 3:6-14          Jn 5:30-47
Judges 16:15-31       2 Cor. 13:1-11       Mk 5:25-34


*Monday*        *106.1-18\*106.19-48*
2 Samuel 17:24-18:8    Acts 22:30-23:11   Mk 11:12-26
Judges 17:1-13         Acts 7:44-8:1a       Jn 5:19-29


*Tuesday*        *120-123\*124-127*
2 Samuel 18:9-18      Acts 23:12-24      Mk 11:27-12:12
Judges 18:1-15        Acts 8:1-13          Jn 5:30-47


*Wednesday*      *119.145-176\*128-130*
2 Samuel 18:19-23     Acts 23:23-35        Mk 12:13-27
Judges 18:16-31       Acts 8:14-25          Jn 6:1-15


*Thursday*        *131-133\*134-135*
2 Samuel 19:1-23      Acts 24:1-23        Mk 12:28-34
Job 1:1-22            Acts 8:26-40          Jn 6:16-27


*Friday*        *140, 142\*141, 143*
2 Samuel 19:24-43     Acts 24:24-25:12    Mk 12:35-44
Job 2:1-13            Acts 9:1-9            Jn 6:27-40


*Saturday*        *137, 144\*104*
2 Samuel 23:1-17,13-17    Acts 25:13-27    Mk 13:1-13
Job 3:1-26               Acts 9:10-19a      Jn 6:41-51


**Proper 16**  *August 21-27  (Aug 24 St. Bartholomew)*
*Sunday*        *146-147\*111-113*
2 Samuel 24:1-2,10-25    Gal. 3:23-4:7      Jn 8:12-20
Job 4:1-6,12-21          Rev. 4:1-11        Mk 6:1-6a


*Monday*        *1-3\*4, 7*
1 Kings 1:5-31        Acts 26:1-23        Mk 13:14-27
Job 4:1;5:1-11,17-21,26-27    Acts 9:19b-31  Jn 6:52-59


*Tuesday*        *5-6\*10-11*

222

| 1 Kings 1:38-2:4 | Acts 26:24-27:8 | Mk 13:28-37 |
| Job 6:1-4,8-15,21 | Acts 9:32-43 | Jn 6:60-71 |

*Wednesday*    *119.1-24\*12-14*
| 1 Kings 3:1-15 | Acts 27:9-26 | Mk 14:1-11 |
| Job 6:1,7:1-21 | Acts 10:1-16 | Jn 7:1-13 |

*Thursday*    *18.1-20\*18.21-50*
| 1 Kings 3:16-28 | Acts 27:27-44 | Mk 14:12-26 |
| Job 8:1-10, 20-22 | Acts 10:17-33 | Jn 7:14-36 |

*Friday*    *16-17\*22*
| 1 Kings 5:1-6:1,7 | Acts 28:1-16 | Mk 14:27-42 |
| Job 9:1-15,32-35 | Acts 10:34-48 | Jn 7:37-52 |

*Saturday*    *20-21\*110, 116-117*
| 1 Kings 7:51-8:21 | Acts 28:17-31 | Mk 14:43-52 |
| Job 9:1;10:1-9,16-22 | Acts 11:1-18 | Jn 8:12-20 |

**Proper 17** *August 28-September 1*
*Sunday*    *148-150\*114-115*
| 1 Kings 8:22-40 | 1 Tim. 4:7b-16 | Jn 8:47-59 |
| Job 11:1-9,13-20 | Rev. 5:1-14 | Mt. 5:1-12 |

*Monday*    *25\*9, 15*
| 2 Chron. 6:32-7:7 | James 2:1-13 | Mk 14:53-65 |
| Job 12:1-6,13-25 | Acts 11:19-30 | Jn 8:21-32 |

*Tuesday*    *26, 28\*36, 39*
| 1 Kings 8:65-9:9 | James 2:14-26 | Mk 14:66-72 |
| Job 12:1,13:3-17,21-27 | Acts 12:1-17 | Jn 8:33-47 |

*Wednesday*    *38\*119.25-48*
| 1 Kings 9:24-10:13 | James 3:1-12 | Mk 15:1-11 |
| Job 12:1,14:1-22 | Acts 12:18-25 | Jn 8:47-59 |

*Thursday*    *37.1-18\*37.19-42*
| 1 Kings 11:1-13 | James 3:13-4:12 | Mk 15:12-21 |

Job 16:16-22,17:1,13-16     Acts 13:1-12     Jn 9:1-17

*Friday*          *31\*35*
1 Kings 11:26-43     James 4:13-5:6     Mk 15:22-32
Job 19:1-7,14-27     Acts 13:13-25     Jn 9:18-41

*Saturday*          *30, 32\*42-43*
1 Kings 12:1-20     James 5:7-12,19-20  Mk 15:33-39
Job 22:1-4,21-23:7   Acts 13:26-43     Jn 10:1-18

**Proper 18** *September 4-10*
*Sunday*          *63, 98\*103*
1 Kings 12:21-33    Acts 4:18-31     Jn 10:31-42
Job 25:1-6,27:1-6   Rev. 14:1-7,13    Mt. 5:13-20

*Monday*          *41, 52\*44*
1 Kings 13:1-10     Phil. 1:1-11     Mk 15:40-47
Job 32:1-10,19-33:1,19-28   Acts 13:44-52  Jn 10:19-30

*Tuesday*          *45\*47-48*
1 Kings 16:23-34    Phil. 1:12-30    Mk 16:1-8(9-20)
Job 29:1-20       Acts 14:1-18     Jn 10:31-42

*Wednesday*     *119.49-72\*49, 53*
1 Kings 17:1-24     Phil. 2:1-11     Mt. 2:1-12
Job 29:1,30:1-2,16-31   Acts 14:19-28   Jn 11:1-16

*Thursday*        *50\*93, 96*
1 Kings 18:1-19     Phil. 2:12-30    Mt. 2:13-23
Job 29:1,31:1-23    Acts 15:1-11     Jn 11:17-29

*Friday*          *40, 54\*51*
1 Kings 18:20-40    Phil. 3:1-16     Mt. 3:1-12
Job 29:1;31:24-40   Acts 15:12-21    Jn 11:30-44

*Saturday*        *55\*138-139*
1 Kings 18:41-19:8  Phil. 3:17-4:7   Mt. 3:13-17
Job 38:1-17       Acts 15:22-35    Jn 11:45-54

**Proper 19** *September 11-17 (Sept 14 Holy Cross)*
*Sunday*        *24, 29\*8, 84*

| | | |
|---|---|---|
| 1 Kings 19:8-21 | Acts 5:34-42 | Jn 11:45-47 |
| Job 38:1,18-41 | Rev. 18:1-8 | Mt. 5:21-26 |

*Monday*        *56-58\*64-65*

| | | |
|---|---|---|
| 1 Kings 21:1-16 | 1 Cor. 1:1-19 | Mt. 4:1-11 |
| Job 40:1-24 | Acts 15:36-16:5 | Jn 11:55-12:8 |

*Tuesday*        *61-62\*68*

| | | |
|---|---|---|
| 1 Kings 21:17-29 | 1 Cor. 1:20-31 | Mt. 4:12-17 |
| Job 40:1,41:1-11 | Acts 16:6-15 | Jn 12:9-19 |

*Wednesday*        *72\*119.73-96*

| | | |
|---|---|---|
| 1 Kings 22:1-28 | 1 Cor. 2:1-13 | Mt. 4:18-25 |
| Job 42:1-17 | Acts 16:16-24 | Jn 12:20-26 |

*Thursday*        *70-71\*74*

| | | |
|---|---|---|
| 1 Kings 22:29-45 | 1 Cor. 2:14-3:15 | Mt. 5:1-10 |
| Job 28:1-28 | Acts 16:25-40 | Jn 12:27-36a |

*Friday*        *69\*73*

| | | |
|---|---|---|
| 2 Kings 1:2-17 | 1 Cor. 3:16-23 | Mt. 5:11-16 |
| Esther 1:1-4,10-19 | Acts 17:1-15 | Jn 12:36b-43 |

*Saturday*        *75-76\*23, 27*

| | | |
|---|---|---|
| 2 Kings 2:1-18 | 1 Cor. 4:1-7 | Mt. 5:17-20 |
| Esther 2:5-8,15-23 | Acts 17:16-34 | Jn 12:44-50 |

**Proper 20** *September 18-24 (Sept 21 St. Matthew)*
*Sunday*        *93, 96\*34*

| | | |
|---|---|---|
| 2 Kings 4:8-37 | Acts 9:10-31 | Lk 3:7-18 |
| Esther 3:1-4:3 | James 1:19-27 | Mt. 6:1-6,16-18 |

*Monday*        *80\*77, 79*

| | | |
|---|---|---|
| 2 Kings 5:1-19 | 1 Cor. 4:8-21 | Mt. 5:21-26 |
| Esther 4:4-17 | Acts 18:1-11 | Lk (1:1-4),3:1-14 |

*Tuesday*        *78.1-39*78.40-72*
2 Kings 5:19-27        1 Cor. 5:1-8        Mt. 5:27-37
Esther 5:1-14        Acts 18:12-28        Lk 3:15-22

*Wednesday*     *119.97-120*81-82*
2 Kings 6:1-23        1 Cor. 5:9-6:8        Mt. 5:38-48
Esther 6:1-14        Acts 19:1-10        Lk 4:1-13

*Thursday*        *116-117*85-86*
2 Kings 9:1-16        1 Cor. 6:12-20        Mt. 6:1-6,16-18
Esther 7:1-10        Acts 19:11-20        Lk 4:14-30

*Friday*        *88*91-92*
2 Kings 9:17-37        1 Cor. 7:1-9        Mt. 6:7-15
Esther 8:1-8,15-17        Acts 19:21-41        Lk 4:31-37

*Saturday*        *87, 90*136*
2 Kings 11:1-20a        1 Cor. 7:10-24        Mt. 6:19-24
Hosea 1:1-2:1        Acts 20:1-16        Lk 4:38-44

**Proper 21** *September 25-October 1  (Sept 29 St. Michael and All Angels)*
*Sunday*        *66-67*19, 46*
2 Kings 17:1-18        Acts 9:36-43        Lk 5:1-11
Hosea 2:2-14        James 3:1-13        Mt. 13:44-52

*Monday*        *89.1-18*89.19-52*
2 Kings 17:24-41        1 Cor. 7:25-31        Mt. 6:25-34
Hosea 2:14-23        Acts 20:17-38        Lk 5:1-11

*Tuesday*        *97, 99*94*
2 Chron. 29:1-3: 30:1-27  1 Cor. 7:32-40        Mt. 7:1-12
Hosea 4:1-10        Acts 21:1-14        Lk 5:12-26

*Wednesday*     *101, 109*119.121-144*
2 Kings 18:9-25        1 Cor. 8:1-13        Mt. 7:13-21
Hosea 4:11-19        Acts 21:15-26        Lk 5:27-39

*Thursday*        *105.1-22\*105.23-45*
2 Kings 18:28-37      1 Cor. 9:1-15          Mt. 7:22-29
Hosea 5:8-6:6         Acts 21:27-36          Lk 6:1-11

*Friday*        *102\*107.1-32*
2 Kings 19:1-20      1 Cor. 9:16-27          Mt. 8:1-17
Hosea 10:1-15         Acts 21:37-22:16       Lk 6:12-26

*Saturday*        *107.33-43, 108\*33*
2 Kings 19:21-36      1 Cor. 10:1-13         Mt:8:18-27
Hosea 11:1-9          Acts 22:17-29          Lk 6:27-38

**Proper 22** *October 2-8*
*Sunday*        *118\*145*
2 Kings 20:1-21      Acts 12:1-17            Lk 7:11-17
Hosea 13:4-14         1 Cor. 2:6-16          Mt. 14:1-12

*Monday*        *106.1-18\*106.19-48*
2 Kings 21:1-18      1 Cor. 10:14-11:1       Mt. 8:28-34
Hosea 14:1-9          Acts 22:30-23:11       Lk 6:39-49

*Tuesday*        *120-123\*124-127*
2 Kings 22:1-13      1 Cor. 11:2,17-22       Mt. 9:1-8
Micah 1:1-9           Acts 23:12-24          Lk 7:1-17

*Wednesday*        *119.145-176\*128-130*
2 Kings 22:14-23:3   1 Cor. 11:23-34         Mt. 9:9-17
Micah 2:1-13          Acts 23:23-35          Lk 7:18-35

*Thursday*        *131-133\*134-135*
2 Kings 23:4-25      1 Cor. 12:1-11          Mt. 9:18-26
Micah 3:1-8           Acts 24:1-23           Lk 7:36-50

*Friday*        *140, 142\*141, 143*
2 Kings 23:36-24:17  1 Cor. 12:12-26         Mt. 9:27-34
Micah 3:9-4:5         Acts 24:24-25:12       Lk 8:1-15

*Saturday*        *137, 144\*104*

| Jer. 35:1-19 | 1 Cor. 12:27-13:3 | Mt. 9:35-10:4 |
| Micah 5:1-4,10-15 | Acts 25:13-27 | Lk 8:16-25 |

**Proper 23** *October 9-15*
*Sunday*        *146-147\*111-113*

| Jer. 36:1-10 | Acts 14:8-18 | Lk 7:36-50 |
| Micah 6:1-8 | 1 Cor. 4:9-16 | Mt. 15:21-28 |

*Monday*        *1-3\*4, 7*

| Jer. 36:11-26 | 1 Cor. 13:(1-3)4-13 | Mt. 10:5-15 |
| Micah 7:1-7 | Acts 26:1-23 | Lk 8:26-39 |

*Tuesday*        *5-6\*10-11*

| Jer. 36:27-37:2 | 1 Cor. 14:1-12 | Mt. 10:16-23 |
| Jonah 1:1-17a | Acts 26:24-27:8 | Lk 8:40-56 |

*Wednesday*        *119.1-24\*12-14*

| Jer. 37:3-21 | 1 Cor. 14:13-25 | Mt. 10:24-33 |
| Jonah 1:17-2:10 | Acts 27:9-26 | Lk 9:1-17 |

*Thursday*        *18.1-20\*18.21-50*

| Jer. 38:1-13 | 1 Cor. 14:26-33a,37-40 | Mt. 10:34-42 |
| Jonah 3:1-4:11 | Acts 27:27-4 | Lk 9:18-27 |

*Friday 16-17\*22*

| Jer. 38:14-28 | 1 Cor. 15:1-11 | Mt. 11:1-6 |
| Ecclus. 1:1-10,18-27 | Acts 28:1-16 | Lk 9:28-36 |

*Saturday*        *20-21\*110, 116-117*

| 2 Kings 25:8-12,22-26 | 1 Cor. 15:12-29 | Mt. 11:7-15 |
| Ecclus. 3:17-31 | Acts 28:17-31 | Lk 9:37-50 |

**Proper 24**    *October 16-22  (Oct 18 St Luke; Oct 23 St. James of Jerusalem)*
*Sunday*        *148-150\*114-115*

| Jer. 29:1,4-14 | Acts 16:6-15 | Lk 10:1-12,17-20 |
| Ecclus. 4:1-10 | 1 Cor. 10:1-13 | Mt. 16:13-20 |

*Monday*        *25\*9, 15*

| Jer. 44:1-14 | 1 Cor. 15:30-41 | Mt. 11:16-24 |

Ecclus. 4:20-5:7          Rev. 7:1-8                Lk 9:51-62

*Tuesday*          *26, 28\*36, 39*
Lam. 1:1-5(6-9)10-12      1 Cor. 15:41-50      Mt. 11:25-30
Ecclus. 6:5-17            Rev. 7:9-17           Lk 10:1-16

*Wednesday*       *38\*119.25-48*
Lam. 2:8-15               1 Cor. 15:51-58      Mt. 12:1-14
Ecclus. 7:4-14            Rev. 8:1-13           Lk 10:17-24

*Thursday*        *37.1-18\*37.19-42*
Ezra 1:1-11               1 Cor. 16:1-9         Mt. 12:15-21
Ecclus. 10:1-18           Rev. 9:1-12           Lk 10:25-37

*Friday*           *31\*35*
Ezra 3:1-13               1 Cor 16:10-24        Mt. 12:22-32
Ecclus. 11:2-2            Rev. 9:13-21          Lk 10:38-42

*Saturday*         *30, 32\*42-43*
Ezra 4:7,11-24            Philemon 1-25         Mt. 12:33-42
Ecclus. 15:9-20           Rev. 10:1-11          Lk 11:1-13

**Proper 25** *October 23-29  (Oct 28 SS Simon and Jude)*
*Sunday*           *63, 98\*103*
Haggai 1:1-2:9            Acts 18:24-19:7       Lk 10:25-37
Ecclus. 18:19-33          1 Cor. 10:15-24       Mt. 18:15-20

*Monday*           *41, 52\*44*
Zech. 1:7-17              Rev. 1:4-20           Mt. 12:43-50
Ecclus. 19:4-17           Rev. 11:1-14          Lk 11:14-26

*Tuesday*          *45\*47-48*
Ezra 5:1-17               Rev. 4:1-11           Mt. 13:1-9
Ecclus. 24:1-12           Rev. 11:14-19         Lk 11:27-36

*Wednesday*       *119.49-72\*49, 53*
Ezra 6:1-22               Rev. 5:1-10           Mt. 13:10-17
Ecclus. 28:14-26          Rev. 12:1-6           Lk 11:37-52

*Thursday*     *50\*59, 60*
Neh. 1-1:11       Rev. 5:11-6:11      Mt. 13:18-23
Ecclus. 31:12-18,25-32:2   Rev. 12:7-17   Lk 11:53-12:12

*Friday*       *40, 54\*51*
Neh. 2:1-20       Rev. 6:12-7:4      Mt. 13:24-30
Ecclus. 34:1-8,18-22     Rev. 13:1-10     Lk 12:13-31

*Saturday*     *55\*138-139*
Neh. 4:1-23       Rev. 7:(4-8)9-17    Mt. 13:31-35
Ecclus. 35:1-17      Rev. 13:11-18    Lk 12:32-48

**Proper 26**   *October 30-November 5*   *(November 1 is All Saints'*
*Day)*
*Sunday*      *24, 29\*8, 84*
Neh. 5:1-19       Acts 20:7-12     Lk 12:22-31
Ecclus. 36:1-17     1 Cor. 12:27-13:13   Mt. 18:21-35

*Monday*      *56-58\*64-65*
Neh. 6:1-19       Rev. 10:1-11     Mt. 13:36-43
Ecclus. 38:24-34    Rev. 14:1-13     Lk 12:49-59

*Tuesday*      *61, 62\*68*
Neh. 12:27-31a,42b-47    Rev. 11:1-19    Mt. 13:44-52
Ecclus. 43:1-22     Rev. 14:14-15:8     Lk 13:1-9

*Wednesday*   *72\*119.73-96*
Neh. 13:4-22     Rev. 12:1-12     Mt. 13:53-58
Ecclus. 43:23-33    Rev. 16:1-11     Lk 13:10-17

*Thursday*     *70-71\*74*
Ezra 7:(1-10)11-26    Rev. 14:1-13     Mt. 14:1-12
Ecclus. 44:1-15     Rev. 16:12-21    Lk 14:18-30
*Friday*       *69\*73*
Ezra 7:27-28, 8:21-36   Rev. 15:1-8    Mt. 14:13-21
Ecclus. 50:1,11-24    Rev. 17:1-18    Lk 13:31-35

*Saturday*        75-76*23, 27
Ezra 9:1-15              Rev. 17:1-14          Mt. 14:22-36
Ecclus. 51:1-12          Rev. 18:1-14          Lk 14:1-11

**Proper 27** *November 6-12*
*Sunday*          93, 96*34
Ezra 10:1-17             Acts 24:10-21         Lk 14:12-24
Ecclus. 51:13-22         1 Cor. 14:1-12            Mt. 20:1-16

*Monday*          80*77, 79
Neh. 9:1-15(16-25)       Rev. 18:1-8           Mt. 15:1-20
Joel 1:1-13              Rev. 18:15-24         Lk 14:12-24

*Tuesday*        78.1-39*78.40-72
Neh. 9:26-38             Rev. 18:9-20          Mt. 15:21-28
Joel 1:15-2:2(3-11)      Rev. 19:1-10          Lk 14:25-35

*Wednesday*   119.97-120*81-82
Neh. 7:73b-8:3,5-18      Rev. 18:21-24         Mt. 15:29-39
Joel 2:12-19             Rev. 19:11-21         Lk 15:1-10

*Thursday*       23, 27*85-86
1 Macc. 1:1-28           Rev. 19:1-10          Mt. 16:1-12
Joel 2:21-27             James 1:1-15      Lk 15:1-2,11-32

*Friday*              88*91-92
1 Macc. 1:41-63          Rev. 19:11-16         Mt. 16:13-20
Joel 2:28-3:8            James 1:16-27         Lk 16:1-9

*Saturday*        87, 90*136
1 Macc. 2:1-28           Rev. 20:1-6           Mk 16:21-28
Joel 3:9-17              James 2:1-13      Lk 16:10-17(18)

**Proper 28** *November 13-19*
*Sunday*          66, 67*19, 46
1 Macc. 2:29-43,49-50    Acts 28:14b-23   Lk 16:1-13

Hab. 1:1-4(5-11)12-2:1  Phil. 3:13-4:1  Mt. 23:13-24

*Monday          89.1-18\*89.19-52*
1 Macc. 3:1-24        Rev. 20:7-15        Mt. 17:1-13
Hab. 2:1-4,9-20       James 2:14-26       Lk 16:19-31

*Tuesday          97, 99\*94*
1 Macc. 3:25-41       Rev. 21:1-8         Mt. 17:14-21
Hab. 3:1-10(11-15)16-18  James 3:1-12  Lk 17:1-10

*Wednesday    101, 109\*119.121-144*
1 Macc. 3:42-60       Rev. 21:9-21        Mt. 17:22-27
Mal. 1:1,6-14         James 3:13-4:12     Lk 17:11-19

*Thursday       105.1-22\*105.23-45*
1 Macc. 4:1-25        Rev. 21:22-22:5     Mt. 18:1-9
Mal. 2:1-16          James 4:13-5:6       Lk 17:20-37

*Friday        102\*107.1-32*
1 Macc. 4:36-59       Rev. 22:6-13        Mt. 18:10-20
Mal. 3:1-12          James 5:7-12         Lk 18:1-8

*Saturday      107.33-43, 108\*33*
Isa. 65:17-25        Rev. 22:14-21        Mt. 18:21-35
Mal. 3:13-4:6        James 5:13-20        Lk 18:9-14

**Proper 29** *November 20-26*
*Sunday          118\*145*
Isa. 19:19-25        Rom. 15:5-13         Lk 19:11-27
Zech. 9:9-16         1 Pet. 3:13-22       Mt. 21:1-13

*Monday       106.1-18\*106.19-48*
Joel 3:1-2,9-17      1 Pet. 1:1-12        Mt. 19:1-12
Zech. 10:1-12        Gal. 6:1-10          Lk 18:15-30

*Tuesday        120-123\*124-127*

| Nahum 1:1-13 | 1 Pet. 1:13-25 | Mt. 19:13-22 |
| Zech. 11:4-17 | 1 Cor. 3:10-23 | Lk 18:31-43 |

*Wednesday    119.145-176*128-130*
| Obadiah 15-21 | 1 Pet. 2:1-10 | Mt. 19:23-30 |
| Zech. 12:1-10 | Eph. 1:3-14 | Lk 19:1-10 |

*Thursday    131-133*134-135*
| Zeph. 3:1-13 | 1 Pet. 2:11-25 | Mt. 20:1-16 |
| Zech. 13:1-9 | Eph. 1:15-23 | Lk 19:11-27 |

*Friday    140, 142*141, 143*
| Isa. 24:14-23 | 1 Pet. 3:13-4:6 | Mt. 20:17-28 |
| Zech. 14:1-11 | Rom. 15:7-13 | Lk 19:28-40 |

*Saturday    137, 144*104*
| Micah 7:11-20 | 1 Pet. 4:7-19 | Mt. 20:29-34 |
| Zech. 14:12-21 | Phil. 2:1-11 | Lk 19:41-48 |

# COLLECTS

## First Sunday of Advent

Almighty God, give us grace that we may cast away the works of darkness, and put upon us the armor of light, now in the time of this mortal life in which thy Son Jesus Christ came to visit us in great humility; that in the last day, when he shall come again in his glorious majesty to judge both the quick and the dead, we may rise to the life immortal; through him who liveth and reigneth with thee and the Holy Ghost, one God, now and for ever. **Amen**.

## Second Sunday of Advent

Merciful God, who sent thy messengers the prophets to preach repentance and prepare the way for our salvation: Give us grace to heed their warnings and forsake our sins, that we may greet with joy the coming of Jesus Christ our Redeemer; who liveth and reigneth with thee and the Holy Spirit, one God, now and for ever. **Amen**.

## Third Sunday of Advent

Stir up thy power, O Lord, and with great might come among us; and, because we are sorely hindered by our sins, let thy bountiful grace and mercy speedily help and deliver us; through Jesus Christ our Lord, to whom, with thee and the Holy Ghost, be honor and glory, world without end. **Amen**.
*Wednesday, Friday, and Saturday of this week are the traditional winter Ember Days.*

**Winter Ember Days**

Almighty God, the giver of all good gifts, who of thy divine providence hast appointed divers Orders in thy Church: Give thy grace, we humbly beseech thee, to all those who are to be called to any office and administration int he same; and so replenish them with the truth of thy doctrine, and endue them with innocency of life, that thy may faithfully serve before thee, to the glory of thy great Name, and the benefit of thy holy Church; through Jesus Christ our Lord. **Amen.**

**Fourth Sunday of Advent**

We beseech thee, Almighty God, to purify our consciences by thy daily visitation, that when thy Son our Lord cometh he may find in us a mansion prepared for himself; through the same Jesus Christ our Lord, who liveth and reigneth with thee, in the unity of the Holy Spirit, one God, now and for ever. **Amen**.

**The Nativity of Our Lord: Christmas Day** *December 25*

O God, who makest us glad with the yearly remembrance of the birth of thy only Son Jesus Christ:  Grant that as we joyfully receive him for our Redeemer, so we may with sure confidence behold him when he shall come to be our Judge; who liveth and reigneth with thee and the Holy Ghost, one God, world without end. **Amen**.

*or the following*

O God, who hast caused this holy night to shine with the illumination of the true Light:  Grant us, we beseech thee,that as we have known the mystery of that Light upon earth, so may we also perfectly enjoy him in heaven; where with thee and the Holy Spirit he liveth and reigneth, one God, in glory everlasting. **Amen**.

*or this*

Almighty God, who hast given us thy only-begotten Son to take our nature upon him and as at this time to be born of a pure virgin: Grant that we, being regenerate and made thy children by adoption and grace, may daily be renewed by thy Holy Spirit; through the same our Lord Jesus Christ, who liveth and reigneth with thee and the same Spirit ever, one God, world without end. **Amen**.

**First Sunday after Christmas Day**

Almighty God, who hast poured upon us the new light of thine incarnate Word: Grant that the same light, enkindled in our hearts, may shine forth in our lives; through the same Jesus Christ our Lord, who liveth and reigneth with thee, in the unity of the Holy Spirit, one God, now and for ever. **Amen**.

**The Holy Name** *January 1*

Eternal Father, who didst give to thine incarnate Son the holy name of Jesus to be the sign of our salvation: Plant in every heart, we beseech thee, the love of him who is the Savior of the world, even our Lord Jesus Christ; who liveth and reigneth with thee and the Holy Spirit, one God, in glory everlasting. **Amen**.

**Second Sunday after Christmas Day**

O God, who didst wonderfully create, and yet more wonderfully restore, the dignity of human nature: Grant that we may share the divine life of him who humbled himself to share our humanity, thy Son Jesus Christ; who liveth and reigneth with thee, in the unity of the Holy Spirit, one God, for ever and ever. **Amen**.

## The Epiphany *January 6*

O God, who by the leading of a star didst manifest thy only-begotten Son to the peoples of the earth: Lead us, who know thee now by faith, to thy presence, where we may behold thy glory face to face; through the same Jesus Christ our Lord, who liveth and reigneth with thee and the Holy Spirit, one God, now and for ever. **Amen**.

## First Sunday after the Epiphany: The Baptism of our Lord

Father in heaven, who at the baptism of Jesus in the RiverJordan didst proclaim him thy beloved Son and anoint him with the Holy Spirit: Grant that all who are baptized into his Name may keep the covenant they have made, and boldly confess him as Lord and Savior; who with thee and the same Spirit liveth and reigneth, one God, in glory everlasting. **Amen**.

## Second Sunday after the Epiphany

Almighty God, whose Son our Savior Jesus Christ is the light of the world: Grant that thy people, illumined by thy Word and Sacraments, may shine with the radiance of Christ's glory, that he may be known, worshiped, and obeyed to the ends of the earth; through the same Jesus Christ our Lord, who with thee and the Holy Spirit liveth and reigneth, one God, now and for ever. **Amen**.

## Third Sunday after the Epiphany

Give us grace, O Lord, to answer readily the call of our Savior Jesus Christ and proclaim to all people the Good News of his salvation, that we and all the whole world may perceive the glory of his marvelous works; who liveth and reigneth with thee and the Holy Spirit, one God, for ever and ever. **Amen**.

## Fourth Sunday after the Epiphany

Almighty and everlasting God, who dost govern all things in heaven and earth: Mercifully hear the supplications of thy people, and in our time grant us thy peace; through Jesus Christ our Lord, who liveth and reigneth with thee and the Holy Spirit, one God, for ever and ever. **Amen**.

## Fifth Sunday after the Epiphany

Set us free, O God, from the bondage of our sins and give us, we beseech thee, the liberty of that abundant life which thou hast manifested to us in thy Son our Savior Jesus Christ; who liveth and reigneth with thee, in the unity of the Holy Spirit, one God, now and for ever. **Amen**.

## Sixth Sunday after the Epiphany

O God, the strength of all those who put their trust in thee: Mercifully accept our prayers; and because through the weakness of our mortal nature, we can do no good thing without thee, grant us the help of thy grace, that in keeping thy commandments we may please thee both in will and deed; through Jesus Christ our Lord, who liveth and reigneth with thee and the Holy Spirit, one God, for ever and ever. **Amen**.

## Seventh Sunday after the Epiphany

O Lord, who hast taught us that all our doings without charity are nothing worth: Send thy Holy Ghost and pour into our hearts that most excellent gift of charity, the very bond of peace and of all virtues, without which whosoever liveth is counted dead before thee. Grant this for thine only Son Jesus Christ's sake, who liveth and reigneth with thee and the same Holy Ghost, one God, now and for ever. **Amen**.

## Eighth Sunday after the Epiphany

O most loving Father, who willest us to give thanks for all things, to dread nothing but the loss of thee, and to cast all our care on thee who carest for us: Preserve us from faithless fears and worldly anxieties, and grant that no clouds of this mortal life may hide from us the light of that love which is immortal, and which thou hast manifested unto us in thy Son Jesus Christ our Lord; who liveth and reigneth with thee, in the unity of the Holy Spirit, one God, now and for ever. **Amen**.

## Last Sunday after the Epiphany

O God, who before the passion of thy only-begotten Son didst reveal his glory upon the holy mount: Grant unto us that we, beholding by faith the light of his countenance, may be strengthened to bear our cross, and be changed into his likeness from glory to glory; through the same Jesus Christ our Lord, who liveth and reigneth with thee and the Holy Spirit, one God, for ever and ever. **Amen**.

## Ash Wednesday

Almighty and everlasting God, who hatest nothing that thou hast made and dost forgive the sins of all those who are penitent: Create and make in us new and contrite hearts, that we, worthily lamenting our sins and acknowledging our wretchedness, may obtain of thee, the God of all mercy, perfect remission and forgiveness; through Jesus Christ our Lord, who liveth and reigneth with thee and the Holy Spirit, one God, for ever and ever. **Amen**.

## Thursday after Ash Wednesday

Direct us, O Lord, in all our doings with thy most gracious favor, and further us with thy continual help; that in all our works begun, continued, and ended in thee, we may glorify thy holy Name, and finally, by thy mercy, obtain everlasting life; through Jesus Christ our Lord, who liveth and reigneth with thee and the Holy Spirit, one God, for ever and ever. **Amen.**

## Friday after Ash Wednesday

Support us, O Lord, with thy gracious favor through the fast we have begun; that as we observe it by bodily self-denial, so we may fulfill it with inner sincerity of heart; through Jesus Christ our Lord, who liveth and reigneth with thee and the Holy Spirit, one God for ever and ever. **Amen.**

## Saturday after Ash Wednesday

Almighty and everlasting God, mercifully look upon our infirmities, and in all our dangers and necessities stretch forth thy right hand to help and defend us; through Jesus Christ our Lord, who liveth and reigneth with thee and the Holy Spirit, one God, for ever and ever. **Amen.**

## First Sunday in Lent

Almighty God, whose blessed Son was led by the Spirit to be tempted of Satan: Make speed to help thy servants who are assaulted by manifold temptations; and, as thou knowest their several infirmities, let each one find thee mighty to save; through Jesus Christ thy Son our Lord, who liveth and reigneth with thee and the Holy Spirit, one God, now and for ever. **Amen**.

*Wednesday, Friday, and Saturday of this week are the traditional spring Ember Days.*

**Spring Ember Days**
O Almighty God, who has committed to the hands of men the ministry of reconciliation: We humbly beseech thee, by the inspiration of thy Holy Spirit, to put it into the hearts of many to offer themselves for this ministry; that thereby mankind may be drawn to thy blessed kingdom; through Jesus Christ our Lord. **Amen.**

**Monday in the First Week of Lent**

Almighty and everlasting God, mercifully increase in us thy gifts of holy discipline, in almsgiving, prayer, and fasting; that our lives may be directed to the fulfilling of thy most gracious will; through Jesus Christ our Lord, who liveth and reigneth with thee and the Holy Spirit, one God, for ever and ever. **Amen.**

**Tuesday in the First Week of Lent**

Grant to thy people, Lord, grace to withstand the temptations of the world, the flesh, and the devil, and with pure hearts and minds to follow thee, the only true God; through Jesus Christ thy Son our Lord, who liveth and reigneth with thee and the Holy Spirit, one God, for ever and. ever. **Amen.**

## Wednesday in the First Week of Lent

Bless us, O God, in this holy season, in which our hearts seek thy help and healing; and so purify us by thy discipline that we may grow in grace and in the knowledge of our Lord and Savior Jesus Christ; who liveth and reigneth with thee and the Holy Spirit, one God, for ever and ever. **Amen.**

## Thursday in the First Week of Lent

Strengthen us, O Lord, by thy grace, that in thy might we may overcome all spiritual enemies, and with pure hearts serve thee; through Jesus Christ our Lord, who liveth and reigneth with thee and the Holy Spirit, one God, for ever and ever. **Amen**.

## Friday in the First Week of Lent

Lord Christ, our eternal Redeemer, grant us such fellowship in thy sufferings, that, filled with thy Holy Spirit, we may subdue the flesh to the spirit, and the spirit to thee, and at the last attain to the glory of thy resurrection; who livest and reignest with the Father and the Holy Spirit, one God, for ever and ever. **Amen.**

## Saturday in the First Week of Lent

O God, who by thy Word dost marvelously carry out the work of reconciliation: Grant that in our Lenten fast we may be devoted to thee with all our hearts, and united with one another in prayer and holy love; through Jesus Christ our Lord, who liveth and reigneth with thee and the Holy Spirit, one God, for ever and ever. **Amen.**

## Second Sunday in Lent

O God, whose glory it is always to have mercy: Be gracious to all who have gone astray from thy ways, and bring them again with penitent hearts and steadfast faith to embrace and hold fast the unchangeable truth of thy Word, Jesus Christ thy Son; who with thee and the Holy Spirit liveth and reigneth, one God, for ever and ever. **Amen**.

**Monday in the Second Week of Lent**

Let thy Spirit, O Lord, come into the midst of us to wash us with the pure water of repentance, and prepare us to be always a living sacrifice unto thee; through Jesus Christ our Lord, who liveth and reigneth with thee and the Holy Spirit, one God, for ever and ever. **Amen.**

**Tuesday in the Second Week of Lent**

O God, who didst will to redeem us from all iniquity by thy Son: Deliver us when we are tempted to regard sin without abhorrence, and let the virtue of his passion come between us and our mortal enemy; through Jesus Christ our Lord, who liveth and reigneth with thee and the Holy Spirit, one God, for ever and ever. **Amen.**

**Wednesday in the Second Week of Lent**

O God, who didst so love the world that thou gavest thine only-begotten Son to reconcile earth with heaven: Grant that we, loving thee above all things, may love our friends in thee, and our enemies for thy sake; through Jesus Christ our Lord, who liveth and reigneth with thee and the Holy Spirit, one God, for ever and ever. **Amen.**

**Thursday in the Second Week of Lent**

O Lord, strong and mighty, Lord of hosts and King of glory: Cleanse our hearts from sin, keep our hands pure, and turn our minds from what is passing away; so that at the last we may stand in thy holy place and receive thy blessing; through Jesus Christ our Lord, who liveth and reigneth with thee and the Holy Spirit, one God, for ever and ever. **Amen.**

### Friday in the Second Week of Lent

Grant, O Lord, that as thy Son Jesus Christ prayed for his enemies on the cross, so we may have grace to forgive those who wrongfully or scornfully use us, that we ourselves may be able to receive thy forgiveness; through Jesus Christ our Lord, who liveth and reigneth with thee and the Holy Spirit, one God, for ever and ever. **Amen.**

### Saturday in the Second Week of Lent

Grant, most merciful Lord, to thy faithful people pardon and peace, that they may be cleansed from all their sins, and serve thee with a quiet mind; through Jesus Christ our Lord, who liveth and reigneth with thee and the Holy Spirit, one God, for ever and ever. **Amen.**

### Third Sunday in Lent

Almighty God, who seest that we have no power of ourselves to help ourselves: Keep us both outwardly in our bodies and inwardly in our souls, that we may be defended from all adversities which may happen to the body, and from all evil thoughts which may assault and hurt the soul; through Jesus Christ our Lord, who liveth and reigneth with thee and the Holy Spirit, one God, for ever and ever. **Amen.**

### Monday in the Third Week of Lent

Look upon the hearty desires of thy humble servants, we beseech thee, Almighty God, and stretch forth the right hand of thy majesty to be our defense against all our enemies; through Jesus Christ our Lord, who liveth and reigneth with thee and the Holy Spirit, one God, for ever and ever. **Amen.**

### Tuesday in the Third Week of Lent

O Lord, we beseech thee mercifully to hear us; and grant that we, to whom thou hast given a hearty desire to pray, may, by thy mighty aid, be defended and comforted in all dangers and adversities; through Jesus Christ our Lord, who liveth and reigneth with thee and the Holy Spirit, one God, for ever and ever. **Amen.**

### Wednesday in the Third Week of Lent

Give ear to our prayers, O Lord, and dispose the way of thy servants in safety under thy protection, that, amidst all the changes of our earthly pilgrimage, we may ever be guarded by thy mighty aid; through Jesus Christ our Lord, who liveth and reigneth with thee and the Holy Spirit, one God; for ever and ever. **Amen.**

### Thursday in the Third Week of Lent

Keep watch over thy Church, O Lord, with thine unfailing love; and, seeing that it is grounded in human weakness and cannot maintain itself without thine aid, protect it from all danger, and keep it in the way of salvation; through Jesus Christ thy Son our Lord, who liveth and reigneth with thee and the Holy Spirit, one God, for ever and ever. **Amen.**

### Friday in the Third Week of Lent

Grant us, O Lord our Strength, to have a true love of thy holy Name; that, trusting in thy grace, we may fear no earthly evil, nor fix our hearts on earthly goods, but may rejoice in thy full salvation; through Jesus Christ our Lord, who liveth and reigneth with thee and the Holy Spirit, one God, for ever and ever. **Amen.**

## Saturday in the Third Week of Lent

O God, who knowest us to be set in the midst of so many and great dangers, that by reason of the frailty of our nature we cannot always stand upright: Grant to us such strength and protection as may support us in all dangers, and carry us through all temptations; through Jesus Christ our Lord, who liveth and reigneth with thee and the Holy Spirit, one God, for ever and ever. **Amen.**

## Fourth Sunday in Lent

Gracious Father, whose blessed Son Jesus Christ came down from heaven to be the true bread which giveth life to the world: Evermore give us this bread, that he may live in us, and we in him; who liveth and reigneth with thee and the Holy Spirit, one God, now and for ever. **Amen**.

## Monday in the Fourth Week of Lent

O Lord our God, who in thy holy Sacraments hast given us a foretaste of the good things of thy kingdom: Direct us, we beseech thee, in the way that leadeth unto eternal life, that we may come to appear before thee in that place of light where thou dost dwell for ever with thy saints; through Jesus Christ our Lord, who liveth and reigneth with thee and the Holy Spirit, one God, for ever and ever. **Amen.**

## Tuesday in the Fourth Week of Lent

O God, with whom is the well of life, and in whose light we see light: Quench our thirst, we pray thee, with living water, and flood our darkened minds with heavenly light; through Jesus Christ our Lord, who liveth and reigneth with thee and the Holy Spirit, one God, for ever and ever. **Amen.**

## Wednesday in the Fourth Week of Lent

O Lord our God, who didst sustain thine ancient people in the wilderness with bread from heaven: Feed now thy pilgrim flock with the food that endureth unto everlasting life; through Jesus Christ thy Son our Lord, who liveth and reigneth with thee and the Holy Spirit, one God, for ever and ever. **Amen.**

## Thursday in the Fourth Week of Lent

Almighty and most merciful God, drive from us all weakness of body, mind, and spirit; that, being restored to wholeness, we may with free hearts become what thou dost intend us to be and accomplish what thou willest us to do; through Jesus Christ our Lord, who liveth and reigneth with thee and the Holy Spirit, one God, for ever and ever. **Amen.**

## Friday in the Fourth Week of Lent

O God, who hast given us the Good News of thine abounding love in thy Son Jesus Christ: So fill our hearts with thankfulness that we may rejoice to tell abroad the good tidings we have received; through Jesus Christ our Lord, who liveth and reigneth with thee and the Holy Spirit, one God, for ever and ever. **Amen.**

## Saturday in the Fourth Week of Lent

Mercifully hear our prayers, O Lord, and spare all those who confess their sins unto thee; that they, whose consciences by sin are accused, by thy merciful pardon may be absolved; through Jesus Christ thy Son our Lord, who liveth and reigneth with thee and the Holy Spirit, one God, for ever and ever. **Amen.**

## Fifth Sunday in Lent

O Almighty God, who alone canst order the unruly wills and affections of sinful men: Grant unto thy people that they may love the thing which thou commandest, and desire that which thou dost promise; that so, among the sundry and manifold changes of the world, our hearts may surely there be fixed where true joys are to be found; through Jesus Christ our Lord, who liveth and reigneth with thee and the Holy Spirit, one God, now and for ever. **Amen**.

## Monday in the Fifth Week of Lent

Be gracious to thy people, we beseech thee, O Lord, that they, repenting day by day of the things that displease thee, may be more and more filled with love of thee and of thy commandments; and, being supported by thy grace in this life, may come to the full enjoyment of eternal life in thine everlasting kingdom; through Jesus Christ our Lord, who liveth and reigneth with thee and the Holy Spirit, one God, for ever and ever. **Amen.**

## Tuesday in the Fifth Week of Lent

Almighty God, who through the incarnate Word dost make us to be born anew of an imperishable and eternal seed: Look with compassion, we beseech thee, upon those who are being prepared for Holy Baptism, and grant that they may be built as living stones into a spiritual temple acceptable unto thee; through Jesus Christ our Lord, who liveth and reigneth with thee and the Holy Spirit, one God, for ever and ever. **Amen.**

## Wednesday in the Fifth Week of Lent

Almighty God our heavenly Father, renew in us the gifts of thy mercy; increase our faith, strengthen our hope, enlighten our understanding, enlarge our charity, and make us ready to serve thee; through Jesus Christ our Lord, who liveth and reigneth with thee and the Holy Spirit, one God, for ever and ever. **Amen.**

## Thursday in the Fifth Week of Lent

O God, who hast called us to be thy children, and hast promised that those who suffer with Christ will be heirs with him of thy glory: Arm us with such trust in him that we may ask no rest from his demands and have no fear in his service; through the same Jesus Christ our Lord, who liveth and reigneth with thee and the Holy Spirit, one God, for ever and ever. **Amen.**

## Friday in the Fifth Week of Lent

O Lord, who dost, out of the abundance of thy great riches, relieve our necessity: Grant, we beseech thee, that we may accept with joy the salvation thou dost bestow, and by the quality of our lives show forth the same to all the world; through Jesus Christ our Lord, who liveth and reigneth with thee and the Holy Spirit, one God, for ever and ever. **Amen.**

## Saturday in the Fifth Week of Lent

O Lord, who in thy goodness dost bestow abundant graces on thine elect: Look with favor, we entreat thee, upon those who in these Lenten days are being prepared for Holy Baptism, and grant them the help of thy protection; through Jesus Christ thy Son our Lord, who liveth and reigneth with thee and the Holy Spirit, one God, for ever and ever. **Amen.**

## Sunday of the Passion: Palm Sunday

Almighty and everlasting God, who, of thy tender love towards mankind, hast sent thy Son our Savior Jesus Christ to take upon him our flesh, and to suffer death upon the cross, that all mankind should follow the example of his great humility: Mercifully grant that we may both follow the example of his patience, and also be made partakers of his resurrection; through the same Jesus Christ our Lord, who liveth and reigneth with thee and the Holy Spirit, one God, for ever and ever. **Amen**.

## Monday in Holy Week

Almighty God, whose most dear Son went not up to joy but first he suffered pain, and entered not into glory before he was crucified: Mercifully grant that we, walking in the way of the cross, may find it none other than the way of life and peace; through the same thy Son Jesus Christ our Lord, who liveth and reigneth with thee and the Holy Spirit, one God, for ever and ever. **Amen**.

## Tuesday in Holy Week

O God, who by the passion of thy blessed Son didst make an instrument of shameful death to be unto us the means of life: Grant us so to glory in the cross of Christ, that we may gladly suffer shame and loss for the sake of thy Son our Savior Jesus Christ; who liveth and reigneth with thee and the Holy Spirit, one God, for ever and ever. **Amen**.

## Wednesday in Holy Week

O Lord God, whose blessed Son our Savior gave his back to the smiters and hid not his face from shame: Grant us grace to take joyfully the sufferings of the present time, in full assurance of the glory that shall be revealed; through the same thy Son Jesus Christ our Lord, who liveth and reigneth with thee and the Holy Spirit, one God, for ever and ever. **Amen**.

## Maundy Thursday

Almighty Father, whose dear Son, on the night before he suffered, did institute the Sacrament of his Body and Blood: Mercifully grant that we may thankfully receive the same in remembrance of him who in these holy mysteries giveth us a pledge of life eternal, the same thy Son Jesus Christ our Lord; who now liveth and reigneth with thee and the Holy Spirit, ever one God, world without end. **Amen**.

## Good Friday

Almighty God, we beseech thee graciously to behold this thy family, for which our Lord Jesus Christ was contented to be betrayed, and given up into the hands of sinners, and to suffer death upon the cross; who now liveth and reigneth with thee and the Holy Ghost ever, one God, world without end. **Amen**.

## Holy Saturday

O God, Creator of heaven and earth: Grant that, as the crucified body of thy dear Son was laid in the tomb and rested on this holy Sabbath, so we may await with him the coming of the third day, and rise with him to newness of life; who now liveth and reigneth with thee and the Holy Spirit, one God, for ever and ever. **Amen**.

## Easter Day

O God, who for our redemption didst give thine only-begotten Son to the death of the cross, and by his glorious resurrection hast delivered us from the power of our enemy: Grant us so to die daily to sin, that we may evermore live with him in the joy of his resurrection; through the same thy Son Christ our Lord, who liveth and reigneth with thee and the Holy Spirit, one God, now and for ever. **Amen**.

*or this*

O God, who didst make this most holy night to shine with the glory of the Lord's resurrection: Stir up in thy Church that Spirit of adoption which is given to us in Baptism, that we, being renewed both in body and mind, may worship thee in sincerity and truth; through the same Jesus Christ our Lord, who liveth and reigneth with thee, in the unity of the same Spirit, one God, now and for ever. **Amen**.

*or this*

Almighty God, who through thine only-begotten Son Jesus Christ hast overcome death and opened unto us the gate of everlasting life: Grant that we, who celebrate with joy the day of the Lord's resurrection, may be raised from the death of sin by thy life-giving Spirit; through the same Jesus Christ our Lord, who liveth and reigneth with thee and the same Spirit ever, one God, world without end. **Amen**.

## Monday in Easter Week

Grant, we beseech thee, Almighty God, that we who celebrate with reverence the Paschal feast may be found worthy to attain to everlasting joys; through Jesus Christ our Lord, who liveth and reigneth with thee and the Holy Spirit, one God, now and for ever. **Amen**.

## Tuesday in Easter Week

O God, who by the glorious resurrection of thy Son Jesus Christ destroyed death and brought life and immortality to light: Grant that we, who have been raised with him, may abide in his presence and rejoice in the hope of eternal glory; through the same Jesus Christ our Lord, to whom, with thee and the  Holy Spirit, be dominion and praise for ever and ever. **Amen**.

## Wednesday in Easter Week

O God, whose blessed Son did manifest himself to his disciples in the breaking of bread: Open, we pray thee, the eyes of our faith, that we may behold him in all his redeeming work; through the same thy Son Jesus Christ our Lord, who liveth and reigneth with thee, in the unity of the Holy Spirit, one God, now and for ever. **Amen**.

## Thursday in Easter Week

Almighty and everlasting God, who in the Paschal mystery hast established the new covenant of reconciliation: Grant that all who have been reborn into the fellowship of Christ's Body may show forth in their lives what they profess by their faith; through the same Jesus Christ our Lord, who liveth and reigneth with thee and the Holy Spirit, one God, for ever and ever. **Amen**.

## Friday in Easter Week

Almighty Father, who hast given thine only Son to die for our sins and to rise again for our justification: Grant us so to put away the leaven of malice and wickedness, that we may always serve thee in pureness of living and truth; through the same thy Son Jesus Christ our Lord, who liveth and reigneth with thee and the Holy Spirit, one God, now and for ever. **Amen**.

### Saturday in Easter Week

We thank thee, heavenly Father, for that thou hast delivered us from the dominion of sin and death and hast brought us into the kingdom of thy Son; and we pray thee that, as by his death he hath recalled us to life, so by his love he may raise us to joys eternal; who liveth and reigneth with thee, in the unity of the Holy Spirit, one God, now and for ever. **Amen**.

### Second Sunday of Easter

Almighty and everlasting God, who in the Paschal mystery hast established the new covenant of reconciliation: Grant that all who have been reborn into the fellowship of Christ's Body may show forth in their lives what they profess by their faith; through the same Jesus Christ our Lord, who liveth and reigneth with thee and the Holy Spirit, one God, for ever and ever. **Amen**.

### Third Sunday of Easter

O God, whose blessed Son did manifest himself to his disciples in the breaking of bread: Open, we pray thee, the eyes of our faith, that we may behold him in all his redeeming work; through the same thy Son Jesus Christ our Lord, who liveth and reigneth with thee, in the unity of the Holy Spirit, one God, now and for ever. **Amen**.

### Fourth Sunday of Easter

O God, whose Son Jesus is the good shepherd of thy people: Grant that when we hear his voice we may know him who calleth us each by name, and follow where he doth lead; who, with thee and the Holy Spirit, liveth and reigneth, one God, for ever and ever. **Amen**.

## Fifth Sunday of Easter

O Almighty God, whom truly to know is everlasting life: Grant us so perfectly to know thy Son Jesus Christ to be the way, the truth, and the life, that we may steadfastly follow his steps in the way that leadeth to eternal life; through the same thy Son Jesus Christ our Lord, who liveth and reigneth with thee, in the unity of the Holy Spirit, one God, for ever and ever. **Amen**.

## Sixth Sunday of Easter

O God, who hast prepared for those who love thee such good things as pass man's understanding: Pour into our hearts such love toward thee, that we, loving thee in all things and above all things, may obtain thy promises, which exceed all that we can desire; through Jesus Christ our Lord, who liveth and reigneth with thee and the Holy Spirit, one God, for ever and ever. **Amen**.

## Weekdays before Ascension Day

Almighty God, Lord of heaven and earth: We beseech thee to pour forth thy blessing upon this land, and to give us a fruitful season; that we, constantly receiving thy bounty, may evermore give thanks unto thee in thy holy Church; through Jesus Christ our Lord. **Amen.**

## Ascension Day

O Almighty God, whose blessed Son our Savior Jesus Christ ascended far above all heavens that he might fill all things: Mercifully give us faith to perceive that, according to his promise, he abideth with his Church on earth, even unto the end of the ages; through the same Jesus Christ our Lord, who liveth and reigneth with thee and the Holy Spirit, one God, in glory everlasting. **Amen**.

*or this*

Grant, we beseech thee, Almighty God, that like as we do believe thy only-begotten Son our Lord Jesus Christ to have ascended into the heavens, so we may also in heart and mind thither ascend, and with him continually dwell; who liveth and reigneth with thee and the Holy Ghost, one God, world without end. **Amen**.

**Seventh Sunday of Easter: The Sunday after Ascension Day**

O God, the King of glory, who hast exalted thine only Son Jesus Christ with great triumph unto thy kingdom in heaven: We beseech thee, leave us not comfortless, but send to us thine Holy Ghost to comfort us, and exalt us unto the same place whither our Savior Christ is gone before; who liveth and reigneth with thee and the same Holy Ghost, one God, world without end. **Amen**.

**The Day of Pentecost: Whitsunday**

Almighty God, who on this day didst open the way of eternal life to every race and nation by the promised gift of thy Holy Spirit: Shed abroad this gift throughout the world by the preaching of the Gospel, that it may reach to the ends of the earth; through Jesus Christ our Lord, who liveth and reigneth with thee, in the unity of the same Spirit, one God, for ever and ever. **Amen**.

*or this*

O God, who on this day didst teach the hearts of thy faithful people by sending to them the light of thy Holy Spirit: Grant us by the same Spirit to have a right judgment in all things, and evermore to rejoice in his holy comfort; through the merits of Christ Jesus our Savior, who liveth and reigneth with thee, in the unity of the same Spirit, one God, world without end. **Amen**.

*Wednesday, Friday, and Saturday of this week are the traditional summer Ember Days.*

## Summer Ember Days

Almighty God, our heavenly Father, who hast purchased to thyself a universal Church by the precious blood of thy dear Son: Mercifully look upon the same, and at this time so guide and govern the minds of thy servants the Bishops and Pastors of thy flock, that they may lay hands suddenly on no man, but faithfully and wisely make choice of fit persons to serve in the sacred Ministry of thy Church; and to those who shall be ordained to any holy function, give thy grace and heavenly benediction; that both by their life and doctrine thy may show forth thy glory, and set forward the salvation of all men; through Jesus Christ our Lord. **Amen.**

## First Sunday after Pentecost: Trinity Sunday

Almighty and everlasting God, who hast given unto us thy servants grace, by the confession of a true faith, to acknowledge the glory of the eternal Trinity, and in the power of the Divine Majesty to worship the Unity: We beseech thee that thou wouldest keep us steadfast in this faith and worship, and bring us at last to see thee in thy one and eternal glory, O

Father; who with the Son and the Holy Spirit livest and reignest, one God, for ever and ever. **Amen**.


## Proper 1 *Week of the Sunday between May 8-14*

Remember, O Lord, what thou hast wrought in us and not what we deserve; and, as thou hast called us to thy service, make us worthy of our calling; through Jesus Christ our Lord, who liveth and reigneth with thee and the Holy Spirit, one God, now and for ever. **Amen**.

## Proper 2 *Week of the Sunday between May 15-21*

O Almighty and most merciful God, of thy bountiful goodness keep us, we beseech thee, from all things that may hurt us, that we, being ready both in body and soul, may with free hearts accomplish those things which belong to thy purpose; through Jesus Christ our Lord, who liveth and reigneth with thee and the Holy Spirit, one God, now and for ever. **Amen**.

## Proper 3 *The Sunday between May 22-28*

Grant, O Lord, we beseech thee, that the course of this world may be peaceably governed by thy providence, and that thy Church may joyfully serve thee in confidence and serenity; through Jesus Christ our Lord, who liveth and reigneth with thee and the Holy Spirit, one God, for ever and ever. **Amen**.

## Proper 4 *The Sunday between May 29-June 4*

O God, whose never-failing providence ordereth all things both in heaven and earth: We humbly beseech thee to put away from us all hurtful things, and to give us those things which are profitable for us; through Jesus Christ our Lord, who liveth and reigneth with thee and the Holy Spirit, one God, for ever and ever. **Amen**.

**Proper 5** *The Sunday between June 5-11*

O God, from whom all good doth come: Grant that by thy inspiration we may think those things that are right, and by thy merciful guiding may perform the same; through Jesus Christ our Lord, who liveth and reigneth with thee and the Holy Spirit, one God, for ever and ever. **Amen**.

**Proper 6** *The Sunday between June 7-18*

Keep, O Lord, we beseech thee, thy household the Church in thy steadfast faith and love, that by the help of thy grace we may proclaim thy truth with boldness, and minister thy justice with compassion; for the sake of our Savior Jesus Christ, who liveth and reigneth with thee and the Holy Spirit, one God, now and for ever. **Amen**.

**Proper 7** *The Sunday between June 19-25*

O Lord, we beseech thee, make us to have a perpetual fear and love of thy holy Name, for thou never failest to help and govern those whom thou hast set upon the sure foundation of thy loving-kindness; through Jesus Christ our Lord, who liveth and reigneth with thee and the Holy Spirit, one God, for ever and ever. **Amen**.

**Proper 8** *The Sunday between June 26-July 2*

O Almighty God, who hast built thy Church upon the foundation of the apostles and prophets, Jesus Christ himself being the chief cornerstone: Grant us so to be joined together in unity of spirit by their doctrine, that we may be made an holy temple acceptable unto thee; through the same Jesus

Christ our Lord, who liveth and reigneth with thee and the Holy Spirit, one God, for ever and ever. **Amen**.

**Proper 9** *The Sunday between July 3-9*

O God, who hast taught us to keep all thy commandments by loving thee and our neighbor: Grant us the grace of thy Holy Spirit, that we may be devoted to thee with our whole heart, and united to one another with pure affection; through Jesus Christ our Lord, who liveth and reigneth with thee and the same Spirit, one God, for ever and ever. **Amen**.

**Proper 10** *The Sunday between July 10-16*

O Lord, we beseech thee mercifully to receive the prayers of thy people who call upon thee, and grant that they may both perceive and know what things they ought to do, and also may have grace and power faithfully to fulfill the same; through Jesus Christ our Lord, who liveth and reigneth with thee and the Holy Spirit, one God, now and for ever. **Amen**.

**Proper 11** *The Sunday between July 17-23*

Almighty God, the fountain of all wisdom, who knowest our necessities before we ask and our ignorance in asking: Have compassion, we beseech thee, upon our infirmities, and those things which for our unworthiness we dare not, and for our blindness we cannot ask, mercifully give us for the worthiness of thy Son Jesus Christ our Lord, who liveth and reigneth with thee and the Holy Spirit, one God, now and for ever. **Amen**.

**Proper 12** *The Sunday between July 24-30*

O God, the protector of all that trust in thee, without whom nothing is strong, nothing is holy: Increase and multiply upon us thy mercy; that, thou being our ruler and guide, we may so pass through things temporal, that we finally lose not the things eternal; through Jesus Christ our Lord, who liveth and reigneth with thee and the Holy Spirit, one God, for ever and ever. **Amen**.

**Proper 13** *The Sunday between July 31-August 5 (August 6 is the Feast of the Transfiguration)*

O Lord, we beseech thee, let thy continual pity cleanse and defend thy Church, and, because it cannot continue in safety without thy succor, preserve it evermore by thy help and goodness; through Jesus Christ our Lord, who liveth and reigneth with thee and the Holy Spirit, one God, for ever and ever. **Amen**.

**Proper 14** *The Sunday between August 7-13*

Grant to us, Lord, we beseech thee, the spirit to think and do always such things as are right, that we, who cannot exist without thee, may by thee be enabled to live according to thy will; through Jesus Christ our Lord, who liveth and reigneth with thee and the Holy Spirit, one God, for ever and ever. **Amen**.

**Proper 15** *The Sunday between August 14-20*

Almighty God, who hast given thy only Son to be unto us both a sacrifice for sin and also an example of godly life: Give us grace that we may always most thankfully receive that his inestimable benefit, and also daily endeavor ourselves to follow the blessed steps of his most holy life; through the same thy Son Jesus Christ our Lord, who liveth and reigneth with thee and the Holy Spirit, one God, now and for ever. **Amen**.

**Proper 16** *The Sunday between August 21-27*

Grant, we beseech thee, merciful God, that thy Church, being gathered together in unity by thy Holy Spirit, may manifest thy power among all peoples, to the glory of thy Name; through Jesus Christ our Lord, who liveth and reigneth with thee and the same Spirit, one God, world without end. **Amen**.

**Proper 17** *The Sunday between August 28-September 3*

Lord of all power and might, who art the author and giver of all good things: Graft in our hearts the love of thy Name, increase in us true religion, nourish us with all goodness, and bring forth in us the fruit of good works; through Jesus Christ our Lord, who liveth and reigneth with thee and the Holy Spirit, one God, for ever and ever. **Amen**.

**Proper 18** *The Sunday between September 4-10*

Grant us, O Lord, we pray thee, to trust in thee with all our heart; seeing that, as thou dost alway resist the proud who confide in their own strength, so thou dost not forsake those who make their boast of thy mercy; through Jesus Christ our Lord, who liveth and reigneth with thee and the Holy Spirit, one God, now and for ever. **Amen**.

**Proper 19** *The Sunday between September 11-17*

O God, forasmuch as without thee we are not able to please thee, mercifully grant that thy Holy Spirit may in all things direct and rule our hearts; through Jesus Christ our Lord, who with thee and the same Spirit liveth and reigneth, one God, now and for ever. **Amen**.

## Autumn Ember Days

O Almighty God, look mercifully upon thy world which thou has redeemed by the blood of thy dear Son, and incline the hearts of many to dedicate themselves to the sacred Ministry of the Church; through the same thy Son Jesus Christ our Lord. **Amen.**

**Proper 20** *The Sunday between September 18-24*

Grant us, O Lord, not to mind earthly things, but to love things heavenly; and even now, while we are placed among things that are passing away, to cleave to those that shall abide; through Jesus Christ our Lord, who liveth and reigneth with thee and the Holy Spirit, one God, for ever and ever. **Amen**.

**Proper 21** *The Sunday between September 25-October 1*

O God, who declarest thy almighty power chiefly in showing mercy and pity: Mercifully grant unto us such a measure of thy grace, that we, running to obtain thy promises, may be made partakers of thy heavenly treasure; through Jesus Christ our Lord, who liveth and reigneth with thee and the Holy Spirit, one God, for ever and ever. **Amen**.

**Proper 22** *The Sunday between October 2-8*

Almighty and everlasting God, who art always more ready to hear than we to pray, and art wont to give more than either we

263

desire or deserve: Pour down upon us the abundance of thy mercy, forgiving us those things whereof our conscience is afraid, and giving us those good things which we are not worthy to ask, but through the merits and mediation of Jesus Christ thy Son our Lord; who liveth and reigneth with thee and the Holy Spirit, one God, for ever and ever. **Amen**.

**Proper 23** *The Sunday between October 9-15*

Lord, we pray thee that thy grace may always precede and follow us, and make us continually to be given to all good works; through Jesus Christ our Lord, who liveth and reigneth with thee and the Holy Spirit, one God, now and for ever. **Amen**.

**Proper 24** *The Sunday between October 16-22*

Almighty and everlasting God, who in Christ hast revealed thy glory among the nations: Preserve the works of thy mercy, that thy Church throughout the world may persevere with steadfast faith in the confession of thy Name; through the same Jesus Christ our Lord, who liveth and reigneth with thee and the Holy Spirit, one God, for ever and ever. **Amen**.

**Proper 25** *The Sunday between October 23-29*

Almighty and everlasting God, give unto us the increase of faith, hope, and charity; and, that we may obtain that which thou dost promise, make us to love that which thou dost command; through Jesus Christ our Lord, who liveth and reigneth with thee and the Holy Spirit, one God, for ever and ever. **Amen**.

**Proper 26** *The Sunday between October 30-November 5; November 1 is All Saints Day*

Almighty and merciful God, of whose only gift it cometh that thy faithful people do unto thee true and laudable service: Grant, we beseech thee, that we may run without stumbling to obtain thy heavenly promises; through Jesus Christ our Lord, who liveth and reigneth with thee and the Holy Spirit, one God, now and for ever. **Amen**.

**Proper 27** *The Sunday between November 6-12*

O God, whose blessed Son was manifested that he might destroy the works of the devil and make us the children of God and heirs of eternal life: Grant us, we beseech thee, that, having this hope, we may purify ourselves even as he is pure; that, when he shall appear again with power and great glory, we may be made like unto him in his eternal and glorious kingdom; where with thee, O Father, and thee, O Holy Ghost, he liveth and reigneth ever, one God, world without end. **Amen**.

**Proper 28** *The Sunday between November 13-19*

Blessed Lord, who hast caused all holy Scriptures to be written for our learning: Grant that we may in such wise hear them, read, mark, learn, and inwardly digest them; that, by patience and comfort of thy holy Word, we may embrace and ever hold fast the blessed hope of everlasting life, which thou hast given us in our Savior Jesus Christ; who liveth and reigneth with thee and the Holy Spirit, one God, for ever and ever. **Amen**.

**Proper 29** *The Sunday between November 20-26*

Almighty and everlasting God, whose will it is to restore all things in thy well-beloved Son, the King of kings and Lord of lords: Mercifully grant that the peoples of the earth, divided and enslaved by sin, may be freed and brought together under his most gracious rule; who liveth and reigneth with thee and the Holy Spirit, one God, now and for ever. **Amen**.

## Holy Days

**Saint Andrew** *November 30*     *Is 49.1-6; 1 Cor 4.1-16\*Is 55.1-5; Jn 1.35-42*

Almighty God, who didst give such grace to thine apostle Andrew that he readily obeyed the call of thy Son Jesus Christ, and brought his brother with him: Give unto us, who are called by thy Word, grace to follow him without delay, and to bring those near to us into his gracious presence; who liveth and reigneth with thee and the Holy Spirit, one God, now and for ever. **Amen**.

**Saint Thomas** *December 21*     *Job 42.1-6; 1 Pet 1.3-9\*Is 43.8-13; Jn 14.1-7*

Everliving God, who didst strengthen thine apostle Thomas with sure and certain faith in thy Son's resurrection: Grant us so perfectly and without doubt to believe in Jesus Christ, our Lord and our God, that our faith may never be found wanting in thy sight; through him who liveth and reigneth with thee and the Holy Spirit, one God, now and for ever. **Amen**.

**Saint Stephen** *December 26*

We give thee thanks, O Lord of glory, for the example of the first martyr Stephen, who looked up to heaven and prayed for his persecutors to thy Son Jesus Christ, who standeth at thy right hand; where he liveth and reigneth with thee and the Holy Spirit, one God, in glory everlasting. **Amen**.

**Saint John** *December 27*

Shed upon thy Church, we beseech thee, O Lord, the brightness of thy light; that we, being illumined by the teaching of thine apostle and evangelist John, may so walk in the light of thy truth, that we may at length attain to the fullness of life everlasting; through Jesus Christ our Lord, who liveth and reigneth with thee and the Holy Spirit, one God, for ever and ever. **Amen**.

**The Holy Innocents** *December 28*

We remember this day, O God, the slaughter of the holy innocents of Bethlehem by the order of King Herod. Receive, we beseech thee, into the arms of thy mercy all innocent victims; and by thy great might frustrate the designs of evil tyrants and establish thy rule of justice, love, and peace; through Jesus Christ our Lord, who liveth and reigneth with thee, in the unity of the Holy Spirit, one God, for ever and ever. **Amen**.

**Confession of Saint Peter** *January 18     Ezk3.4-11; Act 10.34-44\*Ezk 34.11-16; Jn 21.15-22*

Almighty Father, who didst inspire Simon Peter, first among the apostles, to confess Jesus as Messiah and Son of the living God: Keep thy Church steadfast upon the rock of this faith, that in unity and peace we may proclaim the one truth and follow the one Lord, our Savior Jesus Christ; who liveth and reigneth with thee and the Holy Spirit, one God, now and for ever. **Amen**.

**Conversion of Saint Paul** *January 25     Is 45.18-25, Php 3.4b-11\*Eccus 39.1-10, Act 9.1-22*

O God, who, by the preaching of thine apostle Paul, hast caused the light of the Gospel to shine throughout the world: Grant, we beseech thee, that we, having his wonderful conversion in remembrance, may show forth our thankfulness unto thee for the same by following the holy doctrine which he taught; through Jesus Christ our Lord, who liveth and reigneth with thee, in the unity of the Holy Spirit, one God, now and for ever. **Amen**.

**The Presentation** *February 2  1 Sam 2.1-10, Jn 8.31-36*Hag 2.1-9, 1 Jn 3.1-8*

Almighty and everliving God, we humbly beseech thee that, as thy only-begotten Son was this day presented in the temple, so we may be presented unto thee with pure and clean hearts by the same thy Son Jesus Christ our Lord; who liveth and reigneth with thee and the Holy Spirit, one God, now and for ever. **Amen**.

**Saint Matthias** *February 24  1 Sam 16.1-13, 1 Jn 2.18-25*1 Sam 12.1-5, Act 20.17-35*

O Almighty God, who into the place of Judas didst choose thy faithful servant Matthias to be of the number of the Twelve: Grant that thy Church, being delivered from false apostles, may always be ordered and guided by faithful and true pastors; through Jesus Christ our Lord, who liveth and reigneth with thee, in the unity of the Holy Spirit, one God, now and for ever. **Amen**.

**Saint Joseph** *March 19  Is 63.7-16, Mt 1.18-25*2 Chr 6.12-17, Eph 3.14-21*

O God, who from the family of thy servant David didst raise up Joseph to be the guardian of thy incarnate Son and the spouse of his virgin mother: Give us grace to imitate his uprightness of life and his obedience to thy commands;

through the same thy Son Jesus Christ our Lord, who liveth and reigneth with thee and the Holy Spirit, one God, for ever and ever. **Amen**.

**The Annunciation** *March 25  Is 52.7-12, Hb 2.5-10\*Wsd 9.1-12, Jn 1.9-14*

We beseech thee, O Lord, pour thy grace into our hearts, that we who have known the incarnation of thy Son Jesus Christ, announced by an angel to the Virgin Mary, may by his cross and passion be brought unto the glory of his resurrection; who liveth and reigneth with thee, in the unity of the Holy Spirit, one God, now and for ever  **Amen**.

**Saint Mark** *April 25  Eccus 2.1-11, Act 12.25-13.3\*Is62.6-12, 2 Tm 4.1-11*

Almighty God, who by the hand of Mark the evangelist hast given to thy Church the Gospel of Jesus Christ the Son of God: We thank thee for this witness, and pray that we may be firmly grounded in its truth; through the same Jesus Christ our Lord, who liveth and reigneth with thee and the Holy Spirit, one God, for ever and ever. **Amen**.

**Saint Philip and Saint James** *May 1  Job 23.1-12, Jn 1.43-51\*Prv 4.7-18, Jn 12.20-26*

Almighty God, who didst give to thine apostles Philip and James grace and strength to bear witness to the truth: Grant that we, being mindful of their victory of faith, may glorify in life and death the Name of our Lord Jesus Christ; who liveth and reigneth with thee and the Holy Spirit, one God, now and for ever. **Amen**.

**The Visitation** *May 31  1 Sam 1.1-20, Hb 3.1-6\*Zech 2.10-13, Jn 3.25-30*

Father in heaven, by whose grace the virgin mother of thy incarnate Son was blessed in bearing him, but still more blessed in keeping thy word: Grant us who honor the exaltation of her lowliness to follow the example of her devotion to thy will; through the same Jesus Christ our Lord, who liveth and reigneth with thee and the Holy Spirit, one God, for ever and ever. **Amen**.

**Saint Barnabas** *June 11  Eccus 31-3-11, Act 4.32-37\*Job 29.1-16, Act 9.26-31*

Grant, O God, that we may follow the example of thy faithful servant Barnabas, who, seeking not his own renown but the well-being of thy Church, gave generously of his life and substance for the relief of the poor and the spread of the Gospel; through Jesus Christ our Lord, who liveth and reigneth with thee and the Holy Spirit, one God, for ever and ever. **Amen**.

**The Nativity of Saint John the Baptist** *June 24  Mal 3.1-5, Jn 3.22-30\*Is 4.1-6, Mt 11.2-19*

Almighty God, by whose providence thy servant John the Baptist was wonderfully born, and sent to prepare the way of thy Son our Savior by preaching repentance: Make us so to follow his doctrine and holy life, that we may truly repent according to his preaching; and after his example constantly speak the truth, boldly rebuke vice, and patiently suffer for the truth's sake; through the same thy Son Jesus Christ our Lord, who liveth and reigneth with thee and the Holy Spirit one God, for ever and ever. **Amen**.

**Saint Peter and Saint Paul** *June 29  Ezk 2.1-7, Act 11.1-18\*Is 49.1-6, Gal 2.1-9*

Almighty God, whose blessed apostles Peter and Paul glorified thee by their martyrdom: Grant that thy Church, instructed by their teaching and example, and knit together in unity by thy Spirit, may ever stand firm upon the one foundation, which is Jesus Christ our Lord; who liveth and reigneth with thee, in the unity of the same Spirit, one God, for ever and ever. **Amen**.

**Independence Day** *July 4  Eccus 10.1-18, Jas 5.7-10*Mic 4.1-5, Rev 21.1-7*

Lord God Almighty, in whose Name the founders of this country won liberty for themselves and for us, and lit the torch of freedom for nations then unborn:  Grant we beseech thee, that we and all the people of this land may have grace to maintain these liberties in righteousness and peace; through Jesus Christ our Lord, who liveth and reigneth with thee and the Holy Spirit, one God, for ever and ever. **Amen**.

**Saint Mary Magdalene** *July 22  Zeph 3.14-20, Mk 15.37-16.7*Ex 15.19-21, 2 Cor 1.3-7*

Almighty God, whose blessed Son restored Mary Magdalene to health of body and mind, and called her to be a witness of his resurrection: Mercifully grant that by thy grace we may be healed of all our infirmities and know thee in the power of his endless life; who with thee and the Holy Spirit liveth and reigneth, one God, now and for ever. **Amen**.

**Saint James** *July 25  Jer 16.14-21, Mk 1.14-20*Jer 26.1-15, Mt 10.16-32*

O gracious God, we remember before thee this day thy servant and apostle James, first among the Twelve to suffer martyrdom for the Name of Jesus Christ; and we pray that thou wilt pour out upon the leaders of thy Church that spirit of self-denying service by which alone they may have true authority among thy people; through the same Jesus Christ our Lord, who liveth and reigneth with thee and the Holy Spirit, one God, now and for ever. **Amen**.

**The Transfiguration**  *August 6   Ex 24.12-18, 2 Cor 4.1-6\*Dan 7.9-14, Jn 12.27-36a*

O God, who on the holy mount didst reveal to chosen witnesses thy well-beloved Son, wonderfully transfigured, in raiment white and glistening: Mercifully grant that we, being delivered from the disquietude of this world, may by faith behold the King in his beauty; who with thee, O Father, and thee, O Holy Ghost, liveth and reigneth, one God, world without end. **Amen**.

**Saint Mary the Virgin**  *August 15   1 Sam 2.1-10, Jn 2.1-12\*Jer 31.1-14, Jn 19.23-27*

O God, who hast taken to thyself the blessed Virgin Mary, mother of thy incarnate Son: Grant that we, who have been redeemed by his blood, may share with her the glory of thine eternal kingdom; through the same thy Son Jesus Christ our Lord, who liveth and reigneth with thee, in the unity of the Holy Spirit, one God, now and for ever. **Amen**.

**Saint Bartholomew**  *August 24   Gen 28.10-17, Jn 1.43-51\*Is 66.1-23, 1 Pt 5.1-11*

O Almighty and everlasting God, who didst give to thine apostle Bartholomew grace truly to believe and to preach thy Word: Grant, we beseech thee, unto thy Church to love what he believed and to preach what he taught; through Jesus Christ our Lord, who liveth and reigneth with thee and the Holy Spirit, one God, for ever and ever. **Amen**.

**Holy Cross Day** *September 14  Nbr 21.4-9, Jn 3.11-17\*Gen 3.1-15, 1 Pt 3.17-22*

Almighty God, whose Son our Savior Jesus Christ was lifted high upon the cross that he might draw the whole world unto himself:  Mercifully grant that we, who glory in the mystery of our redemption, may have grace to take up our cross and follow him; who liveth and reigneth with thee and the Holy Spirit, one God, in glory everlasting. **Amen**.

**Saint Matthew** *September 21  Is 8.11-20, Ro 10.1-15\*Job 28.12-28, Mt 13.44-52*

We thank thee, heavenly Father, for the witness of thine apostle and evangelist Matthew to the Gospel of thy Son our Savior; and we pray that, after his example, we may with ready wills and hearts obey the calling of our Lord to follow him; through Jesus Christ our Lord, who liveth and reigneth with thee and the Holy Spirit, one God, now and for ever. **Amen**.

**Saint Michael and All Angels** *September 29  Job 38.1-7, Heb 1.1-14\*Dan 12.1-3, Mk 13.21-27*
O everlasting God, who hast ordained and constituted the ministries of angels and men in a wonderful order: Mercifully grant that, as thy holy angels always serve and worship thee in heaven, so by thy appointment they may help and defend us on earth; through Jesus Christ our Lord, who liveth and reigneth with thee and the Holy Spirit, one God, for ever and ever. **Amen**.

**Saint Luke** *October 18  Ezek 47.1-12, Lk 1.1-4\*Is 52.7-10, Act 1.1-8*

Almighty God, who didst inspire thy servant Luke the physician to set forth in the Gospel the love and healing power of thy Son:  Graciously continue in thy Church the like love and power to heal, to the praise and glory of thy Name; through the same thy Son Jesus Christ our Lord, who liveth and reigneth with thee, in the unity of the Holy Spirit, one God, now and for ever. **Amen**.

**Saint James of Jerusalem**  *October 23   Jer 11.18-23, Mt 10.16-22\*Is 65.17-25, Heb 12.12-24*

Grant, we beseech thee, O God, that after the example of thy servant James the Just, brother of our Lord, thy Church may give itself continually to prayer and to the reconciliation of all who are at variance and enmity; through the same our Lord Jesus Christ, who liveth and reigneth with thee and the Holy Spirit, one God, now and for ever. **Amen**.

**Saint Simon and Saint Jude**  *October 28   Is 28.9-16, Eph 4.1-16\*Is4.2-6, Jn 14.15-31*

O God, we thank thee for the glorious company of the apostles, and especially on this day for Simon and Jude; and we pray that, as they were faithful and zealous in their mission, so we may with ardent devotion make known the love and mercy of our Lord and Savior Jesus Christ; who liveth and reigneth with thee and the Holy Spirit, one God, for ever and ever. **Amen**.

**All Saints' Day**  *November 1   2 Esdras 2.42-47, Heb 11.32-12.2\*Wsd 5.1-16, Rev 21.1-22.5*

O Almighty God, who hast knit together thine elect in one communion and fellowship in the mystical body of thy Son Christ our Lord: Grant us grace so to follow thy blessed saints in all virtuous and godly living, that we may come to those ineffable joys which thou hast prepared for those who unfeignedly love thee; through the same Jesus Christ our

Lord, who with thee and the Holy Spirit liveth and reigneth, one God, in glory everlasting. **Amen**.

**Thanksgiving Day** *Dt 26.1-11, Jn 6.26-35\*Joel 2.1-27, 1 Th 5.12-24*

Almighty and gracious Father, we give thee thanks for the fruits of the earth in their season and for the labors of those who harvest them. Make us, we beseech thee, faithful stewards of thy great bounty, for the provision of our necessities and the relief of all who are in need, to the glory of thy Name; through Jesus Christ our Lord, who liveth and reigneth with thee and the Holy Spirit, one God, now and for ever. **Amen**.

# ABOUT THE AUTHOR

David Mathus is a priest in the Anglican Church in North America and founding rector of Holy Cross Anglican Church, Kent, Ohio.

30570794R00168

Printed in Great
Britain
by Amazon